BURIED LIVES

BURIED LIVES

THE PROTESTANTS
OF SOUTHERN
IRELAND

ROBIN BURY

To John, my brother.

First published 2017
Reprinted 2018, 2019, 2021

The History Press
97 St George's Place,
Cheltenahm, Gloucestershire, GL50 3QB
www.thehistorypress.co.uk

British Library Cataloguing in Publication Data.
A catalogue record for this book is available from the British Library.

ISBN 978 1 84588 880 0

Typesetting and origination by The History Press
Printed by TJ Books Limited, Padstow, Cornwall

Contents

Acknowledgements

I am very grateful to my brother, John, for all his encouragement and for starting me on the long journey of writing this book. He was puzzled by our mild apartheid-style lives in east Cork and set me on this road of exploration and discovery some twelve years ago. This led to an M.Phil. dissertation in Trinity College Dublin in 2012/13 when I researched a point of time in history which was pivotal for Protestants in Southern Ireland.

I thank David Dickson for his patience and guidance as my supervisor for the M.Phil. He suggested I concentrate on Protestants in Co. Tipperary during a period of armed conflict, an area not examined in any considerable detail by historians. He sometimes respectfully disagreed with drafts for my dissertation and helped to make me 'keep on my historian's hat', as he put it, to shape and balance my writing.

Thanks to those people in the taught graduate M.Phil course in Modern Irish history who gave support and encouragement to a rather mature student. Eunan O'Halpin encouraged me to apply and accepted my last minute application, for which sincere thanks. Anne Dolan's knowledge of the period is highly impressive, though we did not always see eye to eye. David Fitzpatrick, my examiner, provided me with much valued help for my research on the decline in Protestant numbers.

I am particularly grateful to the very helpful people in the Representative Church Body Library (Milltown, Dublin), particularly Susan Hood and Mary Furlong who met my endless demands for information and leads. Thanks also to Aideen Ireland, Head, Reader Services Division, and the National Archives of Ireland, who helped me to locate Irish compensation archives. Mary Guinan-Darmody in the Tipperary Libraries Study section graciously met my many requests for research material used in the dissertation, particularly newspaper reports. David Griffin in the Irish Architectural Archives has been a friend and inspiration.

Thanks to the various Church of Ireland clergy in Roscrea, Cashel and Nenagh, and to Marjorie Quarton in Nenagh, who gave unstintingly of their time and who introduced me to people who supplied sources of information on local history.

Eoghan Harris has been hugely supportive for many years and I am indebted to him for suggesting the title, Buried Lives, where my surname comes into play. Dr Mark Dooley read early drafts and made a number of suggestions for shaping the book in its early stages: to him sincere thanks. Also to Dr David Butler of University College, Cork.

Donald Wood's excellent research has been invaluable for calculating the reasons for the sharp fall in southern Protestant numbers from 1911 to 1926. His knowledge of local history in west Cork is highly impressive, in particular in identifying the sixteen Protestants targeted, but not killed, by the IRA in April, 1922. Their names appear in the Appendix. I am much obliged to him for all his help and advice.

Gerald Murphy gave me much information on the various cases of Protestant intimidation in the early chapters of the book, adding most valuable insights. His book *The Year of Disappearances: Political Killings in Cork, 1920–1921* was highly revealing and shocking.

Brian Walker more than anyone else, made possible the finalised version of the book. He tirelessly edited it in a gentle and humorous manner. His own book, *A Political History of the Two Irelands*, much quoted by me, is inspirational.

Finally, my family gave me the strength and untiring support to keep going. My siblings Catherine, Richard, John and Anne, and my children Sophie, Emily and Mark. Thank you all. Sophie, and your generous partner Bill, both in Toronto, merit particular thanks for proof reading my dissertation up against a very tight deadline. This dissertation forms the backbone of this book.

Preface

Some 12 years ago my brother, John, told me that he was puzzled by the apartheid lifestyle our Church of Ireland family experienced when growing up in east Co. Cork in the 1950s and '60s. My father was a clergyman, the Dean of Cloyne, the seat of an ancient bishopric and famous for the Irish philosopher, Bishop Berkeley, who once lived there. We lived in isolation, among a small scattering of Church of Ireland people who worshipped in the three little churches in the parishes of Ballycotton, Corkbeg and Inch as well as the ancient Norman cathedral in Cloyne. We mixed with our own faith at whist drives in the Deanery, parish fêtes and private tennis parties. The only Catholics I knew when growing up were the local doctor and shopkeepers. The Church of Ireland members included the once large landlord, the Longfields/Ponsonbys, whose children were educated in England, the now-famous Allen family, who ran a restaurant near Ballycotton, and the Pearces. Philip Pearce was English and his wife, Lucy, was Welsh. He was a pacifist who left England during the Second World War to start a pottery in Shanagarry. His Shangarry pottery brand became a household name in Ireland. So why had this mutually accepted form of apartheid, which had deeply divided the Catholic and Protestant communities and nation, come to be?

It is a long and troublesome story that this book attempts to tell. I have used the subtitle of the Protestants of 'Southern Ireland' rather than 'Republic of Ireland or 'Irish Free State', because this book goes from before 1921 until the present. The early twentieth century saw the transformation of the southern Irish Protestants from a once strong people into an isolated, pacified community. Their influence, status and numbers had weakened greatly by the end of the civil war in

1923 and they were to form a quiescent minority up to modern times.
The historian Patrick Buckland believed that after 1917 there was a
'disintegration' of the Protestant southern unionists. Their numbers
fell sharply, events having 'shattered the confidence of those who
remained in Ireland and undermined their determination to continue
distinctive political activity.[1] They were denied 'a powerful Senate' in
the constitution of the Free State, and a new Ireland emerged based
on blood, religion and – above all – enmity with Britain. A homogenous society came into being, nationalist and Catholic with an
'Anglocentric obsession'.[2] In such a world, those supporting England
were unwanted, their rights as a minority in conflict with the ethos of
the Free State.

In the words of another historian, Marianne Elliott, Irish nationalism
was 'another form of religion in disguise'; Irish Catholics 'became the "real
Irish" in common perception'.[3] In the newly independent Ireland, 'the
prevailing Catholic and anti-English ethos ... has caused real problems,
and the claims that the Protestant minority has been treated well by the
State rather ignores the fact that in that ethos Protestants had been considered England's "garrison" and un-Irish, tolerated rather than accepted'.[4]

In 1911, Protestants in the 26 counties numbered some 300,000
(excluding Protestants in the British Army, which departed in 1922),
or 10 per cent of the total population. By the time of the last census in
2011 there were only 137,000 southern Irish Protestants (excluding
non-Irish Protestants), or less than 3 per cent of the population. They
had become an insignificant minority, having once 'played such a
conspicuous and powerful role in Irish life'.[5] They had been responsible for much of Ireland's finest architecture, both domestic and civic.
In Dublin, once called an English city, the Protestants built superb
buildings, which are 'in all their geometrical simplicity and austerity,
among the glories of domestic architecture ... The Georgian squares,
the Houses of Parliament on College Green ... and the great public
buildings designed by James Gandon had their counterpart in the
country houses of the gentry.'[6] They produced a glittering array of the
world's greatest writers, among them Jonathan Swift, Oliver Goldsmith,
Oscar Wilde, W.B. Yeats, Sean O'Casey, John Millington Synge, George
Bernard Shaw, and, more recently, Samuel Beckett. They produced
important painters in the nineteenth and early twentieth century such
as William Orpen, Paul Henry, Jack B. Yeats and Francis Bacon. They
led the country in manufacturing industries, too: international brands

Guinness, Jacob's Biscuits and Jameson Whiskey, among many others, were dominant in commercial and financing enterprises. Their decline and virtual disappearance was a loss to an independent Ireland.

Protestant disintegration had started in the late nineteenth century, when their economic strength had been fatally eroded by a series of land acts which placed the land of Protestant landlords in the hands of their tenant farmers: Ireland, therefore, quickly became a land of peasant proprietorship. Their once-strong influence at local government level was removed by the Local Government Act of 1898.

The process of their becoming an insignificant silent, even silenced, minority began in the early twentieth century. It accelerated rapidly during the years between 1919 and 1923, a period of armed rebellion and civil war. The period immediately before and after the signing of the Treaty, up to the end of the civil war, saw many Protestants come under attack when they 'felt the threat of harm and dislocation with particular acuteness.'[7] At that time the screws were turned on some of their often isolated and defenceless communities by violent nationalists. Agrarianism played an important part, with land being seized and cattle driven off. Protestant businesses were boycotted and up to 300 'big houses' owned by Protestants were burnt down. During this period, and until 1926, possibly as many as 40,000 people emigrated; Protestants who would otherwise have stayed on had there been neither violence nor the threat of violence. Statistics do not reveal the exact number of those who fled, but 'it is fair to say … that the pressure exercised on unionists … partly accounts for the striking fall in the Protestant population of the 26 counties between 1919 and 1923.'[8]

In the family documentary, *The Other Irish Travellers*, Fiona Murphy touchingly tells the story of her Church of Ireland family in Co. Mayo before and after Irish independence. Her family, termed 'planters', had lived there for hundreds of years and had been given land by the British Crown. They held much affection for the land and people. Yet Fiona Murphy asks at the beginning of the documentary,[9] 'How does a whole community know when it's time to just go away? That their faces don't fit? That they're not wanted?' She points out that, as far as they were concerned, 'you were different anyway because you were a Protestant', and goes on to claim that the exodus of the Protestant community from 1919 in large numbers 'was a polite form of ethnic cleansing'. In some cases, this was perhaps far from polite, as we will see in the early chapters of this book. The violence directed against many Protestants, the burning of their houses and their decline in numbers, will be addressed in the first three chapters in some detail.

What sort of Irish State emerged after 1921? How did this affect the dwindling Protestant minority? The violence directed against them had all but ended in 1923, except for the widespread anti-Protestant riots and assaults in 1935, but the Gaelic, Catholic, nationalist emphasis of the State and its educational system, particularly in terms of the new emphasis on teaching of history in a hibernocentric manner, left little doubt that the ex-Unionist community had become marginalised. Chapter 4 looks at the new Ireland that came into being after 1921.

As well as nationalism of a narrow nature, which isolated Protestants once loyal to the Crown, a Protestant religious affiliation saw to it that 'you were different', as Fiona Murphy asserts. If a Protestant married a Roman Catholic up to 1970, the Roman Catholic *Ne Temere* decree of 1908 seriously eroded Protestant numbers in the many mixed-religion marriages that took place. This is examined in some detail in the infamous Fethard-on-Sea incident in Chapter 5.

How do some Protestants relate to modern Ireland with its many transnational companies and its increased prosperity following membership of the European Union? How did they adapt, or fail to adapt? A series of interviews with Protestants in Chapter 6 and 7 give an account of some contemporary attitudes, including those of Protestants in the Orange Order, and chapter 8 is devoted to the failed attempt in 2000 to commemorate the founding of the Orange Order in Dublin. Finally, the Epilogue looks at some aspects of the position of Protestants in the modern Republic of Ireland post the economic collapse and much weakened position of the Catholic Church. This includes an account of the closure of six Church of Ireland churches in the centre of Dublin on Easter Day 2016 in order to accommodate parades commemorating the 1916 Rising.

1

The Protestant Exodus

What happened to the Protestant minority in the 26 counties of Ireland during the period of revolutionary violence and civil war between 1919 and 1923? We know one thing that is indisputable. There was a dramatic, unprecedented decrease in their numbers between the censuses of 1911 and 1926. Between 1891 and 1901, the Protestant population had decreased by 7.1 per cent and between 1901 and 1911 by 4.8 per cent. However, there was a 33 per cent collapse in the Protestant population of the 26 counties that became the Irish Free State between 1911 and 1926. In 1911, Protestants in these counties numbered 327,179; 10.4 per cent of the population of 3,139,688.[1] By 1926, they made up 7.4 per cent of the population, numbering 220,723, of which 164,215 were members of the Church of Ireland, 32,429 Presbyterians, 10,663 Methodists and 13,416 others. The total decline in Protestant numbers was 106,456.[2] During this period, Roman Catholic numbers remained almost static, falling by just 2.2 per cent in the island. In Northern Ireland, the combined number of Protestant denominations rose by 2 per cent.

In effect, the southern Protestant people suffered a very serious decline in numbers from 1919 to 1923. There was exceptional emigration, particularly during the civil war in 1922. 'Although no reliable figures are available the tendency is clear … unionists of all shapes and sizes were leaving the south of Ireland in 1922 because of the troubles.'[3] Also, their 'political strength and unity evaporated in the south in 1922'[4] and 'the renewed violence of Irish life completed this disintegration. It did so in three ways. It weakened Anglo-Ireland numerically. It shattered the confidence of those who remained in Ireland and undermined their determination to continue distinctive political activity. Lastly, the disorder reacted upon the provisional government's attitude to southern unionists' claims for a powerful Senate.'[5]

Research undertaken by historians has been handicapped by a lack of available data to fully explain the reasons for this sharp decline in numbers. Historians do agree on one thing: the decline was exceptional. According to Patrick Buckland:

> Some families died out but part of the decrease must have been the result of emigration. The ordinary rate of emigration must not be forgotten, but it is reasonable to assume that the quality of life for southern unionists before and after the Treaty increased the ordinary rate of emigration and accounts largely for the decline of the Protestant population.[6]

Peter Hart wrote that this was 'the only example of the mass displacement of a native ethnic group within the British Isles since the seventeenth century'.[7] Hart believes that the widespread attacks on Protestants both before and after the Anglo-Irish truce led to a major exodus and were largely, though not entirely, inspired by sectarian motives, which were 'embedded in the vocabulary and the syntax of the Irish revolution'.[8] There is no doubt that many loyalists left the 26 counties during the violence and turmoil in the period 1920–23. There was a mini refugee crisis in London. The Southern Irish Loyalists Relief Association was formed in July 1922 and had interviewed 9,400 refugees by 1928, assisting many with clothing, accommodation and loans.[9] Many were Catholic members of the RIC, which had been disbanded in 1922. This exodus was at its most dramatic between 1922 and 1923, the time of the civil war.

Kent Fedorowich wrote about this exodus:

> Equally important was the plight of the isolated and beleaguered Protestant community in the southern 26 counties whose population declined by 34 per cent between 1911 and 1926. This included 20,000 refugees who fled to the United Kingdom in 1922 to find sanctuary from continuous and sometimes violent nationalist persecution.[10]

Enda Delaney points out that 'the decline in [Protestant] numbers was a process initiated before the advent of Irish independence in 1921–22'.[11] This is true, as was the decline in the Catholic population. Between 1861 and 1911, the decline in the number of Protestants was 30.2 per cent and Catholic decline 28.5 per cent. The difference was 1.7 per cent, but given the higher growth rate in the Catholic population, it could be argued that Protestant emigration was lower than Catholic. Furthermore, the Protestant percentage of the population was much the same as it was in 1861, so comparative decline, from whatever cause, was small. Not so from 1911 to 1926. The sharp rate of decline of Protestant numbers, particularly between 1921 and 1923, is remarkable compared to previous rates of decline, as Hart points out.[12] Delaney does, however, conclude that 'at the very least over 60,000 Protestants who were not directly connected with the British administration left southern Ireland between 1911 and 1926'.[13] I would suggest that the figure is closer to 80,000, considering that the total decrease 1911–1926 was 107,000 and '… only about one fourth of this decrease can be attributed to the withdrawal of the British Army and the disbandment of the Police Forces and the emigration of their dependents.'[14] In other words, some 27,000 of the decrease of 107,000 were people in the British forces and police.

But how many Protestants left willingly and how many constituted an enforced outflow from the 26 counties? It is impossible to establish the precise number of Protestants who were the subject of an enforced outflow during this period, as statistical information is not available. Nor is it possible to know how many left for 'normal' reasons associated with seeking employment and new opportunities, as they had done for a hundred years before 1926. However, we can make a reasonably credible estimate based on the limited available statistics. It seems certain that there was an exceptional major exodus of Protestants who left for reasons associated with intimidation, fear and concern about being unwanted in the new State. Kurt Bowen points out that '… the newly dominant culture of the majority created a sense of unease and marginality among the Irish Anglicans …'[15]

Looking at the available statistical information, we know that the number of Protestants in the British Army, Navy and Royal Irish Constabulary (RIC) in 1911 in the 26 counties amounted to 21,422[16] with at most 8,000 dependents. The figure for dependents is based on the 1926 census estimate that of 100 men in the forces, 37 were dependents based on 'the known proportion for Dublin city',[17] but we have to consider that outside Dublin and other cities, the number of dependents is likely to have been lower, as numbers of eligible Protestant women were lower than in Dublin. Also, 'many [British soldiers] were married to Catholic women, with Catholic children'.[18]

Let us therefore estimate that at most 30 per cent, not 37 per cent, of the 21,422 Protestants in the armed forces were Protestant dependents, namely 6,420. We then arrive at a total of 21,422 plus 6,420, or approximately 28,000 Protestants, who left with the Forces and RIC. We can take it that some civil servants left after the Treaty. There was a total decline in Protestant civil service numbers of about 733 between 1911 and 1926. Of these perhaps 200 were born outside Ireland and returned to their countries post independence, with dependents making a total of 300. But it has to be said this is a tentative figure as no statistical information is available to inform us how many civil servants left the Free State 1922–26.

How many Protestants fell in the First World War? Some 27,400 people from the island fell, according to the Registrar General. However, the figure of about 40,000 has been put forward by Kevin Myers in his recently published book *Ireland's Great War*.[19] Sexton and O'Leary estimate that 'about one half of the total was from the counties of the Republic'.[20] Deducing that 13,700 fell from the 26 counties and that a third were 'from the minority religious communities this suggests a war deaths figure of about 5,000'.[21] I would argue, however, that this figure errs substantially on the high side. If over a third of those who fell from the 26 counties were Protestants, this is disproportionately high in relation to the 10 per cent of Protestants making up the population of the 26 counties. There is no evidence that Protestants enlisted in much greater numbers than other religious groups except in urban areas. Also, on a pro rata basis, it is likely that there were 7,200 Protestant fatalities from the island out of the 27,400 total (there were 1.16 million Protestants on the island of a total population of 4.4 million) and 66 per cent were 6 county Protestants. A figure of 2,800 southern Protestant fatalities seems realistic, and this may err on the high side. Ian d'Alton has asked in relation to the Protestants who fell: 'how many of these who served died?[22] We don't know, but applying an average fatality rate to the participation number gives a figure of some 1700.'[23] This is much lower than the figure given by Sexton and O'Leary but is probably too low in relation to the national average. Let us take a figure of 2,800.

Some 28,000 Protestants left with the British forces and administration, and at most 2,800 fell in the Great War, leaving approximately 75,000. Of this 75,000, we need to know how many were voluntary emigrants, but these statistics are not available. We know that Protestants emigrated voluntarily from 1901 to 1911, as they had done during the previous decade. There was a decrease in Church of Ireland Protestants of 7.9 per cent from 1891 to 1901 and 5.6 per cent between 1901 and 1911.[24] So we can say the Church of Ireland population decreased by an average of 6.7 per cent in these two decades and the average for other religions was similar, namely 5.9 per cent.[25] If we apply this 6.7 per cent figure to the total number of Protestants, excluding the British forces and Protestants of the RIC and Dublin Metropolitan Police, in 1911, namely 300,000, we get a decrease of 20,100. However, the intercensal period 1911–26 was a fifteen-year one, not the normal ten-year period, so account must be taken of an extra five years. The Great War accounts for four of these years when emigration figures are not available but we can state normal emigration was not possible and of those who enlisted, almost all who did not fall would have returned. Perhaps we can add 4,000 emigrants for the years 1914–18 and this is likely to be on the high side. A figure of 24,100 seems realistic for emigrants from 1911–1926.

The number of Protestants in 1911 was 327,000. Of these, some 28,000 left with the British Forces, 2,800 fell in the First World War and perhaps 300 civil servants born outside Ireland left with dependents after 1921, giving a total of 31,100. Add 24,100 who left as emigrants based on the percentage who emigrated 1891 to 1911 and this gives a total of 55,200.

We do not know how many Protestants died in the influenza epidemic of 1918–19. Based on correspondence with Ida Milne,[26] who has recently written a PhD on this subject, a total of perhaps as many as 1,400 Protestants died in this epidemic.[27] This must be a rough estimate, as Dr Milne made clear, because the religions of those who died are not given.

Lastly, the question of natural increase has been raised by various historians, most recently – and controversially – by David Fitzpatrick, who argued that 'if any campaign of "ethnic cleansing" was attempted, its demographic impact was fairly minor', and 'the inexorable decline of southern Protestantism was mainly self-inflicted'.[28] Fitzpatrick attributes the main cause of the Protestant decrease in numbers (he uses the word 'malaise') to 'low fertility and nuptiality, exacerbated by losses through mixed marriage and conversion'.[29] However, the evidence he produces does not seem to substantiate these arguments. The reports of the Irish Registrar General, 1923–27 show the marriage rate for Protestants was higher in 1920 than in 1913 and then fell rapidly.[30] His study is based on the Methodists, who were only a small section of the Protestant population. Eugenio Biagini, in his review of Fitzpatrick's book *Descendancy Review: The Decline of Irish*

Protestantism, questioned the conclusion 'that Protestant demographic decline had little to do with violence, or the threat of violence or other forms of sectarian behaviour by the Catholic majority. This may work for the Methodists, but Fitzpatrick does not convincingly establish whether their experience was representative of the Protestant community as a whole.'[31] Biagini finds Fitzpatrick's conclusions 'somewhat startling' and points out that Brian Walker, when 'working with evidence from both Anglican and "nonconformist" communities ... reach[es] different conclusions.'[32] This was also the case with R.B. McDowell,[33] Kent Fedorowich (see above), Patrick Buckland and Andrew Bielenberg, who probably underestimated the number of Protestants who were involuntary emigrants, as Biagini points out.

Fitzpatrick gives statistics that need challenging. He quotes a total of 1,953 deaths amongst Methodist members between 1911 and 1926. In the 1911 census, quoted by Fitzpatrick, there were 2,520 Methodists under the age of 9 in the 26 counties in 1911. That translates into some 3,300 to 3,500 Methodists under the age of 16 in 1911. To suggest that 3,300 young Methodists in 1911 were not sufficient on their own to keep natural change neutral or positive is hardly credible. In the words of Don:

> His infertility case seems to depend on such a migration occurring if net outward migration is not to be considered the major factor of Methodist decline. But he presents no evidence to quantify how much inward Methodist migration there was and how it might have been distributed between the five triennia. His inward migrant numbers are hidden in his 'new membership' totals, but he does not break that total down into the various sources of new membership – e.g. young Methodists graduating to full membership, immigrants, conversions from other faiths.
>
> It is unlikely that many foreign Methodists viewed Ireland as an attractive place to go and live in the 1919–23 period. If there was inward migration of Methodists during 1911–26, it is more likely to have occurred in the 1911–14 period. But such an idea might undermine Fitzpatrick's argument about emigration then being higher before the First World War than in the violent revolutionary period and with it his argument about the limited effect of violence on migration.

Similarly, we do not know what the balance was between conversions from and defections to other faiths. So, based on his own evidence, or lack of it, his plumping for infertility seems somewhat premature. It seems that most of Fitzpatrick's extra recruits were from free association with Episcopalians, and this free association does not tally with his multiplier of 20 to estimate all Protestant behaviour from the behaviour of Methodists.

The reality is that from 1920–23, there was an exodus of Church of Ireland members induced by intimidation, fear of both loss of identity and being ostracized in an independent Irish state that was Anglophobic. The United Empire Loyalists in the USA at the end of the eighteenth century were in a similar situation, many leaving to go to Canada and Britain rather than remain in an independent USA. So with many southern Irish Protestants who left for new lives in countries which shared their allegiances. The synods of the Church of Ireland in this period make this clear, as do the protests by various bishops and the *Church of Ireland Gazette*. Examples of these statements and concern will be given in the next chapter.[34]

Protestant civilian decline, the sum of emigration and natural decline, was 6.5 per cent between 1901 and 1911. As emigration was not negative in this period, natural decline was in the order of 5 per 1,000 or less. So for natural decline to be the major reason for the decline of Protestants between 1911 and 1926, it would have had to jump from its usual 5 per 1,000 to 14 per 1,000 per annum. From 1936 to 1971, the natural decline was between 5.5 and 3.3 per 1,000. So if fertility was the main issue between 1911 and 1926, birth rates would have had to decrease to around a quarter of their usual level from 12 to 13 to 3 or 4 per 1,000 per annum. This is highly unlikely. Even if they had, this could not have led so quickly to such a large natural decrease. Also, Kurt Bowen points out that the decline in Anglican numbers post-1926 'was largely due to emigration' and that their fertility rate was not low compared to European countries and America' in 1946, when comparative figures became available.[35]

In her study of Protestants in Killala and Achonry, Miriam Moffitt concluded that 'emigration was the principal cause of population decline in the years after 1922'.[36] There is no evidence that this was not the case in the rest of the 26 counties. This was followed by a 'lower or later rate of marriage and secondly a growing prevalence of mixed marriages, where the offspring were generally brought up outside the Church of Ireland.'[37] This was 'the national Protestant norm' after 1922.[38] Before 1922, low fertility was not the major cause of natural decrease.

Andrew Bielenberg argues that marriage rates among Protestants 'had fully recovered after the First World War, slightly exceeding the levels achieved in 1911–12.'[39] He concludes that Protestant marriage rates fell sharply in 1922 in the non-garrison counties due to an increase in Protestant emigration during the 'period of the nationalist revolution'.[40] It seems, therefore, that the exceptional decline in Protestant numbers was caused by emigration rather than the effects of lower nuptuality and fertility, which decreased after 1921. David Fitzpatrick's Methodist figures show Methodist decline tracking emigration very closely throughout each triennium between 1911 and 1926.

Bielenberg quoted 'a huge drop in the number of Protestant accountants' countrywide. This had little to do with economic decline or even political change. In 1911 all sorts of book keepers and other clerical staff described themselves as accountants. In 1926, only Chartered Accountants could describe themselves as accountants. Net result was a huge drop in the number of accountants of all religions. Accountancy was one of the very few, maybe the only profession, where the percentage drop in Catholics was greater than that of Protestants. Furthermore, Bielenberg argues that 'permanent emigration was not higher than normal between 1911 and 1920'. But what was 'normal'? It would surely be logical to assume he meant emigration of the imme-diately preceding years – i.e. 1901–11. But then he estimates 'normal/ economic' emigration for the entire 1911–26 period as being at the same rate or above 1926–36 rates. That is arguably illogical. To calculate the number who can be accounted for by economic or voluntary emigration, he uses a figure of their emigration in the next period, rather than reflecting what happened in the earlier period, as emigration of Protestants 1926–36 would have been lower as we know Protestant numbers had declined sharply by 1926.

Sexton and O'Leary estimate that the natural decrease of Protestants between 1911 and 1926 was 10,000. But this figure is based on the natural decrease of 'the minority communities in 1926–36 and 1936–46'.[41] There is no data 'on age structure of the population by religious denomination … until 1926' and Delaney thinks the estimate of Sexton and O'Leary 'appears quite high'.[42] The natural decrease from 1926 to 1946 is likely to have been quite high compared to that between 1911 and 1926, as Protestants were fewer in numbers and nuptiality was lower. Let us then take a high figure of 8,000 natural decrease instead.

To sum up:

Protestants who left with the British forces and RIC including dependents according to the 1926 census	28,000
Estimate of Protestants who fell in the First World War	2,800
Estimate of decrease in Protestant numbers due to emigration 1911–1926	24,100
Estimate of Protestants who died in the influenza epidemic post First World War	1,400
Estimate of Protestant public servants who left at the end of the union with Britain 1921	300
Estimate of natural decrease in Protestant numbers 1911–26	8,000
Total	64,600

As mentioned, the total decline in Protestant numbers between 1911 and 1926 was 106,456, so subtracting the above total of 64,600 generates a figure of 41,856 Protestants who were exceptional emigrants between 1911 and 1926. As I have indicated, this estimate is based on limited, insufficient figures. Delaney points out, '… establishing a direct causal link between sectarian intimidation or harassment and migration is problematic.'[43] What we can say is that without doubt there was a sharp and exceptional exodus of Protestants between 1911 and 1926, some of which was caused by intimidation, some by apprehension following the end of the union and some due to Protestants concerned about their future in the new Catholic, Anglophobic Free State.

When the 1926 census is released, it will be possible to formulate a more accurate picture of the identity of the Protestants who left. The subject has become highly controversial, but there seems little doubt that some 20,000 people fled to the United Kingdom after 1921, as stated by Kent Fedorowich, and most of these were southern Protestants, as well as RIC-disbanded men with their families. Reports from Church of Ireland synods, 1920–23, Brian Walker has recorded, unequivocally show that violence or threat of violence was a major factor in the large outflow of Church of Ireland people at this time.[44] There are some historians who are not persuaded that there was a major, exceptional involuntary exodus of Protestants between 1911 and 1926, but it does seem that the evidence is sufficiently overwhelming. Dr Bielenberg argues that the flight was largely for economic reasons, but does not take into account the lack of a corresponding exodus among Catholics for economic reasons.[45] There certainly was Catholic emigration in this period, turning a substantial natural increase into a decline. But the various professions that Dr Bielenberg quotes for Protestant decline nearly all show an increase in Catholic numbers. In the words of Don Wood, 'Between 1911 and 1926 Catholic emigration was at an historic low and Protestant emigration was at an historic high. How might economic factors drive out Protestants rather than Catholics, particularly when Protestants were in general better equipped to ride out a harsh economy.'[46]

In Dublin city and suburbs, the Protestant population fell by 31.3 per cent in 1911–26, by 50 per cent in Cork city, by 50 per cent in Limerick and 45 per cent in Waterford. In 62 towns with populations of between 1,500 and 5,000 inhabitants, there was a decrease of 47 per cent.[47] Some of these decreases were, however, largely accounted for by the departure of the armed forces, particularly in Dublin and Cork and to a lesser extent in Limerick and Waterford. In many other counties where there was no British Army presence, though, there was still a significant drop in the Protestant population.

It is unclear where these Protestants went. In the new border counties of Donegal, Monaghan and Cavan, there was an expectation that a significant number of Protestants would go to Northern Ireland. The Rt Revd Dr Moore, Bishop of Kilmore diocese, in his address to the Diocesan Synod in July 1923, referred to the previous twelve months, when 'one of the saddest features of the situation is that so many of our communion have been driven from the country'.[48] Moore did not say where they had gone. His Cavan/Roscommon diocese bordered on Co. Fermanagh, yet the Church of Ireland population also declined slightly between 1911 and 1926 in the latter county.[49] In the border counties of Tyrone and Derry, the Protestant population also declined.[50] However, Protestant farmers from the south did buy up land in Fermanagh between 1920 and 1925.[51] In Northern Ireland as a whole, the 1926 census 'estimated that roughly 24,000 immigrants from the Irish Free State had taken up residence in the preceding fifteen years'.[52] The majority of these immigrants were registered as members of the Church of Ireland, 'with east Ulster accounting for the largest share of the settlement.'[53] Most went to Belfast where employment opportunities were reasonable. It seems that of the others, most went to England.

This exodus took place sometime after 'Westminster statutes knocked Protestants off their public pedestals', in the colourful words of David Fitzpatrick.[54] However, it should be noted that most rural Protestants lived simple lives, owning small farms, while in urban areas they were shop-keepers, solicitors, bank officials and clerks. By 1920, Protestant landlords had sold most of their lands to their tenants under the 1903 Wyndham Land Act. The Reform Act of 1884 had 'placed electoral power in most constituencies in the hands of the small farmers and labourers ... In 1898 the gentry lost control of county government. The Local Government Act of that year ... transferred local administration from grand juries, landed oligarchies to elected county, urban and rural councils'.[55] Protestants had, in effect, lost political power and the economic power that goes with the ownership of large estates, though they remained strong in the financial, business, industrial and legal sectors. As an editorial in *The Irish Times* put it when the 1926 census was published:

> Although the Protestant population of the Free State constitutes only seven and a half percent of the whole, its social and economic status is most important ... they form 38 per cent of the barristers, 37 per cent of the solicitors ... of the higher bank officials, 53 per cent are Protestants. They are represented strongly also in insurance, brewing, shipping and virtually all the commercial trades.[56]

Fergus Campbell has made it clear that there was no major greening at the top levels of the civil service before 1922. He notes that over a third of 'the senior membership' was Catholic in 1911 and that no 'systematic "greening" process was underway'.[57] In the RIC, only 9 per cent of 'the senior police officers'[58] were Catholics in 1911.

It was a period of guerrilla warfare, followed by civil war character-ised by 'ethnic violence' and 'terrorism, communal conflict, displaced people, assassins, gunmen, and gun-runners'.[59] It was a period of change and turmoil in which the small Protestant community in southern Ireland, largely supportive of the British connection, found itself increasingly isolated and undefended. It was a crisis; a funda-mental turning point at which those who chose to stay on tended to withdraw into the comforts of their own world, mindful of earning the goodwill of their huge Catholic majority neighbours.

Many Protestants went because they felt unwanted and estranged in the new Ireland. Lloyd George wrote to Andrew Bonar Law about the position in which Protestants found themselves in 1918: 'the little Protestant community of the south, isolated in a turbulent sea of Sinn Féinism and popery'.[60] While there was no policy of ethnic cleansing

by the Free State government, Peter Hart and Gerard Murphy
have concluded that, at least in Co. Cork, a substantial number of
Protestants were targeted and murdered by the IRA in what can only
be considered sectarian murders. Hart has written at length about a
mini pogrom of small farmers, ordinary businessmen and a Church of
Ireland clergyman, who were targeted in the Bandon Valley in April
1922.[61] He is clear about the motivation:

> The atmosphere of fear and polarization provided the communal
> context of the massacre. One could not have taken place without the
> other. Protestants had become 'fair game' because they were seen as
> outsiders and enemies. Not just by the IRA but by a large segment
> of the Catholic population as well … Their [Protestants'] status was
> codified in the political language – or mythology – of the day in
> terms such as landlord, land grabber, loyalist, imperialist, Orangeman,
> Freemason, Free Stater, spy, and informer.[62]

Southern Protestants were almost all loyalists, opposed to separation and
anxious to be part of the multi-national, multi-racial two islands with
representative government based in London. But they were a tiny minority.
When religion was part of social status, land holdings and a willingness to
serve in the British forces, this encouraged ethnically directed violence,
particularly after the Treaty and during the civil war, leading to an exodus.

Sexton and O'Leary point out in *Building Trust in Ireland* that: 'There
can be little doubt that the main causation underlying this exodus
was a sense of apprehension in certain of these communities associated with the transition to national independence in 1922 and the
upheavals which attended the event.'[63]

Diarmaid Ferriter goes on to suggest that sectarianism played an
influential role in the behaviour of the IRA:

> Sectarianism too played its part and there was no shortage of abusive
> political language to identify enemies ('land grabber', 'loyalist', 'impe-
> rialist', 'Orangeman', 'Freemason') and assert the need for their killing.
> In the same manner, labeling one an informer could in fact cover a
> multitude of sins, agrarian and domestic included.[64]

The editorial in the *Church of Ireland Gazette* reported on 9 September
1921 that, according to a rector from an urban area in the West, his

congregation had been reduced by half. Another clergyman expressed 'little hope that this exodus will be stopped and less that those who have gone will return'. It was a 'most grave matter' for finances and there was a 'large breakdown in parochial finance in many dioceses, consequent on the exodus of the people.'[65]

The *Gazette* reported on 7 October 1921 that the Church of Ireland congregations were 'vanishing' and that:

> Over a large part of the country the already sparse congregations are being reduced to vanishing point – memories of the "terror" have burnt very deep – anyone who knows Southern Ireland knows also *the undercurrent of feeling urging the elimination of Protestantism* [my italics]… the fact remains that a migration of younger clergy has begun.

So young clergy, the lifeblood of the Church of Ireland, were protesting with their feet in some dioceses. In 1920, there were 911 clergy in the Church of Ireland in the 26 counties, excluding the diocese of Clogher, which contained parts of Donegal, Monaghan and Louth, but by 1930 the number had reduced by almost a third, to 647.[66]

The violence directed against the Protestants in some parts of the South between 1919 and the Truce of July 1921 was largely the by-product of the guerrilla war between the IRA and the British Army and the Royal Irish Constabulary, augmented in 1920 by the RIC Special Reserve (RICSR) and the Auxiliary Division RIC (ADRIC). After the Treaty, however, violence against the minority increased following the withdrawal of the Crown forces and the disbandment of the RIC. A breakdown of law and order quickly followed with the outbreak of civil war, leading both Catholics and Protestants to flee.

The situation became so serious that the Archbishop of Dublin, Dr Gregg, accompanied by the Bishop of Cashel, Dr Miller, and a leading Protestant businessman, Sir William Goulding, went to see Michael Collins in May 1922, following the murders of thirteen Protestants in the Bandon valley, to ask whether the Protestant minority should stay on. Collins 'assured them that the government would maintain civil and religious liberty'.[67] However, Collins was in no position to protect Protestants and was shortly afterwards killed in an ambush near Bandon. Dr Miller's dioceses in south Tipperary had suffered by then but in north Tipperary, the Bishop of Killaloe 'had warned in the summer of 1921 that the Church of Ireland population of his diocese had slumped to 5,876 – down by two-thirds from its Victorian heyday and a decline the Bishop described as "almost staggering"'.[68]

As far as sectarian motive was a factor in this decline, the historian Richard English has pointed out in *Irish Freedom*:

> If Catholic Ireland defined itself as the nation, then historically the process had also worked the other way, as Protestant Britain had effectively defined itself in exclusive ways too. Thus it was that the 1919–21 IRA (and their enemies) on occasions exhibited an ugly sectarianism of word and deed.[69]

Apart from sectarianism, land hunger was a powerful motivation for violence and intimidation of Protestant 'planters' in the period 1921–23. By 1921, much land had been transferred from landlords to tenants, thanks to legislation from Westminster. Various land acts since 1885 had made it possible for tenants to purchase land, the price being fixed on a number of rental years. In total, almost 2.5 million acres were sold under the land acts from 1881 to 1896, for which landowners received almost £24 million.[70] However, 'it was not until the passage of the Wyndham Land Act of 1903 that a revolutionary transfer of landownership began'.[71] Dooley, however, makes it clear that:

> While the Land Acts of 1903 and 1909 had made a major contribution to the transfer of land from landlords to tenants they did not end landlordism in Ireland. Prior to the enactment of the 1923 Land Act, there were approximately 114,000 holdings on three million acres that had not been sold.[72]

Marianne Elliott points out that the safety valve of emigration had been closed during the First World War, leading to young men being landless, and some resorted to burning out Protestant landowners:

> Given the land hunger, the resentment of Protestant privilege, and the unusual numbers of impoverished young males in the country because the First World War had closed off emigration, it would have been surprising had sectarianism not been an element in the burning of almost 300 'big houses'. Expectations raised by the Land Acts had not been satisfied.[73]

However, a number of 'big houses' were burnt for reasons not in any way associated with land hunger, but instead as retaliation for Black and Tan house burnings, theft of contents and for military reasons to prevent occupation by British forces. A separate chapter will examine the 'big house' burnings.

The question of compensation for those who fled, lost property or land and suffered malicious injury soon became a dominant issue. Initially, a voluntary body, the Irish Registration Bureau in London, offered to help refugees with accommodation and with prosecuting claims for compensation. It reported in May 1922 that: 'the list of the poorer people who have had to fly is very bad, as they have arrived in London without means of subsistence and are dependent on the charity of friends. A number of these refugees have come together and formed a committee.'[74]

The British Government eventually accepted that it had to come to the rescue of the refugees. The Irish Distress Committee, an official body, was formed in May 1922 to deal with the 20,000 or so people who arrived in London in the spring of 1922, who were given refugee status. These people were largely made up of disbanded members of the RIC, British ex-servicemen and civilians loyal to the British regime in Ireland. Sir Samuel Hoare was the first chairman, followed by Lord Eustace Percy, and in March 1923 it was reconstituted as the Irish Grants Committee (IGC). In the first six months it received 3,349 applications. By November 1922, 598 Protestants and 1,063 Roman Catholics had been helped with loans and grants. By 1923, 4,330 applications were approved for loans and grants and advances 'amounting to £52,000 on compensation decrees and on arrears of rent'.[75] The second interim report of the IGC for 1923 declared that £11 million in grants had been supplied to refugees and £7.8 million loans advanced. The IGC reported that it had 'in this way resettled a considerable number of refugees in this country and have been able to arrange for the emigration of others to the Dominions'.[76]

An advocacy body, the Southern Irish Loyalists' Relief Association (SILRA) helped with information and recommended cases for compensation. This Association was very active from 1922, with Lord Linlithgow as chairman with the support of many conservative MPs. Major White was the secretary, thorough and sympathetic, with a network of informants in Ireland. The files of the Irish Grants Committee make it clear that Major White referred many cases to them for compensation.

Another advocacy body was the London-based Irish Compensation Claims Association (ICCA), representing loyalists who felt that they had been hard done by, and it was quick to point out that much more was needed. Robert Sanders, from the Glen of Aherlow in Co. Tipperary, was chairman and another Tipperary man, Lord Dunalley, whose mansion was burnt in 1922, was an active lobbyist.

Under the heads of working arrangements agreed on 24 January 1922, the British and Provisional governments agreed that each would be responsible for payment of compensation to its own supporters and that awards already given should stand. As for damage to property, 'in the pre-Truce period each side was to pay for the losses it had inflicted.'[77] Awards made by county councils prior to the Truce under the Criminal and Malicious Injuries Acts which had not been paid or defended, were to be suspended, and a new commission was established with three members: one from the Free State, Senator J.C. Dowdall; one from England, C.H.J. Thomas from the Inland Revenue; and Lord Shaw, the chairman, a lawyer from Scotland, agreed by both governments.

The commission was to consider claims for damages from 1 January 1919 to 11 July 1921. However, as time went on, many claims were made for post-Truce compensation for damages to property and for personal injuries. The Free State government enacted the Damage to Property (Compensation) Act in 1923 to deal with such claims. All unpaid awards under undefended decrees between 21 January 1919 and 11 July 1921 were annulled. 'Injuries committed after the 11th July 1921 on which a decree had been made prior to the passing of the act were to be re-opened and re-heard on the application of the applicant or the minister of Finance.'[78]

Significantly, compensation did not cover consequential losses, theft of money, jewellery and furniture 'if it could be proved they had not been taken by the members of an unlawful association'.[79] In effect, this referred to the Irregulars in the civil war and, as Terrence Dooley has pointed out, because of 'the amount of looting that took place by locals who … more often than not belonged to no such association, big house owners were to be hard pressed to prove the legitimacy of their claims.' Lord Dunalley's original claim was for £100,000 but his 'claim for compensation for the loss of contents was dismissed by the county court judge in May 1924'[80] because he could not prove that property was stolen by the Irregulars.[81] Dunalley's mansion was situated in Dolla, Co. Tipperary, and his solicitors thought goods were stolen 'by the "mountainy" people [locals around the Silvermines area] after the burning' of his mansion in August 1922.[82]

R.B. McDowell tells us that:

> The workings of the Shaw Commission, the land act of 1923 and the Damage to Property (Compensation) Act, 1923, left loyalists in the 26 counties disappointed and with a strong sense they had been badly treated. Acting 'under the mantle' of the Shaw Commission the sub-commissioners had reduced the judges' awards on average by 40 per cent.[83]

The ICCA objected to the Damage to Property (Compensation) Act as, under its terms, no compensation was allowed for personal injuries.

Compensation for damage to buildings was to be based on full or partial reinstatement. Full reinstatement meant the restoration of the old building as it stood before, while partial reinstatement was awarded for building a smaller house on the same site or anywhere in the Free State. The judge had power to award a further sum to defray architectural and legal expenses. Some owners of big houses, fearing they might be attacked again, chose to build new houses far from their old ones, moving to Dublin and Wicklow. Terrence Dooley took a random sample of 50 big houses throughout the 26 counties and concluded that awards came to only 26 per cent of the claims made.[84] There was little or no compensation for the valuable furniture, silver and pictures often stolen and which found their way into small houses in the neighbourhood of the burnt mansions.

In Dublin, the Shaw Commission worked in Ely Place, but when Sir Samuel Hoare visited Dublin in September 1922, he was 'shocked by how slowly the Commission was working' and urged that 'it should immediately revise its methods and increase its staff'.[85] Shaw resigned in November and Sir Alexander Wood-Renton, a prominent lawyer, replaced him. The work was soon undertaken with much more effect, two valuators being appointed for each of the 26 counties 'to assess claims, with claimants having the right to appeal to the commissioners.'[86]

There was much criticism of the reduced awards made by the ICCA. In July 1924, Edward Carson dramatically said in the House of Lords: 'Commission's inspectors … used the most tyrannical methods towards claimants to come to an agreement out of court.' On the restitution awards it meant:

You, sir, have been driven out of Ireland, your house and your furniture has been burned; you have probably been shot; your wife and family have been in danger, but you must go back and rebuild your house and live among the people who drove you out.[87]

The Shaw Commission wound up its activities in February 1926, when Wood-Renton wrote to President Cosgrave, advising that he was returning to London and thanking him 'for the courtesy and assistance that have been extended to us during the whole period of our work by the Free State Government and its officers'.[88] Cosgrave acknowledged this letter on 24 March, stating that he 'was fully sensible of the tact, resource and hard work demanded by your own especially difficult position as Chairman'.[89]

There were awards made in 17,792 cases, of which 22,682 were not 'within the ambit of the Commission',[90] and £7,048,332 was paid out of £19,107,281 claimed.[91] The sum of £7 million was considerably lower than the budgeted amount of £10.3 million mentioned by the Minister for Finance in the Dáil in April 1925. He then estimated the British Government was due to pay £3.6 million of the total £10.3 million to cover damage inflicted by Crown forces from 1919 to the Treaty on 11 July 1921. In addition to this amount, in August 1924 it was controversially agreed that the British Government would pay £900,000 for claims from 1919–22. Lord Danesfort raised this in the House of Lords in June 1925, saying that it had not been sanctioned by the House of Commons and was in breach of the terms agreed by heads of government in 1922. Carson thought the reason behind the agreement was that the Free State had informed 'the British Government that they could never prevent a republic unless more money was given away to recompense men who used the property that was destroyed in Ireland to murder British troops and police'.[92]

David Fitzpatrick paints a different picture. Writing about the sack of Balbriggan in September 1920, he condemns the reprisals of the RIC, Black and Tans and Auxiliaries when they went on a rampage, destroying properties of suspected Sinn Féin supporters in the town:

Episodes such as Balbriggan undermined Britain's credentials as a liberal democracy, negated the gains from decades of reconciliation and reform, persuaded nationalist doubters and many former unionists

that Irish terrorists were less arbitrary and malign than the forces of the
Crown, and conferred moral legitimacy on the emerging republic.[93]

One wonders who Fitzpatrick had in mind when including 'many
former unionists who post-Balbriggan thought Irish terrorists were
less arbitrary and malign than forces of the Crown'? The IRA had
killed 66 members of the RIC by September 1920, wounded 79 and
destroyed 351 barracks and 33 courthouses. The behaviour of the
Crown forces between 1919 and 1921 was perhaps often 'arbitrary
and malign', but it was the IRA who took the guerrilla war to the
RIC and the British response of maintaining law and order through
the RIC, the RIC Special Reserve sent to bolster the regular RIC,
and the demonised Auxiliaries became inevitable. Attempts at 'reconciliation and reform' had not brought peaceful negotiations post-1918
for a settlement. The RIC, their families and friends became the main
target. The subject is controversial, but Fitzpatrick's interpretation is
perhaps questionable. Southern unionists were under siege by the IRA
in many parts of the country by September 1920 and most would have
wished for the suppression of the IRA. The evidence for their malign
treatment is to be found in the files of the Irish Grants Committee and,
to some extent, in the Shaw-Renton awards.

Some records of the Shaw-Renton Commission have been destroyed,
though there is a possibility that there are copies in the National
Archives in London.[94] However, a substantial number of awards were
regularly published in *Iris Oifigiúl*, the *Dublin Gazette*. Many were very
small. But it seems that the large amounts were paid for by Westminster
covering the burning of Cork, the sacking of Balbriggan and Granard.[95]

The IGC in London in its second report recommended that
further and larger compensation should be given to people who had
fled from Ireland and did not wish to return, even though peace had
been restored with the ending of the civil war. There was 'a need for
more permanent compensation, which had not been satisfactorily
provided for under the Free State's Damage to Property Act, the Shaw
Commission and land act of 1923'.[96]

Both lobbying groups, the ICCA and SILRA, brought the British
Government's attention to the inadequate compensation paid to
loyalists by the Free State. They forcibly argued that most, if not all
claims were substantially reduced by the Shaw-Renton Commission.
Carson gave details to the House of Lords of some hardship cases

and Northumberland, the chairman of SILRA, informed Amery, the Colonial Secretary, that much more had to be done. Amery was initially reluctant to act but he was eventually prevailed on by Salisbury and appointed a committee to look into what might be done. The chairman, Lord Dunedin, recommended that loyalists who had supported the British in the period before the Truce 'should be compensated for the hardships they had endured "beyond the inevitable dislocation" resulting from the change of regime'.[97]

Thus the British Government eventually accepted responsibility for the losses suffered by its supporters who had received inadequate compensation from the fledgling Irish State. The Irish Grants Committee was formed in 1925 and first met in January 1926 under the chairmanship of Wood-Renton, who had gained experience of Irish cases in Dublin when acting as chairman of the Compensation (Ireland) Commission. The terms of reference laid emphasis on loyalists in the 26 counties who suffered hardship or loss between 11 July 1921 and 12 May 1923. The names of two people were required for reference purposes (Bank Managers, Solicitors, Ministers of Religion).[98] Major Reid Jamieson acted as secretary. He wrote thorough reports and recommendations for the attention of the committee, being fair and often demanding more information from referees and back-up material from claimants where detailed accounts were required..

Jamieson's reports were generally supportive and generous in their recommendations for claimants but he was quick to dismiss excessive claims not supported by accounts or reports from valuers. In cases where there was contention or doubt, the claimant was invited to an oral hearing, generally with his or her solicitor. Major White of SILRA was often called on to comment on claims that had been sent to him before the IGC started and his network of Irish informants in Ireland proved useful. Details of any awards made by decrees in Irish courts or by the Shaw Commission had to be given, and often claimants asked for compensation for inadequate awards made by the Irish courts, the Shaw Commission and indeed the Land Commission. Land sold in Co. Tipperary at a loss to the Land Commission was often referred to the IGC.

Dunedin had made it clear in his report that 'all claimants under the new committee must be able to prove that they had first explored all possible avenues under the 1923 act'.[99] In many cases, claimants from Co. Tipperary had looked to the Shaw Commission for compensation. However, they became aware that the new Damage to Property Act gave less compensation than was available in Ireland under the old acts before the Treaty and that the IGC tended to look sympathetically at consequential losses and looting where the claimant could not prove that the culprits were Irregulars. Furthermore, *ex gratia* payments were not permitted by the Shaw Commission, unlike the IGC, which paid a number of these to Tipperary claimants.

Initially, compensation was limited in full for awards up to £250 and 50 per cent on awards 'between £250 and £1,000 and 30 per cent on awards above £1,000.'[100] This was 'the policy taken up by Lord Sumner's commission for sufferers from air-raids during the Great War.'[101] SILRA protested, pointing out that 'much of the suffering had been caused by the British Government's swift withdrawal of the army and police, "leaving the countryside at the mercy of rough bands".'[102] Eventually, following further lobbying by some peers and MPs, including Howard-Bury, an MP from Tullamore, the government gave way in February 1927, fearful of defeat. Amery announced that payment in full would be made on all recommendations. A limit of £400,000 was agreed in December 1927. When the IGC finished its work in March 1930, its awards amounted to £2,188,549. However, in the words of Sir William Davison, Conservative MP for Kensington, it was a matter of 'a debt of honour … recognised by successive governments of all parties in this country for years past.'[103]

The IGC processed 4,032 cases between October 1926 and November 1930. Most came from Cork, Tipperary and Clare. Of these, 2,237 were compensated, 895 were deemed outside its scope, 840 were given an oral hearing, and 900 were refused. A wide range of cases was considered, including claims from landlords, shopkeepers, farmers, disbanded RIC men and their dependents, ex-servicemen, shopkeepers, business people and some Church of Ireland clergy. In many cases money was paid in advance. It is not possible to know how many of those compensated stayed on in the Free State to build new lives but, from reading a cross-section of some 400 files, it seems a quite small minority left. The main outflow occurred in the spring and summer of 1922, as mentioned, when the Irish Distress Committee came into being to help Irish refugees and other victims of violence and intimidation.

In the following chapter, a cross-section of IGC claims will be looked at throughout the 26 counties, with particular emphasis on County Tipperary, during this period of turmoil, intimidation and often brutal attacks on the Protestant community.

2

Personal Stories: 1919 to 1923

There is a growing awareness among Irish historians that many Protestants left the 26 counties as involuntary emigrants between 1920 and 1923. My estimate is some 40,000, as detailed in the previous chapter. The files of the Irish Grants Committee, the applications for financial assistance sent to SILRA and cases submitted to the Shaw-Renton Commission in Dublin in the 1920s show the real terror expressed by many Protestants. These reports detail widespread attacks on southern Protestants. While targeting southern Protestants was never government policy, claims by the IRA that they were non-sectarian appear to have been a fig leaf to cover complacency. Peter Hart has suggested that there was a sectarian thread running through the harassment and murders of Protestants. Had the IRA been non-sectarian, might it not have dealt with their sectarian-motivated members who killed thirteen Protestants in the Bandon valley in 1922? Might not the Free State have been more generous to those Protestants who applied for compensation to the Shaw-Renton Commission, as highlighted in the previous chapter by Terence Dooley? Indeed it is likely that the weakening of the unionists in the south was a motivating factor for advanced nationalist Catholics during much of the nineteenth and early twentieth centuries. As we have seen, these centuries saw a major exodus of Protestants, who increasingly felt homeless. Today they form a tiny, quiet minority: a former people.

In the context of the period between 1916 and 1924, Irish Protestants, with few exceptions, were seen by many nationalists to be the embodiment of the English in Ireland. They were its supporters, who had played a major part in building the Empire with their Catholic fellow countrymen, staunch supporters of the Crown, enemies of romantic Catholic nationalism, and upholders of the Reformation with its emphasis on individualism.

Irish Protestants were subjected to widespread attacks and persecution, from Cork to Sligo to Monaghan, led by local IRA battalions and commandants. It is clear that these Protestants, who saw themselves as Irish – as Irish as Theobald Tone and Davis and Mitchel – had come to be regarded as a foreign race to be harassed, boycotted and even murdered in many parts of the country. Charles Townshend argues when writing about the republicanism espoused by such national icons as Irish Protestants Theobald Wolfe Tone and Thomas Davis:

> Though the rhetoric of Irish republicanism was (and remains), secular, yet the actual behaviour of the IRA in 1919–23 was fairly nakedly sectarian … Thus the War of Independence was to some extent a religious civil war … Even if we do not go the full distance with Peter Hart in characterising the IRA campaign as systematic persecution and massacre, it is clear that the automatic identification of Protestants as actual or potential enemies of the republic had repeatedly deadly results … It was inevitable that the revolution would generate a settlement in which, in Fitzpatrick's words, 'the victors self-consciously embodied the religion as well as the political ideology of the majority'; in the Free State 'the new rulers blatantly identified Catholic with national values' … It may indeed be that the central function of the Irish revolution was to give political embodiment to the 'devotional revolution' of the nineteenth century.[1]

In order to survive, Protestants needed to keep quiet during the War of Independence; the penalty for giving information to the British and RIC security forces could be – and was – execution by the IRA, as happened to Mrs Mary Lindsay in 1921, and James Clark, her Protestant chauffeur, from Broadstreet, Cork. This story is well known to historians. Mrs Lindsay overheard a conversation about an IRA conspiracy to ambush British troops. To prevent lives being lost, she alerted the British Army, but she also entered into an agreement with Father Shinnick, a local priest, who soon told the IRA that the British forces had been alerted about their planned ambush. However, the local IRA commander ignored this, the ambush went ahead, a member of the IRA was shot, while others were captured and put on trial. Mrs Lindsay and James Clark were captured and held as hostages. Following the execution of some of the IRA insurgents, both were shot and Mrs Lindsay's house was burnt. Their bodies have never been found. Her chauffeur had had nothing to do with the plot and Peter Hart suggests that 'his death was purely revenge', as he was an Ulster Protestant.[2]

What is revealing is that Fr Shinnick was spared, though he was 'virulently anti-republican'. Mrs Lindsay and James Clark 'were more vulnerable because they were outsiders'. As Wall rightly makes clear, these vulnerable outsiders, 'ex-soldiers and retired RIC men formed a large proportion of those accused of "informing" ... Tramps and vagrants were also vulnerable, as were Redmondites and Hibernians who remained politically active'.[3]

There was a widespread 'sense of insecurity of life and property' and 'with the Anglo-Irish war none could consider themselves safe'.[4] The case of the de Burgh family of Drumkeen, Co. Limerick is typical of the treatment suffered by some Irish Protestant landowners. The de Burghs were driven out in 1924 and found a new, fulfilling life in Canada on Prevost Island off the coast of British Columbia. I use this case as it is well documented and their descendants have given me the historical background; also because their suffering and intimidation covered both pre-Treaty and post-Treaty periods.

The family was descended from Anglo-Norman stock, who had acquired land in 1420 in Dromkeen, Co. Limerick, when John de Burgh of Shrule defeated The O'Brien and married his sister. By 1920, they had only 230 acres, on which there were two fairly large houses and some farm buildings. No doubt their once considerably larger landholding had been reduced by various land acts, especially the Wyndham Act of 1903. The owner in 1920 was John Digby Hussey de Burgh; his eldest son, Ulick, born in 1900, was an Officer Cadet at the Royal Military Academy at Sandhurst.

In September 1920, some fifty armed IRA men came to find Ulick. However, as he was in Sandhurst at the time, the men missed him. In Digby's own words in the application he made to the Irish Grants Committee:

> Immediately afterwards your Suppliant applied to Your Majesty's police officer at Pallas Green, Co. Limerick, who was in charge of the district in which Drumkeen is situated for protection and offered to defend himself and the said premises if he were given either two soldiers or policemen to assist him. The police officer said he could not give protection or

even the two soldiers or policemen and advised your Suppliant to leave Drumkeen and take his family away. About the same time your Suppliant got a letter threatening to shoot him if he did not clear out immediately and accordingly he left Drumkeen on or about 24th September 1920.

By reason of the failure of Your Majesty's forces to give your Suppliant any protection, his losses were greatly increased by a conspiracy which had been developing to seize all your Suppliant's property and said conspiracy was in progress during 1921 and until the events hereinafter mentioned.

Your Suppliant with his wife returned to Drumkeen in February 1922 but he had been disarmed along with all other Irish Loyalists by orders of your Majesty's Government and could only get one revolver for which the Irish Government refused him a licence [the Irish Free State came into being in December 1921 which no doubt motivated de Burgh to return to clear up his affairs]. During the Spring of 1922 an attempt was made to seize your Suppliant's lands but your Suppliant managed to keep possession. The conspiracy to take your Suppliant's land was actively supported by one Clancy a member of Dáil Éireann. When your Suppliant sold part of his lands in April 1924, armed men threatened to murder the purchaser and he was prevented from completing the purchase. On your Suppliant complaining to the police at Pallas Green, they promised to guard him but in fact gave no protection. On the morning of 10th April 1924 your Suppliant's house at South Dromkeen was set on fire in two different places and the stables were also set on fire. The damage done on this occasion by the fires was proved to be £1,600 in addition to which £500 worth of property was looted and on your Suppliant applying to the Irish Courts for compensation the Judge there refused to hear the evidence as to the damage and in view of the Damage to Property Compensation (Ireland) Act 1923 only allowed the Suppliant the sum of £750.[5]

On 5 September 1924, the IRA returned. Hubert, Digby's second son, then aged 17, described what happened in an account kept by his granddaughter, Susan de Burgh in British Columbia, Canada:

Dad was fixing the fence in front of the house across the ditch. He had a hammer, staples and nails in a can … a loaded .45 Colt in one pocket of his coat, extra bullets in the other. James McCarthy had left to go to the farmyard for tea. The dogs had barked but he did not see anyone.

As he got to the monkey tree near the corner of the house, two men rushed at him, one behind the other.

Tim O'Donnell shouted – give up the gun. Dad just got his hand in the pocket of his coat and pressed it against O'Donnell and pulled the trigger. At that moment, a man standing to the South on the lawn fired at Dad and hit him across the chest. Dad fired at him but missed. The man behind O'Donnell did nothing. Dad ran to the garden gate, the laurel trees gave him cover. When about twenty feet inside the gate he was hit twice in the left arm, flesh wounds. He fired again and hit a man named Troy in the hand. He then ran across the top of the garden and out into the orchard field. He was almost down to the sunken ditch when he heard a shot. Turning round, he saw Ryan standing about 60 yards away, trying to work his gun … Dad fired and knocked him cold. That was the last shot. He left his white hat on the top of the ditch for them to fire at. He walked along under cover till he got to Philip Berkery's farm. Then into McCarthy's workshop. I had stayed there later than usual talking to Paddy in the shop … Mick was outside and told me afterwards that he heard the shooting and did not know what to do. When he saw Dad and old Philip he rushed in and told me. We got him in the house and wrapped a big towel around him. He was not bleeding hardly anything and luckily nothing serious was hit … We got Dad to Dr Fogarty and then to hospital for three weeks.

O'Donnell [had] got across the back field and out on the road at Quilty's. He then got up to Burke's house, where the police got him. He was in hospital and jail for a while but never really got a sentence. Ryan was carried around by the silos and on to that back road and picked up by an old Ford car. He was buried at night near Abington. He was the man who helped in shooting two unarmed officers, the Barrington girl and her friend. [The Barrington 'girl' referred to above.] With Ryan were Troy, O'Donnell, and a man called Hannan, I think from beyond Pallas and maybe four or five others.

When the two men came in the house, they told Mary [presumably the housemaid] they knew Dad was out at the fence. They could have shot him there.

O'Donnell claimed he had no intention of shooting Dad. Only wanted the guns. I had a small automatic with me.

It was a lucky day for the de Burgh family. Next day I got all the silver packed up and taken to Woodville. Soldiers and police all over the place. One soldier said to Fitz, 'Mr de B must be a wonderful shot'.

'Well,' said Fitz, pointing at the old family church, 'if there was a bumblebee on that steeple, he could hit it from here.'

Dad was in hospital for three weeks. I stayed there with him. Went back to Dromkeen for about one month. We packed up all the furniture and stuff and it was carted to Limerick, from there to Liverpool to Vancouver, to Port Washington, to Prevost Island … We had a police guard at all times till we left on October 24th 1924 and went to Dublin and on to Kingstown.[6]

Hubert stayed with various relatives in Wales and London and then sailed to Vancouver and on to Prevost Island. His sisters, Evelyn and Elizabeth, went to join him.

Digby de Burgh continued in his submission to the Irish Grants Committee:

> By reason of the matters aforesaid, the said conspiracy to drive your Suppliant out of his lands has to a large extent succeeded and your Suppliant has been driven out of Ireland. Such portions of his land as he was able to sell have had to be sold at prices representing merely a fraction of their true value. He has been unable to obtain the profits of said lands since the commencement of said conspiracy and by reason thereof has become involved in debt and much reduced in circumstances and has suffered losses which he estimates at £6000.[7]

De Burgh received many cards and letters from local farmers while he was in hospital, congratulating him on shooting his assailants and escaping to tell the story. The descendants of the de Burghs believe that the attack was brought on by a 'personal grudge stemming from his being a Justice of the Peace',[8] but many Justices of the Peace were left untouched.

Being tough and resilient, he managed to sell some of his land and finally left Ireland for good, although he complained that the Irish Land Commission did him 'a lot of mischief … £1,200 was kept from me for a year'.[9] He ended up with his family at the other side of the world, where he bought over 1,000 acres of land. It was mostly rough forestland, but undaunted and tireless as ever, he fenced and seeded 300 acres of grassland, complaining about the effect of his wounds when he was undertaking this hard manual work.

Impressed by his story, the Irish Grants Committee awarded him £8,080 in February 1928. Hubert declared that his father thought the 'shooting was the best thing that ever happened to him in the long run, as with the money he got in compensation was able to buy more land out in Canada'.[10] He had been thinking of emigrating to Canada before 1924 and had visited British Columbia in 1896, where he stayed with the Ruttle family on Salt Spring Island. A German Palatine family, they were friends he had known in Ireland who had lived there for a few generations.

The story has a happy ending. Susan, Hussey de Burgh's grand-daughter, told me that she feels 'welcome and free in a new country. It would never occur to me to ask what religion someone was: most Canadians take people for their worth without prejudice'.

In time, Lieutenant Colonel Ulick de Burgh retired to Drumkeen after army service in Sudan in the Second World War, and lived there with his American wife, Dorothy Spencer, until the 1970s. They had no children and the land is no longer in the hands of the family. The house, however, still stands.

There are many cases of Protestant landowners being the subject of violent campaigns aimed at seizing their lands. In Co. Roscommon on 7 April 1920, a Mr Levin was attacked and the windows and doors of his house were smashed, as he had refused to divide his land among the attackers. In Rockview, Co. Westmeath, Col. J.D. Fetherstonhaugh had his cattle driven on 12 April, while on 23 April in King's County, now Offaly, a deputation called on H.L. King of Ballyline to give up his land. In Co. Galway, Lord Ashtown's estate was attacked and several cattle drives took place. Graziers were asked to remove their stock.[11] 'There are assassinations, attempted assassinations, house burnings (sometimes to prevent its use by the military), housebreakings for arms; there is land-grabbing and cattle driving.'[12]

An interesting explanation for the widespread outbreak of violence was given by James Campbell, 1st Baron Glenavy:

> The stoppage of emigration since 1914 has shut up in Ireland about 200,000 of the ablest and most enterprising of our youths [sic]. They can find no answer of employment here but owing to the profits made by their fathers in the war they can afford to live in idleness and have thrown themselves heart and soul into the work of conspiracy and crime. For the first time in Irish history they have got out of hand so far as their church is concerned and their bishops are afraid to openly defy them lest they may be courting defeat.[13]

In many incidents, the motivation of the attackers was often land greed, using revenge as a cloak. In Co. Clare, R.F. Hibbert, a member of the Irish Unionist Association, reported that during the Anglo-Irish War, 'when there was a sense of insecurity of life and property',[14] 'the conditions of affairs in my neighbourhood in Co. Clare is [sic] beyond description; there is no protection whatsoever for life and property'.[15] He was raided by forty masked men with guns and axes, but they left after Hibbert fired on them with a repeating rifle. The local barracks was closed, so there was no local police protection. His boathouse and outhouses were raided and the houses of most of his neighbours were attacked. Meanwhile:

> ... every night gangs of armed men assemble in different houses and walk the countryside, terrorising the respectable inhabitants – from dark to dawn law-abiding people scarcely dare to sleep. Owing to the withdrawal of police all regulations are disregarded, and the public houses remain open night and day, consequently, as may be imagined, the state of drunkenness and robbery is appalling. Even the farmer's crops are stolen out of the ground to buy drink.[16]

Eventually, Hibbert and his family were forced to leave the country after disposing of their furniture. It has been estimated that 'since 1919, seventy from a total of eighty Protestant landed families had left [the] county'.[17] This is astonishing and may constitute the largest outflow of Protestants in percentage terms from any county in the Free State. Today Protestants have all but disappeared in Co. Clare, constituting just over 1 per cent of the population in the 2011 census of Ireland.

Many Protestants in Co. Cork were subjected to intimidation and murder. Peter Hart has written in detail about this subject, stating that between 1919 and 1923, the IRA shot 44 Protestants accused of being 'spies and informers' out of a total of 122 people who were shot.[18] Hart goes on to write:

> Of 113 private homes burned by the guerrillas, 96 (or 85 per cent) belonged to Protestants. None of the more than two dozen farms seized from 'spies' in 1921 and 1922 was owned by a Catholic. Protestants who wished to sell up and leave were presumed to have 'guilty consciences.' Their sales were often boycotted, fined or stopped altogether ... Those who stayed were frequently subjected to a regime of boycotts, vandalism,

and theft. Many had their property commandeered by neighbours or Volunteers and nearly all those who lived in rural areas had to put up with IRA squatters. Some indication of the severity of the terror is given by the scores of Protestant men and women who suffered nervous breakdowns, even to the point of insanity and suicide.[19]

James Donnelly tells us that 'close to 50 Big Houses and suburban villas were burned there [Co. Cork] before the Truce in July 1921'.[20] Co. Cork was deprived of much of its finest domestic architecture in a matter of a few years.

Some Protestants were murdered for spying, or being suspected of spying. In Co. Cork, one such case is the 1921 murder of Lieutenant Colonel Warren John Peacocke DSO, from Innishannon, for supposedly assisting search parties of the Essex Regiment to capture IRA men. Lieutenant Colonel Peacocke was one of the best officers of the Ulster Division (9th Skins) and rallied the men in the Schwaben redoubt in France near the village of Thiepval, Picardie, on the afternoon of 1 July 1916. Tom Kelleher took credit for murdering Peacocke, on the orders of Tom Barry. But the report of the murder in the *Cork Examiner* states that he was out in his workshop cutting wood 'when two men entered and fired several shots, two of which took effect in the stomach. It is stated the deceased ran into his house about thirty yards away and said he was shot'.[21] Regardless of the exact circumstances, he died in agony on the morning of 1 June 1921. Richard Russell in his statement (BMH 1591) repeats the story of Peacocke being suspected of spying and gives details of his own spying on Peacocke without apparently finding any incriminating evidence. One trip by Peacocke to Dunmanway area, ostensibly on a fishing trip, was closely followed by Russell. It was a waste of time as Peacocke did just that – fished. Russell did this spying in May 1921, yet the IRA had already decided that he was guilty in March 1921.

A few weeks after Peacocke's murder, his widowed mother was burnt out following the looting of her house, Skevanish House, a Victorian Tudor-style building that had been altered at much expense. Mrs Peacocke left with her other son and his wife to settle in Somerset before the house was burnt. The contents were auctioned by local men and she complained that 'Her cattle, horses, and farm stock were stolen, and since the Truce … everything in her garden, all her farm implements, carriages, electric engine, etc.,' had been sold off by the IRA 'by public auction without any interference by the British Government.'[22]

The family had a peacock motif on their crockery and cutlery, and many republican homes throughout the district soon had peacock crockery and cutlery on their sideboards. The local Catholic priest condemned this, saying 'what had peacocks, was Peacocke's', and ordered people to return the crockery to Mrs Peacocke, but she had already departed in fear for her life.

In his book, *Guerrilla Days in Ireland*, Tom Barry wrote:

> [Peacocke] guided in person raiding parties of the Essex Regiment. He wore a mask and was dressed as a civilian during many of his early expeditions with the raiders, but one night, in the house of one of his victims, his mask slipped. From that night in December, 1920, we wanted him very badly, but he knew he was in danger and practically lived with the British Officers in barracks.

Since he had been away at war for years, how could he have known IRA faces in the area around Innishannon? He had returned after July 1920, when his father died. What use would he have been to the RIC?

After Peacocke was shot in late May 1921, Tom Barry boasted that six houses – five owned by Protestants – were set on fire in Innishannon, excluding Peacocke's. The houses were Mrs Stephenson's Cor Castle; Brigadier Caulfield's Innishannon House; Mr Dennehy JP's Prospect House; River View House, which was unoccupied for some time but had been occupied before the burning; the Stennings' house, which had been occupied by the widow of F.C. Stenning, her husband having been recently shot dead, and lastly the Hungerfords' house. It must have been terrifying for Protestants in the area. These houses were burnt because they were 'British Loyalists' houses'.[23] It was an act of vengeance. The Essex regiment had been burning houses of IRA activists in the area, so houses of local loyalists were burnt 'to teach the British a lesson, and once and for all end their fire terror.'[24]

The IRA was at war with the British Army, the RIC and the Auxiliaries, so could expect strong retaliation, but local loyalist citizens were uninvolved, so why punish them? Presumably because they were loyalists.

Ken Loach's film, *The Wind that Shakes the Barley*, supports the actions of the IRA against a Protestant landlord in Co. Cork, but the cardboard

portrayal of the Anglo-Irish landlord, Sir John Hamilton, misses the
point. Irish landlords were a broken force by 1920, both in ownership
of land and political power. They avoided reporting IRA activists to
the army and police, fearing retaliation. Hamilton is portrayed as stiff-
necked, arrogant and spiteful; a snob who disdained his farm workers,
seeing them as rebellious, difficult bogmen. The film also portrays the
Auxiliaries in an extremist light that is not in keeping with modern
historical reassessment. David Leeson has revealed that Irish Catholic
members of the Royal Irish Constabulary, as well as the Black and Tans,
took reprisals against their fellow Irishmen.[25] Their friends and family
were often boycotted and intimidated; people were told by the IRA not
to sit beside RIC families in church; the court system was falling apart
as jurors were intimidated; Summer Assizes could not be held; police
barracks had been burned in outlying parts of the country, resulting
in the closure of many and Republican insurgents were assassinating
policemen throughout the South. The RIC saw itself as a target for
what it considered to be a collection of cowardly terrorists. In such an
environment, some Irish policemen turned to violence and vigilantism
in frustration. The sacking of Balbriggan and Fermoy are examples of
such undisciplined behaviour under provocation.

Loach's portrayal of the landlord in *The Wind that Shakes the Barley*
was assessed by *Irish Examiner* columnist and former UUP advisor,
Steven King: 'The only Irish Protestant character [in the film]
conforms to every worst stereotype of the gentry. Loach allows no
subtlety. Protestant equals rich, equals bastard, equals asking to be
murdered.' Yet very few Protestant landlords were murdered. There
were the attempted murders of Lord Dunalley and Robert Sanders in
Co. Tipperary, and Hibbert in Co. Clare, but the IRA men involved in
these attempted murders proved to be poor shots.

Refusal of tenants to pay rent was another reason why some
Protestants left. Lieutenant Colonel Cooke-Collis lived in Castle
Cooke on the River Funcheon near Fermoy, Co. Cork. Cooke-Collis,
a large-scale farmer, was 'a kind and tactful man'[26] who exhibited
successfully at agricultural shows. According to James Donnelly: 'There
is some evidence that his extensive agricultural operations aroused
local hostility and inspired covetousness among local farmers.'[27] He
decided to leave Ireland after his tenants refused to pay their rent and
the IRA burnt his house and belongings on 8 June 1921. He received
compensation from the Shaw-Renton Commission in 1923.

Cooke-Collis was a man who tried to facilitate the locals as much as possible and claimed he had only a small amount of land left, although Patrick Lyons and his son Thomas tried to take 50 acres from him. This was likely to have been one of the factors that led to Castle Cooke being burned down. James S. Donnelly Jr claimed that Cooke-Collis' 'extensive agricultural operations' aroused local hostility.[28] This seems to contradict the claim in the Irish Grants Committee file. Cooke-Collis is also described as being 'extreme anti-Irish', as an ex-officer, in one of the Bureau of Military History statements. This would sound strange to anyone who knew him – or read the Irish Grants Committee file.[29]

Some suffered for giving evidence to the police. Two Protestant farmers near Skibbereen, William Connell and Matthew Sweetnam, were murdered on 23 February 1921 in front of their wives. They were accused of having 'given evidence against a man who had been levying subscriptions for the IRA'.[30] Richard Draper, who lives in Skibbereen, informed me that Connell had mentioned that he was opposed to the IRA and would not give them any donations, unlike some of his Protestant neighbours, who wanted to be left in peace. Cattle were taken from their herd in lieu of monetary contributions and Connell and Sweetnam reported the theft to the RIC. They were under duress from the police to give evidence against some men arrested for the theft and they were shot for informing. They had received written warning to leave the country, which Connell showed to a solicitor, Willie Kingston. However, Kingston advised them to ignore the letter. That proved to be a mistake. A revealing aspect of this story is that a young IRA man named Daly was instructed to murder Connell. But as he liked Connell, he refused. Daly was later murdered by the IRA for refusing to obey orders and years later his body was exhumed and buried in Abbeystrewry graveyard, outside Skibbereen.

Draper's father lived outside Skibbereen when these murders took place and he was told by a neighbour that it would be best if he and his entire family changed their religion. Draper, the church warden of Abbeystrewry Church of Ireland church at the time, said he would give the matter serious consideration, but decided to do nothing.

Particularly harsh treatment was meted out to the Good family from Timaleague near Bandon, Co. Cork. John Good, murdered on 10 March 1921, was a parishioner of Revd Fleming of Timoleague parish, Co. Cork, where the most charming Church of Ireland church stands by the edge of the sea at Courtmacsherry Bay, close to the ruins of the Franciscan friary. He was the fifth Protestant victim within a few weeks. Good was a farmer with a medium-sized estate in Barryshall who took no interest in politics. Fleming's son Lionel wrote movingly of him: 'He was a good employer, and got on well with his neighbours, but one evening armed men came to his door and shot him.' The Revd Fleming wrote in his diary:

> His son and daughter came for me about 11 p.m., and I drove back with them and stayed until John Good died – as a brave and Christian man can die, without a word of complaint or wish for vengeance on his murderers. I got home – walked home – about one in the morning. My brave wife neither by word nor sign tried to stop me going, though I know what those hours of waiting for my return must have meant to her.

Following the murder of his father, William Good was murdered by the IRA on 26 March 1921 when he came home from Dublin to attend his father's funeral. He had been a captain in the British Army in the Great War, a soldier who had been awarded the Military Cross. He was studying Engineering in Trinity College, Dublin. As Fleming recalled: 'A pony drawing an empty trap was seen galloping along the Bandon Road. It had been driven by John Good's son, his body was found in a ditch a few miles back, with a bullet through the head.'

The mother and her daughter stayed on but were told to leave Ireland by the IRA and on 3 May, they fled. 'They were unable to take any of their furniture or belongings, which had to be left in the house and were of course promptly stolen.'[31] Both father and son were buried in the Church of Ireland graveyard in nearby Clonakilty. According to a local Protestant, their graves have been desecrated quite recently; we do not know where the mother and daughter ended up. Lionel Fleming said that he heard 'long afterwards, that Good was thought to have given the soldiers information about some "wanted" men, but I do not know what truth there was in this.'[32]

Another son of John Good, Thomas William Good, had to flee with his family. Good farmed some 25 miles away from Timoleague in Rosemount, Farran. He applied to the Irish Grants Committee for compensation, having been forced out of the country. He stated in his claim that 'rebels entered his house by day and by night in 1922', to the extent that he had to supply food and lodging free of charge. His wife broke down 'as a result of the strain of keeping an open house'. He was constantly threatened and, fearing he would be murdered, finally sold his farm and house in 1923 for £3,100, much less than the market value. He took his family to England, where he had to take out a mortgage to buy a farm for £4,600 in Westfield, Steeple, Oxfordshire.[33] He was not compensated; however, as the Irish Grants Committee thought he has not lost out on the sale of his farm. Significantly, there is a note in his file that Good was a 'strongly pro-British and on intimate terms with CF intelligence officers'.[34] It seems Thomas Good had been in contact with the Crown Forces before they left in early 1922 and he was targeted after this and forced to leave. But why intimidate and terrorise him and his family well after the Crown Forces intelligence men had left?

The worst atrocity in the 26 counties during 1921 to 1923 occurred in the Bandon Valley in west Cork, when thirteen Protestants were murdered in April 1922. Peter Hart writes at length about this mini pogrom[35] and surprisingly is the first historian to research this atrocity in depth, for which he has attracted a lot of sometimes ugly and personal criticism. A highly controversial and acrimonious debate resulted, the latest development being an article in *Éire-Ireland*.[36] The descendants of the Protestants murdered at that time were willing to tell a Canadian, Peter Hart, what happened and his reporting in detail of these murders has raised a storm of controversy. Why there has been such a controversy about their telling these stories is surely a comment on the refusal of some historians, both professional and amateur, to accept that 'the nationalist revolution had also been a sectarian one'.[37] Hart's arguments have proved highly contentious, and his work has become the subject of a protracted and sometimes bitter dispute unique in recent Irish history-writing.'[38]

Gerard Murphy has suggested that for southern Protestants, 'suppression was the price of survival', and as Townshend has written, this 'rings truer than the argument of those who hold that the failure of Protestant public bodies to protest against the killings proves that they did not happen'.[39] At the Protestant Convention meeting in Dublin in May 1922, a leading Dublin Protestant, Sergeant Hanna, told the convention that 'we are a defenceless minority in Southern Ireland, and all we ask, or have ever asked, is for liberty to live our ... lives ... But unless this campaign of murder, exile, kidnapping, confiscation and destruction of property comes to an end in Southern Ireland an exodus of Protestants must ensue.'[40]

Brian Walker has accumulated a substantial body of evidence, gathered from Church of Ireland synods in 1921–23, dealing with attacks and murders and intimidation of members of the Church of Ireland indicating religion as a factor – even a sometimes determining factor – in hostility towards Protestants. Walker has also made the point that much of the worst violence against Protestants came after the War of Independence, in the early years of the Free State.

The Dunmanway victims included small farmers, businessmen, shopkeepers, a clergyman (wounded), a 16-year-old lad, a farm servant who was mentally handicapped and a post office clerk. It is still not clear why these murders took place. Joseph O'Neill in *Blood-Dark Track* suggests that there may have been old resentments about land but, as he points out, none of the men murdered were associated with the landlord class. Undoubtedly there had been tensions for some time between some Protestants and their neighbours, but this was before the Treaty. The directive issued by IRA headquarters to all brigades at the time of the Truce made it clear that there were to be no attacks on civilians. The Truce had brought hostilities to a close.

Meda Ryan maintains that these men had been informers and spies. But Kevin Myers has pointed out in an article in the *Irish Independent*:

How could members of the little Protestant communities of the Bandon valley possibly know anything about the activities of a clandestine terrorist army? Moreover, since the main attack on Protestants in Cork occurred in May 1922, nearly ten months after the Truce which ended the lunacy of the 1919–21 war, to whom and about what were the unfortunate Protestants informing? If the IRA targets were simply 'informers' why did no Catholics perish in the murderous purge of that terrible week? And since there was a lawful government in Dublin, by what right did the IRA go around killing anyone, never mind a dozen or so defenceless Protestant men?

Meda Ryan's claim that those killed had once informed on the IRA is based largely on 'unrecorded evidence – folk memory'.[41] Ryan tells us of an 'informers' dossier' left behind in a workhouse in Dunmanway by K Company of the ADRIC (Black and Tans) in 1922. This dossier purports to contain the names of 'helpful citizens' who were spies. This list (if it existed) has not been kept and a list in the Bureau of Military Archives in Dublin, reference CD 31, gives no indication of any loyalists who were 'helpful'. Furthermore, there is no evidence of a Loyalist Action Group in the area that, she informs us, was mentioned in the alleged document. As Bielenberg, Borgonovo and Donnelly tell us: '… these documents are not publicly available. Unfortunately, if they cannot be reviewed, they cannot be considered as evidence in this debate.'

The 'Anti-Sinn Féin Society' explanation for the 1922 killings is also at variance with republican evidence. With the exception of Michael O'Donoghue's Bureau of Military History statement, IRA sources do not link the 1921 Anti-Sinn Féin group with the civilians killed in 1922. No such counterintelligence justification emerged from the IRA at the time of the 1922 killings.[42]

In his 1990 biography of Michael Collins, Tim Pat Coogan characterised the Bandon Valley killings as one of the worst outbreaks of sectarian homicide during this period. Peter Hart's conclusion that the killings were sectarian therefore echoed a perception that had been circulating among historians, republicans, churchmen and unionists since April 1922.

When Archbishop Gregg, the Archbishop of Dublin, and Bishop Miller of Cashel – both acting for the General Synod – saw Michael Collins and William Cosgrave in Dublin after these murders, Collins said 'the murders in Belfast had an effect on the present situation but that the Belfast massacres could not be considered any justification for the outrages [notice Collins did not use the word 'massacres'] to which the deputation had alluded'.[43] However, Peter Hart has pointed out that west Cork Protestants had publicly condemned the Belfast murders.

The debate continues. A recent contribution from the historian John Regan conjectures that Hart failed to take into account that four British soldiers had been held by the IRA during the period of the killings and executed, the implication being that they may have given names of Protestant spies to their captors, two of whom were intelligence officers.[44] The suggestion is that the Bandon Valley Protestants who were murdered were on the list of informers extracted from the intelligence officers. But if this is so, and there is no evidence it is, why were Catholic informers not killed? This unsubstantiated intervention by Regan is dismissed by Bielenberg, Borgonovo and Donnelly, who state: 'Their abduction in Macroom is unlikely to have directly influenced the subsequent ten killings, other than to increase anxiety within the IRA.'[45]

More tellingly, Gerard Murphy has questioned John Regan's arguments in his blog of 23 October 2011.[46] There is the difficulty of Regan not providing facts to support his suggestion that the intelligence officers gave the names of informers pre-Treaty to the IRA, and his criticisms of Peter Hart are based on speculation. In addition, the timings do not convince. The first murders of Protestants took place on 26 or 27 April, and the British officers were captured at about 4 p.m. on April 26. It is not credible that the names of Protestant spies were extracted in such a short time and that the men from the 1st Brigade who interrogated the intelligence officers could have gone on to shoot three Protestants in Dunmanway that night, not knowing the layout of the town.

John Regan is quick to criticise Peter Hart and in the words of Gerard Murphy:

> His basic argument is that Hart's research is flawed because he was guilty of 'elision', that is to say of 'ignoring problematic evidence' when it did not suit his thesis – his thesis according to Regan being that the Bandon valley massacre was primarily motivated by sectarianism. 'Others said that the killing had nothing to do with religion and everything to do with spying against the IRA. Hart dismissed this,' Regan states. Now if this is true it is a very serious allegation. If Hart ignored evidence that those shot were 'spies' or 'informers' then he would indeed be guilty of 'elision' and worse than that, he would be guilty of gross manipulation of data.[47] But Hart did not ignore the capture of four British Army men by the IRA. He considered it had no bearing on the murders.

The eminent historian Eric Hobsbawn believed that academic history 'was correct in opposing generalisation insufficiently supported by fact, or backed by unreliable fact.'[48] There seem to be 'unreliable fact' to support Regan's speculative interpretation of events and the evidence to support Peter Hart's interpretation of events is strong.

Hart judged that these killings constituted 'ethnic cleansing', something one of his critics has denied, stating the murders were 'controlled military violence'.[49] However, the total of people targeted was twenty-eight or more,[50] not thirteen, indicating an intent to murder more unarmed Protestant civilians on a large scale, arguably constituting 'ethnic cleansing' on a minor scale. If this was 'controlled military violence' then the killings had an undeniably sectarian motive: only Protestants were targeted, with the exception of retired RIC man Thomas Sullivan, who managed to escape and flee Dunmanway. However, the Protestants who were murdered and targeted posed no military threat to the anti-Treaty IRA. So it seems that it was a spontaneous outbreak of unapproved IRA revenge killings, triggered by the killing of Michael O'Neill. The evidence for spying is weak and even if soundly based, why did the IRA carry out revenge killings for alleged spying in the period 1921–22, approximately three months after Dáil Éireann had accepted the Treaty?

Although thirteen people died, attacks with varying degrees of murderous intent were made on twenty-nine men during this period.[51] The IRA attempted to murder Irish curate Revd Ralph Harbord outside the Church of Ireland rectory in Murragh, near Bandon, whilst he was visiting his father, Richard Harbord, rector of Murragh.

He was shot on the rectory steps when his back was turned. He was lucky to live, but ill health plagued him for the rest of his life. His daughter described him as a kindly man who gave what he could to people in trouble, including his own clothes. But silence descended on the family, as on all Protestant families who had suffered. No apology was made, nor explanation given, by the IRA for this attempted murder. Harbord's daughter wrote: 'I don't know why anyone would have wanted to kill my dad, he always considered he was Irish.'[52]

She pointed out in a letter to the author that 'Ralph was with his brother Charlie when the incident occurred. They were returning from a fishing trip. Charlie was on leave from the British Army. He must have seen the IRA men approaching and jumped over the railings into the basement of the rectory. He was fitter than Ralph.' Perhaps Ralph was mistaken for Charlie or shot in frustration that their man had got away? Was it Charlie they were after? We do not know.

What started this killing campaign? Most of the facts are now well known. Michael O'Neill, the acting commandant of the Bandon battalion, visited the house of loyalists in Ballygroman. He was accompanied by Stephen O'Neill – not a relative – and colleagues Charles O'Donoghue and Michael Hurley. The owner of the house was Thomas Hornibrook, an outspoken loyalist, who lived with his son Sam Hornibrook and Captain Herbert Woods, the nephew of Thomas Hornibrook's son-in-law. They were in the house when the IRA party arrived at 2.30 on the morning of 26 April.

It is not clear why they visited. But when refused entrance at the front door, they entered by a window and Michael O'Neill mounted the stairs seemingly not saying the purpose of his unwanted visit. Herbert, having had military training as part of his service in the First World War, shot O'Neill and he was taken away in the car in which he had arrived and driven back to Bandon, dying on the laneway from Ballygroman House, where a monument to him has since been erected. Later, O'Donoghue returned with two colleagues and the three men surrendered on the condition that their lives would be spared. Perhaps Woods would have been prepared to shoot it out with the Hornibrooks (if they were armed) had they not got a promise of their lives being spared. Woods admitted he had fired the shot that killed O'Neill, was beaten unconscious and one story is that he was dragged by a car until dead. The Hornibrooks were shot and buried and their graves remain undiscovered to this day.

There is a mystery about why O'Neill went to Ballygroman. He was 'acting OC' of Bandon Battalion, and the Hornibrooks were in an area under the Ovens Battalion of Cork No.1 Brigade. If he was acting on brigade orders, which brigade, and with brigade leaders in Dublin, at that time, under whose orders? His own Cork 3 Brigade or Cork 1 Brigade?

One theory is that O'Neill had come to get a magneto for his car, or borrow the Hornibrook car. Yet when he was dead, O'Donoghue was able to drive him back to Bandon in their car. Michael O'Regan of the Ovens IRA was on friendly terms with the Hornibrooks and regularly borrowed their car, so if O'Neill wanted a car, surely all he had to do was to talk to O'Regan.

Perhaps O'Neill wanted Herbert Woods. He had worked after demobilisation in the Victoria barracks in Cork and may have had information that led to the arrest of some IRA members, but this is conjecture. If he had been wanted by the IRA, why did the Cork 1 Brigade not take action?

The killings outside Dunmanway around Ballineen were probably conducted by the local leading members of the IRA and were copycat. It is extremely unlikely that the Dunmanway Irish Republican Police was unaware of what was happening in the town on Tuesday night, given the amount of gunfire and screaming. In Clonakilty, the local battalion commander may have directed the murders there but if not, he would have been aware of what was going on. In Skibbereen, local

IRA leader Neilus Connolly supported the Treaty, so would not have ordered attacks on Protestants.

What is known is that the killings were carried out by the IRA, but it stretches the imagination too far to attribute the murder of thirteen men and attempted murder of sixteen more to revenge for the killing of one IRA man, Michael O'Neill. Resentments had no doubt accumulated over past incidents during the War of Independence, when Protestants were opposed to IRA activities and may well have given information to the RIC, Auxiliaries and Black and Tans. This may have played a part in the sudden planned outbreak of violence, unsanctioned by the IRA command of Tom Barry and Tom Hales, the commander of the West Cork Brigade. Some have suggested that old scores were being settled. Michael Collins, for example, thought that the Belfast sectarian murders had inspired a tit-for-tat response. This makes it clear that, in Collins' opinion, the murders were inspired by sectarianism, a reaction to the murders of Catholics in Northern Ireland. Many saw these killings in this way, but the Belfast murders had nothing to do with Southern Protestants at the other end of the island. It is unlikely that the prime motivation was retaliation for the thirty-five Catholics murdered in Northern Ireland in April 1922. As mentioned earlier, the Protestant communities in west Cork distanced themselves from the sectarian murders in Northern Ireland: 'The Protestant communities of Schull and Clonakilty publicly dissociated themselves from sectarian violence in Ulster, insisting that such tensions were absent in the South.'[53] Perhaps this was glossing over the reality that the Protestant and Catholic communities in Ireland and west Cork were not without tensions on both religious and political grounds. However, 'undoubtedly, the Northern situation heightened ethno-religious tensions in West Cork and other parts of Ireland. Nevertheless, no evidence has yet emerged that events in the North provided a primary motive for the West Cork killings.'[54]

Much has been made of the orders of Barry and Hales to have guards placed on Protestant houses on their return from Dublin but, as Hart points out, 'these statements were not issued until it was all over and had little practical significance'.[55] However, John Bradfield was killed some 36 hours after Hales issued his orders. What was more telling is that those who committed the murders were not investigated nor punished by Barry and Hales, indicating they were respected for their past loyalties and opposition to Michael Collins. Whatever the reasons for not punishing them, it can hardly to be doubted that they were untouchable.

The only law enforcement agency at that time, the Irish Republican Police (IRP), was composed of the IRA. It was their responsibility to investigate the murders. However, it is not impossible that the crimes committed under their noses were done without their connivance. Michael O'Neill's brother, Danny, was charged with finding out who killed John Bradfield of Killowen. He was in charge of the republican police in the Bandon area and has now been directly implicated in the murders. So it seems unlikely that the IRP was ever going to punish the killers. The IRA is more known for punishing its enemies and so-called spies than those who killed Protestant civilians at a time when the British Army and police had withdrawn.

Tom Hales, the IRA West Cork brigade commander, as well as Sean Buckley, a leader of the anti-Treaty side, condemned the murders, having moved too late to put a stop to them. A local Protestant, J.L.B. Deane, wrote to *The Irish Times* in 1994, stating that: 'Sean Buckley was on the 'anti-Treaty side ... [he] was elected to the Dáil in 1938 and at subsequent elections until his retirement, and many Protestants ... voted for him, not because they supported the policy of Fianna Fáil, but as a mark of gratitude and respect for what he had done in 1922'.

Deane is clear on why Protestants were murdered. He writes: 'Protestants were murdered because of their religion and without any suggestion of wrongdoing on their part.'[56]

Cristoir de Baróid claimed:

> The two-day outrages against Protestants by a maverick IRA group in south-west Cork in April 1922 were stamped out immediately by the local IRA leadership. The Northern IRA raised a storm of protest with the West Cork Brigade over the killings. [57]

De Baróid is a well-known figure from the Bandon area, who was aware of what had happened. But the 'local IRA leadership' did nothing to stop the murders and attempted murders at the time, being absent in Dublin. But why did they not thoroughly investigate and punish the perpetrators?

One theory is that of the grandson of Jasper Wolfe, a Methodist from Skibbereen who became a President of the Law Society of Ireland in 1940, who was targeted by the IRA at the time of the murders. He wrote: 'It seemed that some Volunteers had slipped the leash of Republican discipline and were running wild. What would happen next was anybody's guess.'[58] But if they had 'slipped the leash', they had done so in the knowledge that they were a close part of the IRA family, had served in Barry's flying column and were not going to be disciplined later on by Barry and Hales.

What is clear is that there was a widespread breakdown of discipline in the west Cork IRA at a time when there was a split over those who opposed the Treaty and those who supported it. The widespread nature of the attacks in four different battalion areas of the IRA from Killowen to Skibbereen indicates a lack of central leadership, but also varying degrees of enthusiasm for the attacks. After all, almost all of those murdered were unarmed and by April 1922, part of a former, defeated and leaderless people.

The reaction of some the Catholic bishops was strong:

> We have seen too many instances … of barbarous treatment of our Protestant fellow countrymen. Not only has their property been at times unjustly seized and they themselves occasionally driven from their homes and their lives have in some cases been murderously attacked. We condemn unsparingly these manifestations of savagery… our own Catholic people we solemnly warn against that might bring any of them to imbrue their hands in the blood of a fellow man.[59]

Later in February 1923, the Bishop of Cork, Dr Cohalan, said that 'Physical force has always been a curse in Ireland … Protestants have suffered severely during the period of civil war in the South'. He called on 'Republicans in arms … to seek reconciliation with their fellow countrymen who have accepted the Free State Constitution …'[60]

The reaction of Erskine Childers, a Protestant anti-Treaty supporter who had changed his mind, having been one of the signatories to the Treaty in 1921, was strong and clear: he thought the killings were sectarian, and so wrote: 'Sectarian crime is the foulest crime, and it is regarded as such in the tradition of our people, for it violates not only every Christian principle but the very basis of nationality as well.'[61]

There was an exodus of Protestants from the Bandon Valley following these outrages. The Royal Navy commander in Queenstown, now

Cobh, feared that there would be a major exodus and planned to mount an evacuation by sea. It is likely that between 100 and 200 people fled, some staying away, others eventually returning. Most fled by train.

It has been suggested that a major reason for the departure of the Protestant community throughout the 26 counties, not just in west Cork, was their loyalty and ties to the local Protestant peer, or landlord. When the landlord departed for England, his faithful supporters went with him. But by 1921, landlords had little of their original estates left and their Protestant tenants were generally no longer tied to them by land rents. Thus Lord Bandon, whose house was burnt in 1921, wrote of local Protestant farmers in the Bandon area: 'The Sinn Féiners are trying to drive all the Protestant farmers out of the country – a great many of them are selling their farms and leaving – they are warned not to sell their farms to other Protestants'.[62] What Lord Bandon did or did not do had little or no effect on the attacks on local Protestant farmers around Bandon.

In what was then Queen's County, Frank Meehan tells a story about his mother's persecution for sectarian reasons. Frank comes from an Irish Parliamentary Party background; his grandfather, Patrick A. Meehan, was a Redmondite MP for the Leix division of Queen's County and, on his death in 1916, was succeeded by his son, Patrick J. Meehan, who lost his seat to Sinn Féin in the 1918 election 'through intimidation and personation' (interview, June 2007). Members of Sinn Féin beat up his uncle, John Meehan, who was reported as being autistic, tied him to the bed and broke all the furniture and crockery in the house. They wrote 'Up the republic, up Sinn Féin' on the walls and drove the cattle off the farm.

In Frank's words:

When growing up, the three children had a pony between them but the only one interested was Eileen [Frank's mother]. She disliked riding the pony along the roads so rode it in Emo Court estate, with the permission of the Earl. One day, when riding through Emo Court, she came across some young IRA men robbing Smiths of Mountmellick's grocery van. Recognising them she said, 'I know you'. One pulled her off the pony and shot the pony dead. Another said, 'That's the daughter of the widow Cobbe of Clonterry', not knowing Mrs Cobbe had re-married. They presumed she was a Protestant because of the name Cobbe. One of the men said, 'Go home, you Orange bitch, to your old one and if you even mention this, we will kill you and burn you out of it'. She went home crying and had a deep hatred for Irish republicanism all her life.

Further north, in Drumgarra, Co. Monaghan, more Protestants – the Fleming family – were involved in an IRA incident at the end of March 1921. They were attacked by no less than forty IRA men, who demanded that they evacuate their house. William Fleming, aged 64, had been a marked man by the IRA since he had shot one of their members a year earlier during an attack on his farm. He surrendered, but that did not save him. He and his son were shot dead in the road and their bodies thrown in a ditch. Their house was set on fire. While the raid was taking place, another son and daughter hid in an outhouse with Fleming's aged mother and survived. But several weeks later, Mrs Fleming died of shock in the workhouse in Monaghan, leaving two grandchildren behind with no father or mother to raise them. Clearly these were vengeance killings, but perhaps there was also an agrarian motive?

The murder of an elderly clergyman, John Finlay, took place on 12 June 1921. The 80-year-old retired Dean of Leighlin Cathedral, and one time chaplain to a Lord Lieutenant, was taken from his house in Bawnboy, Co. Cavan, and murdered in the early hours of Sunday morning. The IRA took him out on the lawn, shot him in the head and then battered his head to a pulp. The *Church of Ireland Gazette* commented that 'one can only grieve at the awful sight of one's native land lapsing into a condition of moral degradation to which modern history affords no parallel'.[63] The papers recorded the murders of Protestants, but little effort was made to explain why so many were shot. What had they done to deserve their fates? What offence had Dean Finlay committed?

The Rt Revd Robert Miller, Bishop of Cashel, Emly, Lismore and Waterford, preached a sermon in Christ Church, Dublin on 8 October, 1922 at a time when the civil war was at its height. He said:

> … during the past few years the whole Church has passed through experiences which caused grave apprehension regarding our future in this land. Many of our people were driven from their homes, many others left through fear of violence, with the result that many of our parishes, especially where numbers were small, were unable to meet their financial responsibilities.

It is only fair to say that the Government have done their utmost to protect our people from injustice, but owing to the fact that neither police nor military forces were available, the Government have been unable to prevent brutal tyranny to many of our people, and wholesale destruction of property.[64]

He went on to urge members to stay, as 'they are attached to their native land', and claimed that 'while it is true that many people have had no choice as to leaving the country, there are others who have left, and who contemplate leaving, without sufficient reason'. He believed the new Provisional Government was doing its best to restore law and order and had a 'broad spirit of toleration' and 'excellent intentions.'[65]

A month later, Dr Miller addressed the annual Synod of his dioceses as follows:

We have done our duty as peaceful and law-abiding citizens, and we again ask for increased immediate effort to ensure protection and security. We acknowledge that much has been done. We appreciate the courtesy of our rulers, and their evident desire to protect our interests but yet we have still very good cause for complaint. The feeling of insecurity continues, and the causes which have led to it are still daily manifest. Burning of property, refusal to pay just and lawful debts, gross and public interference with the rights of private property ... Honest, brave men will face physical violence, the destruction of their property, but such deed as we are now speaking of chill the hearts of strong men and fill them with an overmastering desire to get away from a country where, in their opinion, civilization is losing its hold.[66]

Bishop Miller did not mince his words. It is significant, as mentioned earlier, that he had been one of the delegation of three called on at a secret meeting of the Church of Ireland General Synod some six months earlier, in May 1922, to meet Michael Collins and William Cosgrave 'in order to lay before them the dangers to which Protestants in the 26 counties were daily exposed.'[67] It seems that the Synod must have thought Bishop Miller's diocese was being subjected to much violence and intimidation and needed protection and assurances. The meeting took place on 12 May and Gregg records the outcome as 'satisfactory,' but the relevant page in his diary detailing discussion that took place is – significantly – missing.[68]

Some 100 people from Miller's dioceses of Cashel, Emly and Lismore applied to the IGC for assistance, petitions including cases of intimidation from ex-RIC members or relatives. South Tipperary was particularly violent during the civil war. Michael Hopkinson tells us that 'British military reports frequently dwelt on the lawlessness of South Tipperary and regarded it as the prime example of the Provisional Government's failure to assert its authority'.[69]

Bishop Miller was installed in 1919. In 1922 he was 56 years old, having served as Dean of Waterford between 1916 and 1919. Prior to that, he had been rector of Donegal. His dioceses took in most parts of the South Riding of Co. Tipperary, including Cashel, Tipperary, Templemore, Thurles, Clonmel and Carrick-on-Suir. Insights into the sufferings of Church of Ireland members in his dioceses in this period can be found in the compensation awards of the Irish Grants Committee in the National Archives in London.

A sectarian attack took place in Newport, west of Cashel. In 1921, the rector of Newport parish, west of Cashel, was the Revd Leonard Henry. Bishop Miller gave him as an example when addressing the synod:

> It was difficult to speak with calmness of the brutal treatment of this worthy man. They deeply sympathized with Mr Henry in his unmerited suffering, and earnestly trusted that he might have a happy future in a land other than his birth. It was pleasant to be able to acknowledge the readiness of the Government to give immediate payment to cover the financial losses that Mr Henry has sustained.[70]

Revd Henry and family were forced to leave Newport parish in 1922 after a period of intense intimidation by the local Brigade of the IRA and then the Irregulars. His application to the IGC gives a vivid account of why he was forced out. The incident was not reported at the time in the local press or *The Irish Times*.[71]

Henry was born in 1864, graduated with a BA from Trinity College in 1899 and was curate of Dunmore East parish near Waterford from 1901 to 1903 and then again from 1906 to 1912. He moved to Grean in Tipperary in 1912 and then as rector to Newport in 1915, aged 51, along with his wife and three children. He was vigorous in his opposition to physical force nationalism and supported the British forces and RIC operating with the Auxiliaries in his parish. The IRA was highly active in the Newport area, where the RIC and Auxiliaries had a strong counter-insurgency presence.

Revd Henry applied to the IGC on 2 November 1926. His case is interesting in that it spans the period 1921 to 1922, pre- and post-civil war. In a lengthy, handwritten claim from Bournemouth, where he then lived with his family, he made it vividly clear why he was intimidated and eventually forced to leave. Pre-Treaty, he and his wife 'assisted the British soldiers and the RIC stationed in my parish in every way possible'. They supplied the RIC with food when they were being boycotted.

Henry 'frequently denounced disloyalty and murderous deeds from the pulpit'[72] even though he was warned 'by several of his parishioners'[73] not to do so as he was asking for trouble. Trouble came when the 'Church in Newport was twice attacked … many of the windows being smashed'.[74]

Henry claimed that 'ten murders took place in my parish and immediate district',[75] though he does not identify the people murdered or when. He reported activities of the local IRA on several occasions, once passing on information to the RIC about the whereabouts of an IRA safe house in his parish, resulting in 'imprisonment and heavy fines'.[76] The IRA got to know Henry had informed and he believed that 'it was largely as a result of this incident I suffered'.[77]

Significantly, he was not personally attacked while the RIC was present in Newport but soon after it was disbanded in early 1922, perhaps partly because he supported the Treaty. He was forced to leave Ireland following an attack on the rectory in June 1922. It is not clear what threat he posed to the local brigade of the anti-Treaty IRA at that time, but they demonstrated their dislike for him and his church by burning the Church of Ireland rectory a few days after his departure. Henry claimed £2,970 and was awarded £1,218 by the Irish Free State in 1924 'for loss of my possessions',[78] which included his furniture. He claimed for the difference of £1,752, believing he had been hard done by, plus £2,372 for the loss of a free house and loss of earnings (strangely he had not taken up a posting in the Church of England by the time he applied, saying he was too unwell to work). He maintained that he was almost destitute.

The IGC picked up the fact that Henry's wife had an income of £525 per annum 'and it is difficult to understand why they are therefore subjected to live in such discomfort'.[79] He was awarded £500 on 3 December 1926, while the rectory was restored with money from the Shaw-Renton Commission and later sold by the Church of Ireland. Henry lived on in Bournemouth for the rest of his life. It appears that he died in 1936 aged 71 or 72 as he is mentioned in *Crockford's Clerical Directory* in 1936 but not 1937.[80]

There was a dispute of a different nature in the scenic Glen of Aherlow, where Robert Sanders had a major commercial enterprise. Sanders owned 4,000 acres, which he had acquired from the Massy Dawson family in 1916. The Sanders were originally from Charleville, Co. Cork, and in the nineteenth century had married into the Massy Dawson family, large landowners in Co. Tipperary. Robert had been active in the Landlord's Defence League, which opposed the Land League, and was a JP for both Cork and Tipperary for many years, as well a magistrate from 1918. He claimed that the latter position had put his name on 'the black list by the Rebel Party'.[81] Clearly something had aroused the enmity of the IRA: in 1920 Sanders was ambushed while with his wife in a car, but they escaped unharmed.

Sanders ran 'a dairy farm, dry cattle, thousands of sheep on the Galtees, a nursery, and sawmills, among many things'.[82] On 28 August 1920, as members of the Transport and General Workers Union, the sawmill employees and herd farm hands went on strike. Sanders refused to recognise the Union, saying that he would negotiate with the strikers himself. The police were called in and, after some demonstrations, the strike was settled.

The Glen of Aherlow was occupied by the Irregulars until October 1922. They moved into Ballinacourtie House, the residence of Sanders, and, as the Free State army approached the area in late 1922, they burnt the house, destroyed the sawmills, burnt the unoccupied Church of Ireland Clonbeg rectory and destroyed the school house. Sanders put in a claim for £77,000 to the IGC for everything he could think of, including the burning of Ballinacourtie House, the schoolhouse, outhouses, gardener's and steward's houses, furniture, sawmills and the rectory. In 1924 he received a decree from the Tipperary court for £28,700. The County Court Judge Sealy said in summing up:

> In the revolution such as Ireland had just passed through, many of the inhabitants of a country saw red and did things, which in their saner moments they would not do. This was common to every country and Ireland was not worse than any other country. Terrible things were done which in a few years would be forgotten.[83]

Perhaps the judge was right, but that would have been cold comfort to
Sanders. In October 1926, he told the IGC that 'not one penny of money
in compensation has been paid to me by the Free State'.[84] Sir Alexander
Wood-Renton, chairman of the IGC, wrote to Sir John Oakley, one of
the three committee members, in November 1926 to suggest that any
decision on the large claim from Sanders should be delayed until more
details were supplied. Oakley, a past president of the Surveyors' Institute,
agreed.[85] Sanders' solicitors were advised of this decision and challenged
it at length, advising that Sanders would attempt to obtain a cash payment
from the Irish Free State and claim the difference of the total claimed from
the IGC. Reid Jamieson replied dismissively that he could not comment
on the action Sanders intended to take with the Irish Free State. At this
point Sanders decided to go over the head of the IGC and wrote to the
Colonial Secretary, Leo Amery, on 10 June 1927, expressing his surprise
that after an oral hearing with two members of the committee, the IGC
decided to wait 'until I had come to terms with the Free State over my
awards'.[86] The Free State had so far only paid him £10 in cash and £400
in land bonds, deducting rates and income tax from what he was due.
Sanders claimed that he was living off bank overdrafts.

Following further contentious correspondence, an award was made
for £15,475 in August 1927. Ballinacourtie House was not rebuilt
and, in 1946, the Land Commission bought 10,000 acres for £10,000.
Thus came to an end the presence of the Massy Dawson-Sanders
connection to the Glen of Aherlow.

Sanders was a victim of the times. He was a successful entrepreneur,
a Protestant loyalist targeted by the IRA, and a large landholder: he
owned extensive forestry plantations, which were purchased by the
Land Commission.

One of the largest claims in Co. Tipperary came from Charles
Neville-Clarke, whose family lived at Craigance mansion near Thurles,
situated on a 1,500-acre farm on the River Suir. They had lived there
for some 100 years. In February 1923, 'armed men forced their way
into the house, drove out five servants, soaked the house with petrol
and destroyed buildings and contents'.[87] The next day, they returned and
stole goods left outside the house, such as harnesses, garden tools and
gates. The Neville-Clarkes had left the house before the burning took
place and stayed away for 4 years. They sold their cattle, sheep and horses
in a 'forced sale'.[88] Neville-Clarke claimed that he could not return, as
he would have been attacked and possibly killed. As it was, his manager

was 'fired at in his own house and had a narrow escape'.[89] He tried to sell the property privately but claimed he was boycotted.

Why the burning of the house and occupation of the land? Neville-Clarke thought the reason was simple: 'to have his land confiscated'.[90] But there seemed more to it than that. It did not help that he had been DL and JP and one of his sons had fought against the IRA when in the British Army in 1920–21. The Land Commission purchased the land for £11 an acre, while Neville-Clarke claimed it was worth at least £40 an acre. Jamieson of the IGC denied it, stating in his report that land was worth £12 an acre in Ireland. Neville-Clarke claimed for a loss of £20,000 on this sale to the Land Commission, £26,000 for the burning of the mansion and furniture and various other items including the forced sale of livestock, making up a total of £49,000.

He had obtained a decree for £8,700 from the county court in Tipperary in 1924. The decree was based on a rental value of £200 a year for 15 years. Clarke had a second house in England where he went to live and Jamieson found out through his contacts that his wife had 'a very large income'.[91] An award for £11,500 was made by the IGC in December 1927.

The *Tipperary Star* reported this burning: 'Thurles and its surroundings have been fortunately very free from burnings … with the exception of the conflagration yesterday (Thursday) morning at Holycross, the picturesque residence of Mr Clarke, a great employer of labour and popular in the county'.[92] Bishop Miller mentioned the incident at the Church of Ireland Synod on 5 July 1923:

> Mr Clark, of Holycross, a fine churchman, a good Irishman, a large and liberal employer of labour, kind, hospitable, generous, has been driven from the country; his beautiful home has been reduced to ashes. It is acts of this kind – stupid, senseless, brutal – which make us almost despair.[93]

During the occupation of Clonmel by the local Irregulars in 1922, the Sweetnam family was forced to leave for Suffolk in December 1922 after a period of boycotting and intimidation. This is an interesting case of a family business being transferred from Ireland to England; unfortunately it failed, and the husband and wife retired.

Sweetnam 'had a good Drapery business in Clonmel until 1921', when 'the people ceased to buy from us owing to a strict boycott being placed on us in consequence of I being formally a member of the Royal

Irish Constabulary, besides we were Protestants and not in sympathy with their actions'.[94] The sectarian nature of the boycott is thus noted by Sweetnam. He had left the RIC in 1919 due to ill health, 2 years before the boycott started. He been forced to pay the IRA a levy and they billeted on his family. Unable to sell his stock in Ireland, he took it to England and sold at a big loss, getting £250 for goods for which he had initially paid £1,250. This is an exceptional case as no claims were made for travel and setting up a new business in Brighton.

Jamieson interviewed Sweetnam in London and was convinced that 'this is a genuine case of hardship and loss'.[95] An award of £800 was made and it seems the Sweetnams joined the many Irish involuntary emigrants in England, some of whose cases have been detailed. Sweetnam and his wife lived on an RIC pension of a mere £105 a year.

In April 1921, the Stone brothers, Protestant farmers near Clonmel, were attacked and the young Robert Stone 'was shot dead'.[96] 'The shooting of young Stone was condemned in the Catholic churches of the district on Sunday.'[97] Crossley Boyle, a 40-year-old Protestant farmer from Dargan, was also shot dead on 14 June and his body was found in the same place as Robert Stone's. He occupied an evicted farm and had 'received messages from Sinn Féiners telling him that they would clear him out of his farm.'[98] Earlier in January 1921, land agent George Frend of Silverhills, Cloughjordan, was murdered on his way home. He was a JP in Moneygall and Cloughjordan. His murderers escaped and their motivation is unknown, perhaps connected with Frend's work as a land agent. George Sackville Wallis, a Protestant civil bill officer, was 'found shot dead near Cashel'[99] on 18 April 1921.

Lastly, on 30 May 1923, Protestant farmer Henry Colclough was shot dead by an unknown assailant. He bred 'Prize winning Hunters'[100] near Clogheen on a 200-acre farm. A previous tenant had been evicted some 25 years earlier. He was subjected to attempts to damage him commercially when twelve of his hunters had their tails cut off in June 1922, rendering them unsaleable. His wife left the farm, put in a claim to the Irish Grants Committee which was turned down as the murder took place just after the closing date for incidents to be considered for compensation.

Some cases of intimidation, boycotting and enforced emigration have been examined in the South Riding of Co. Tipperary. How far this intimidation and harassment led to an outflow of Protestants in this period is impossible to gauge with any degree of accuracy. From 1911 to 1926, the number of Protestants in the South Riding of Tipperary, roughly the diocese of Cashel, Emly and Lismore, fell by 37.5 per cent, from 2,987 to 1,867.[101] Of this fall in number of 1,120 people, however, we must take account of the 1,200 'persons engaged in the Defense of the county'[102] in 1911. They were based in Clogheen, Tipperary, Cashel and Clonmel in the South Riding. In 1911, there were 1,213 Protestants in the British forces based in Co. Tipperary, made up of 1,091 Episcopalians, 59 Presbyterians and 63 Methodists,[103] almost all based in the South Riding. This figure of 1,213 is more or less the equivalent of the fall in numbers of Protestants in the South Riding between 1911 and 1926. So we can conclude that there does not seem to have been a flight of Protestants in the South Riding during the Irish War of Independence and the civil war.[104]

The North Riding was different: there was a fall in Protestant numbers of 29 per cent,[105] particularly the area around Nenagh, where there was an enforced exodus of Protestants. In this areas in the west of the county, the Irish Grants Committee received some thirty claims, including the burning of mansions and houses, boycotting of farms and shops, cattle driving and non-payment of rents by tenant farmers, looting and billeting. The Church of Ireland Gazette, in its editorial of 23 June 1922, mentioned Nenagh specifically:

> ... the fact remains that in certain districts in southern Ireland inoffensive Protestants of all classes are being driven from their homes and shops and their farms in such numbers that many of our little communities are in danger of being entirely wiped out ... Mullingar, Athenry, Loughrea and Nenagh ... the rights of life and property are not being upheld.

At a meeting in Nenagh in April 1922, the Rt Revd Sterling Berry, Bishop of Killaloe since 1913, told the Church of Ireland audience, 'We come together as Irishmen – deeply concerned for the welfare of our land and deeply grieved at occurrences which bring reproach and dishonour upon our country'.[106]

A little later in June, Berry wrote to the Minister of Home Affairs:

> There is scarcely a Protestant family in the district which has escaped molestation. One of my Clergy has had his motor car and a portion of his house burned. (This was Revd Henry). Some other houses have

been burned. Cattle have been driven off farms. Protestant families
have been warned to leave the neighbourhood. Altogether a state of
terrorism exists.[107]

Some three months after Sterling expressed concern, Kilboy House in
Dolla, south of Nenagh – one of three mansions in the same area to
suffer the same fate – was burnt. It is hard to know what the motivations were. The Dunalleys had been in Ireland since the 1660s and
had been rewarded about 20,000 acres of land in the barony of Upper
Ormond for services rendered during Cromwell's Irish campaign.
They were the Prittie family, raised to the peerage in 1800 at the time
of the Union. By 1922, they held some 2,000 acres at the foothills of
the Silvermine Mountains. The then Lord Dunalley was 81 years old
at the time. A conservative with a strong dislike of Gladstone's Irish
policies, he had had a distinguished university career, gaining a double
first at Trinity College, Cambridge. The Dunalley family had a long
history of service in the British Army and one of the lord's sons was
killed in the First World War.

According to the man who is now responsible for the care of the
property, Declan Mullen,[108] Dunalley was not considered an unpopular
landlord. Mullen thought that at a time of chaos during the Civil War,
there was no police protection for Dunalley, nor anyone else. Small,
poor farmers and landless unemployed men in the Silvermines area
took advantage of local conditions to raid the Dunalley estate, take
cattle and burn Kilboy House. Several attempts had been made on
Dunalley's life; on one occasion when he was going to the Church
of Ireland church on his estate with his family, nine shots were
fired at him.[109] He had been raided prior to that and, according to
Mullen, kept loaded guns at all corner windows on the ground floor.
In mid-1922, he moved to England with his wife, shortly before his
mansion was burnt when the out-offices and farmyard were looted.
His steward, Doupe, was living on the premises and wrote to tell
Dunalley, 'It breaks my heart to see the place now.' He went on to say, 'I
suppose we will have to go to England now on the refugees system'.[110]
He was given three months to leave.

Doupe kept in touch with his master, the correspondence now in
the keeping of the National Library of Ireland.[111] He did what he
could to sell off the cattle and sheep before leaving for Fivemiletown
in Co. Tyrone. His family broke up; one son went to start a new life

in Canada under an orphanage scheme, Doupe apparently having abandoned his children.

Both Doupe and the head keeper, Mollison, applied to the IGC for compensation for loss of employment. Doupe had worked for Dunalley for 25 years. He had been shot by those who raided his house, and sustained an injury to one of his fingers.[112] He claimed £840 for loss of earnings and was awarded £150.

Dunalley's solicitor, Dudley of Nenagh, made a claim for £100,000 (about £4.5 million in today's money) in the local court for damage done under the Damage to Property (Compensation) Act of 1923. In July, a county court judge awarded only £17,395 (about £780,000 today) for reinstatement of Kilboy, with £5,105 for damages to the outbuildings. In addition, the new Land Commission paid him £16,000 in land bonds for 1,277 acres of untenanted land (i.e. demesne).

At the same time as Kilboy was burnt, the nearby Castle Otway went up in flames. The Otways and Pritties had been neighbours for several centuries, both families having been awarded lands in the same area as payment for serving in Cromwell's army. Otway was a lieutenant and his descendants went on to serve in the British Navy. An application for a claim to the IGC came from Robert Otway-Ruthven on board HMS *Excellent* in Portsmouth in December 1926. He was the eldest son of William Otway-Ruthven, who died in 1907. Robert had previously applied to the County Court and was awarded £7,235 in July 1924.[113] This award was for partial reinstatement, full reinstatement being turned down as the government valuer offered £8,000, which was considered inadequate to restore the castle.

Robert Otway-Ruthven applied to the IGC as well as to the Irish court, unlike Lord Dunalley. The Dublin court did not compensate him for furniture that was stolen some months before the castle was burnt, nor for a rectory that was burnt on Otway-Ruthven property. The Irish courts required proof that robberies were committed by the Irregulars before compensating claimants, unlike the IGC. For the rectory, £1,600 was awarded which was 'quite insufficient to enable the reconstruction to be effected'.[114] No explanation was given as to why the rectory was burnt.

The IGC awarded Otway-Ruthven £2,550, of which £1,125 was paid in advance. When added to the compensation of the Irish court, the total amount was inadequate to build a new home, restore the rectory and meet the cost of stolen furniture. The Otway-Ruthvens therefore left the area they had lived in for almost 3 centuries.

In her pamphlet, Miriam Lambe quotes from an extract from the Primary School Folklore Collection:

> The Otways were always looked upon as good landlords.
> They gathered no tithes from the people …
> Otway's ancestors were captains in Cromwell's army in 1649.
> There were no people evicted in this district.[115]

A group of men (around ten in number) entered the house of Mr Samuel Biggs at Hazel Point, Dromineer, Nenagh on 16 June 1922. They locked up Mr Biggs, who had only one arm, and an old man, a Mr Thomas Webb, and proceeded to ransack the house. The gang also consumed a quantity of whiskey and tied up and raped Mrs Biggs. They then warned the family that if they reported the matter, they would all be shot. The men stole some jewellery and clothes from the house before departing. Webb stated of Mrs Biggs that 'when she was liberated she was in a frightful condition, almost unconscious'. He could not identify any of the men, though two of them were in uniform. Subsequently four men – Michael Grace, Patrick and Edward Hogan of Drumineer and James Grace of Dunaboy – were charged with the rape (referred to throughout as being 'outraged') and fined £100 each in lieu of 4 months in jail.

Another 'outrage' took place in Sopwell Hall, Cloughjordan, on 29 July 1922, when five armed men attempted to rape two Protestant girls, Alton and Stringer, who were separated by them from the Catholic girl, Flaherty. All three girls were employed by the owner, Cosby G. Trench, 'a generous and dynamic landlord'.[116] The Catholic girl was not abused. The house was looted and the gang of men raided the cellar and drank much alcohol before attempting to assault the girls, whom they knew were Protestants as they had met them previously at local dances. It is recorded that three of the five men were sentenced to 10 years' penal service, a far more severe sentence than that handed down to the four men who raped Mrs Biggs.

There are a number of cases of robbery and boycotting of Protestant shopkeepers in Nenagh, once called an English town. An example is the claim of Cecil Henry Burchett, an Englishman married to the daughter of Mrs Hodgins, the owner of a shop in Nenagh. He was active in recruiting in 1914/15, enlisted in August 1915 and 'was discharged in broken health'.[117] Returning to Nenagh, he found his 'wife's health completely gone'.[118] She had been intimidated during his absence; he attributed this to his recruiting activities and to the fact that he had enlisted in the British Army. Matters deteriorated in 1922 when the shop windows were smashed and the family was told to leave the country. They lost business and Burchett claimed 'nearly all the County – families [sic] who were the back-bone [sic] of our business were between 1920 & 1923 driven from the country'.[119]

The solicitor supporting Burchett's claim, Dudley of Nolan and Dudley, Nenagh, suggested in a long, emotional letter to the IGC of 1 April 1927 that much of his losses were attributable to the fall away in support of the loyalist community whose mansions were burnt: 'Their effects were looted, their cattle stolen, and their lives made unbearable generally with the result that of course many of them had to flee the country leaving their land waste and their business derelict.'[120] Once the British forces had left, loyalists were 'at the mercies of the Irregulars who wandered about the Country in armed bands often without officers doing desperate deeds.'[121] Dudley thought that part of the reason why Burchett had been intimidated and boycotted was that after the 1916 rebellion, he served with the 18th Royal Irish in Fermoy and had been sent to Limerick to arrest suspected insurgents in an area which extended to Nenagh. The IRA Brigade in Nenagh was aware of this and warned Burchett not to return.

In 1924, the business was sold to the bank. Burchett ended up living in a soldier's cottage near Nenagh with an army pension, his solicitor drawing attention to the generous compensation paid by the Irish courts to 'those who were in armed opposition to the British Government during the years of trouble.'[122] Despite Dudley's strenuous advocacy, Burchett was only awarded £1,500. He had requested £5,000.

Both Dudley and Burchett thought there had been a significant exodus of loyalist families from the baronies of Upper and Lower Ormond during this period. It looks as if they are correct. The 1911 census shows 233 Episcopalians, 21 Presbyterians and 2 Methodists in Nenagh,[123] a total of 256, whereas the 1926 census shows 132 Episcopalians, 7 Presbyterians and 2 Methodists,[124] a total of 141, a sharp drop of 45 per cent. Presbyterian numbers fell by two-thirds.

It is worth looking at some compensation claims in the barony of Ikerrin, north-east Co. Tipperary, where Roscrea is the major urban centre. In contrast to Nenagh, however, the number of claims made to the IGC from the Roscrea area was small: only fourteen compared to twenty-nine from the Nenagh area. A Roscrea resident, Adrian Hewson, maintains that relations were generally good between the Catholic and Protestant communities during the period 1920–23, partly because the Cistercian Order outside Roscrea, Mount St Joseph, exercised a calming influence.[125] The Free State Army, based in Roscrea, also helped to maintain law and order during the Civil War.

But not everyone enjoyed a peaceful life. An elderly woman, Elizabeth Vaughan – who was aged 78 in 1926 – lived at Golden Grove, Roscrea. Between May 1922 and January 1923, her out offices and greenhouse, crops, trees and gatehouse were damaged. She believed that these incidents occurred because her husband had been a JP and DL. She claimed £4,000 in the Birr circuit court in November 1925, when Judge Roche observed that 'it is a sad thing that the people of the locality should indulge in such a debauch of savagery towards such a defenseless old man and woman'.[126] The destruction and 'savagery' occurred partly because of a dispute with the Vaughan farm workers. The Transport Union backed a seven-week strike. Mrs Vaughan made it clear in court there was no agrarian motive. She was awarded £1,320 and the IGC awarded an additional £1,500.

There is the exceptional case of two Orange Order members – a father and son – being forced out of the Roscrea area, the only Orange Order claim I found in the IGC files for Co. Tipperary. William McKenna was 72 when he applied for an IGC grant in November 1926. He was employed as a steward on the Vaughan estate, where he arrived in March 1922 with his wife and son, who had been in the Ulster Volunteers. In June, he received a warning letter telling him to leave within 24 hours. This was at the time that his employer, the Vaughan family, was under severe attack. McKenna wrote that 'he could not get away at the time'.[127] Subsequently the family was robbed, and McKenna's wife and son were taken into a wood and tied up. He only found them the following morning. Thereafter, to avoid being attacked at night, they slept outdoors and then left for the Isle of Man. McKenna's wife was 75 when this attack took place and he later stated that she had 'lost her health ever since'.[128]

He returned to Belfast, where his wife was 'an invalid',[129] aged 75 in 1928. He initially claimed £50 for loss of employment, travel expenses and goods stolen, but the IGC considered that he had not presented his case 'to the claimant's best advantage'.[130] and encouraged him to reapply for fuller compensation, which he did, receiving £350 in October 1928. This is a rare case of an applicant being asked to increase the amount of a claim.

It seems there was no significant exodus of Protestants in the Ikerrin barony. The Church of Ireland preachers' book for St Cronin's church, Roscrea, gives a congregation of 216 on Easter day 1915 and 177 in 1924, a decline of 18 per cent, but it seems that 26 Church of Ireland men fell in the First World War in the Roscrea parish, accounting for the reduced numbers. The censuses of Ireland 1911 and 1926 reported that there were 233 Church of Ireland people in Roscrea in 1911 and 202 in 1926.[131] However, in 1911, there were 56 Methodists in Roscrea and by 1926 there were 36, a fall of 36 per cent. Dudley Cooney, the Methodist historian of the Irish midlands, has commented:

> The upheavals of the War of Independence and the Civil War between 1919 and 1923 created difficulties for the Methodist people as well as for others, and some people found it difficult to adjust to the new regime. In particular, those who had served in the security forces during the British administration felt insecure, and emigrated.[132]

In the dioceses of Cashel and Emly, which includes parishes in the South Riding of Co. Tipperary, there were 16 Church of Ireland primary schools in 1915–16 with 246 pupils on the roll. In 1925–26 there were 11 schools with only 154 pupils in the roll, a fall of 62 per cent in pupils in 10 years.[133] The 1924–25 report stated:

> ... the numbers in attendance are for the most part small ... The finances of the Board are much depleted and unless more generous help is given by Church people in future years, the work of our young people will be greatly hampered.[134]

Looking at the decline in civilian Protestant numbers in Co. Tipperary from 1911 to 1926, there were 8,088 Episcopalians, 432 Presbyterians and 435 Methodists in Co. Tipperary in 1911, making a total of 8,088 and 4,143 in 1926, the drop being 3,637.[135] Of this 3,637, there were 1,213 in the British Army who were Protestants.[136] These army men had dependents, possibly 20 per cent[137] so we have 250 dependents and certainly not all were Protestants, perhaps 200. So we are looking at 1,400 British Army Protestants in Co. Tipperary in 1911. The total number of Protestants (Episcopalians, Presbyterians and Methodists) in Co. Tipperary was 8,088, so if we take away 1,400, we get 6,688 civilian Protestants in 1911. In 1926 there were 4,143 civilian Episcopalians, Presbyterians and Methodists, so there was a drop in the number of civilian Protestants of 2,545, or 38 per cent in the county.

Why the widespread persecution, intimidation and looting? The Church of Ireland identified 'covetousness' as a motive, as well as 'personal dislike', and there can be no doubt that anti-British sentiment was sometimes used as a cloak for land-grabbing. Tom Garvin thinks that 'land hunger and communal hatreds commonly led to sectarian and agrarian murders'[138] 'Communal' hatreds included 'the traditional Anglo-Irish (meaning Protestant Irish) and British Ascendancy'.[139] But as we have seen, by 1921 various land acts had seen to it that landlordism had been abandoned and there was little ground for 'hatred' on agrarian grounds. Land had been transferred to ex-tenants on a national scale, but the small Protestant community nevertheless felt insecure and fearful, and with reason. They suffered intimidation, arson, land seizures, boycotting and cattle driving at a time when there was no police force or army and when there was much poverty, unemployment and landlessness during the post-war depression. R.B. McDowell thought 'it was hard to say' whether the motives were 'political, religious or purely agrarian' and 'victims seem to have believed it was a compound of all three.'[140] Opportunism played a part as well as association with the British forces, RIC and service as DLs and JPs which led to many cases of harassment. There can be little doubt that some Protestants lost the goodwill of their neighbours because they were loyal to the Crown. A distant relative of mine, Lady Emily Bury of Charleville Forest, Tullamore, Co. Offaly, expressed the view to the Irish Grants Committee in 1926 that: 'It is quite clear a conspiracy started in 1920 to drive all loyalists out of Ireland to make their places absolutely no use to them with the object of getting hold of their land as being aliens in the country'.[141]

In the neighbouring King's and Queen's Counties, there was a 'forcible ejection of large numbers of Protestants'.[142] In south Donegal, some Protestants similarly received notices ordering them to leave.

On 16 June 1922, the *Church of Ireland Gazette* reported that Protestants had been evicted at Ballinasloe, Co. Galway:

The system which is usually followed is, first, the dispatch of an anonymous letter giving the recipient so many days, or hours, to clear out. If this notice be disregarded, bullets are fired at night through his windows, bombs are thrown at his house, or his house is burnt down … In one case an old man and his crippled son were left destitute … a large number of Protestants have left and others are under sentence of expulsion … A large number of Protestants throughout the County Westmeath got notice to quit.[143]

In Mullingar, 'disgraceful scenes' were reported 'when business premises of nearly all the Protestant residents were attacked … Furthermore, a large number of the Protestants throughout the County Westmeath got notice to quit … the windows of all the Protestant houses in the town were riddled with bullets'.[144]

In the area of Stradbally, Co. Laois (then Queen's County), John Salter, a Protestant, wrote of 'a body of republicans encamped in the hills adjoining the village … they descended upon the Protestant traders in the adjoining villages and looted whatever they required for their purposes. They were well aware that none of the Protestant farmers nor shopkeepers in the neighbourhood were in the least in sympathy with or would have anything to do with their movement and they then proceeded to punish them in this way'.[145]

Leigh-Anne Coffey wrote at some length about the background to the sectarian attacks around Luggacurran and Stradbally, Co. Laois, in her book *The Planters of Luggacurran*. There was a history of agrarian agitation going back as far as 1870 on lands owned by Lord Lansdowne. Local Catholics resented the Protestants, who replaced Catholic tenants evicted by Lansdowne's agent. They were branded 'Orange', though they were not from Northern Ireland. By 1922, with the new State involved in a civil war, the enforcement of law and order had become difficult, if not impossible, in many rural areas, thus giving an opportunity for the law to be taken into the hands of local agitators. Consequently, in certain areas old resentments were given expression through acts of persecution and occasional violence.

Robert Stanley of Stradbally was forced out of his home and farm in April 1922, meaning that he was unable to sell his crops.[146] Henry Sydhes received similar treatment. In March 1922 he was given notice by republicans to leave. He ignored the demand, so on 20 April armed men turned him out, throwing his furniture on the ground outside his home. He only had 9 acres. His son, meanwhile, was forced to leave the country, sailing to make a new life in Canada.[147] In May, Thomas Stone, also from Stradbally, was driven from his home for 3 months in March. The house and garden were damaged.[148]

In nearby Mountrath, Co. Laois, 'all loyalists in Ballyfin were boycotted'. William Bloomfield, a small farmer in the same area, complained that no one was allowed to plough for him, machinery on his farm was wrecked and 3 acres were spiked.[149] In nearby Ballycarney, Annie Wilkinson, a Protestant widow, was attacked. In July 1922 her cattle were removed and her crops were destroyed. She had 56 acres. Colonel Hutcheson Poe, once the Lieutenant for Queen's County, wrote that:

> A number of decent Protestant farmers received notice to give up their lands and had their cattle driven off and in some areas had their houses occupied by landgrabbers … people suffered in that area because they were Protestant.[150]

Four small Protestant farmers were persecuted near Fethard, south Tipperary. Alfred Stephenson was a tenant farmer with 72 acres in Cramps Castle. The IRA ordered him to leave in June 1920 and on 19 July, part of his house was burnt. In March and April 1921, three neighbouring Protestant farmers, named Lysaght, Stone and Boyle, were shot. Stephenson asked the local British military to protect him, but after spending two days in their barracks, he was taken by soldiers to the train and travelled to Belfast, leaving all he had behind. His lands were 'seized and confiscated' when the British Army withdrew in 1922 so, aged 50, he decided to make a new life in Canada, emigrating in July 1924 to Spring Lake, Grand Prairie, Alberta. The Grants Committee awarded him £1,500.[151]

Walter Kelly, a small farmer with 16 acres near Glassan, Co. Westmeath, was punished for being a loyalist who had relations serving in the British Army, who stayed with him when they were on leave. He sold milk to the RIC, something the IRA forbade. In May 1922, three armed men informed him that they were going to take possession of his land. He succeeded in finding a buyer, a Mr Killian, but when the news got out some 100 IRA men called to his house and burnt it, along with the hay barns. He fled to Dublin, where he started a boarding house. This failed, and he emigrated, ending up as a farmhand in New Zealand in 1926. The Irish Grants Committee awarded him £1,500.[152]

Nearby, in Waterstone, Co. Westmeath, Arthur Harris–Temple was driven from his land, his house having been attacked repeatedly. His steward, who had served in the British Army, was attacked twice and left unconscious. Harris–Temple was 'obliged to leave in August 1922 … my house was greatly damaged and I was obliged to dispose of furniture, pictures and china at great sacrifice.' He had been a JP and his family had been in Westmeath since Elizabethan times. His house, built in 1773, stood on about 1,000 acres. The Free State Army occupied the building and badly damaged the woodwork. Harris–Temple was unable to sell privately as his tenants, who had not paid rent during the Troubles, wanted to divide his land. It was 'owing to the kindness of friends have we been able to live at all'. He eventually found himself living in lodgings in London on £2 a week. The Grants Committee gave him £5,000.[153]

In Birr, Co. Offaly, a prosperous Protestant businessman, Michael Tilford, was ruined by a prolonged boycott from 1921 to 1922. He had enjoyed a successful auctioneering business for years but Roman Catholics would not use him; even some Protestants, intimidated by the IRA, boycotted his business when selling their houses. On fair days men were posted at the four corners of the square in Birr and warned people not to buy from him.[154]

Alan Stanley tells a moving story of the cold-blooded murder of the two Pearson sons, Richard and Abraham, on 30 June 1921 in Coolacrease, Co. Offaly. Both were shot in the groin and back and left to bleed to death. Their mother, three sisters and two cousins witnessed the murders. The Pearsons' house was burnt and some of the family ended up in Australia, some in England. The family belonged to a Christian sect called 'Cooneyites'. Founded by Edward Cooney in Fermanagh, this group was accused of helping the British military, though there seems to be no evidence to support this accusation. They were accused of wounding a local IRA man who was with a party of men felling trees on their land to prevent the Black and Tans using a road. Again there seems to be no evidence this happened. The story can be found in Stanley's book, *I Met Murder on the Way.* RTÉ made an award-winning documentary of these murders, shown on 25 October 2007 and directed by Niamh Sammon.

The *Church of Ireland Gazette* reported on 6 October 1922 that 'Protestants and loyalists are being expelled from their homes, which are being ransacked and destroyed … undoubtedly a campaign of persecution is in progress'. It also noted that 'there is a large exodus to England.' On 20 October the *Gazette* observed that 'it would be better that her (the church's) messages should be delivered to living souls than to empty pews in Ireland.' The Protestant churches were emptying. As one clergyman pointed out, the parishes of Munster and Connaught were almost deserted, for 'there is no use sticking to Ireland when our parishioners are not any longer with us. If the laity are driven out, why need we stick to Ireland?'[155]

The Most Revd Dr Fogarty, the Roman Catholic Bishop of Killaloe, came to the defense of the Church of Ireland community in May 1923, noting that 'Protestant fellow countrymen had been persecuted and dealt with in a cruel and coarse manner'.[156]

In view of all this widespread and prolonged intimidation, it is not surprising that many Protestants left. Marcus Tanner commented: 'Practically the whole of the Protestant working class – perhaps 10,000 – fled from Dublin in the early 1920s'.[157]

This estimate is speculative; however, there is no doubt that there was an exodus, which was of concern to the Church of Ireland as pointed out by the *Church of Ireland Gazette* on 15 April 1921: 'From Dublin there is beyond dispute a considerable exodus of Church people. Whole families of the best type are quietly slipping away, and these represent a net loss, since others do not come to take their vacant places.'

The professional middle-class Protestants in Dublin mostly stayed on as barristers (38 per cent), doctors (21 per cent), solicitors (37 per cent), chartered accountants (45 per cent) and civil engineers (30 per cent).[158] However, for the 26 counties as a whole, Protestant numbers in the middle-class professions declined by over 30 per cent between 1911 and 1926. This indicates that the professional middle class left in the same numbers as the rest of the Protestant population.

In 1871, the Protestant population of Dublin city was 18.8 per cent, with 27.5 per cent in the county. By 1926, numbers had declined to 8.7 per cent in the city and 19.4 per cent in the county. In all wards of Dublin, there was a decline of 40 per cent between 1911 and 1926. Protestants were mainly an urban population and of those in Dublin many suffered from poverty and distress; Sean O'Casey's biography bears this out. Though there was a solid educated Protestant middle class with its own schools and university, it is a myth that Protestants were solely middle class and comfortably off.

By 1923, some native-born Protestant Irish loyalists were dead and thousands had been driven out of their homes and homeland. They did not fit in the new Ireland. Irish Protestants who stayed on soon learnt, in the words of the late Professor W.B. Stanford, to 'lie low and say nothing.' As the historian F.S.L. Lyons put it, the tiny Protestant minority 'was, or seemed to be, enervated by the almost repressive tolerance shown to it by the majority'.[159]

By 1939, 'Protestants enjoy toleration at the moment but that is largely because they no longer possess anything, either power or property, which others want. It is the toleration we all accord to the dead', reported the *Christian Irishman*, the paper of the Home Mission, perhaps over dramatically.[160]

There seems to be an unwillingness by Irish historians to shine a light on this dark period of Irish history. Little analysis has been done on the reasons for the exodus. One historian in Trinity College, Dublin, corrected me for pointing out that there had undoubtedly been a major exodus of Protestants who had been persecuted for sectarian reasons, for their allegiance to the Crown, for their service with the British forces and for holding land; a mixed bag of reasons, as this chapter makes clear. This historian told me all had suffered in this period. True, but this period saw the exodus of many unionist Protestants and few Catholic nationalists.

The message was clear: they were no longer wanted. Most Irish historians seem to take a benign view of this fate: one of historical determinism, seeing Protestants as the victims of the inevitable march of victorious Catholic Gaelic nationalism and the defeat of British imperialism. David Fitzpatrick, in his admirable study of Co. Clare during the violence of 1920–23,[161] omits to mention that since 1919, seventy out of eighty 'Protestant landed families had left county Clare'.[162] This was an overwhelming exodus. The eminent Irish historian Roy Foster, who edited the *Oxford Illustrated History of Ireland*, seems not to have understood the deep feeling of abandonment southern Protestants felt after 1921. He is taken to task by Miriam Moffitt for not acknowledging the effects of partition on southern Protestants, rather highlighting the negative results for Catholics in Northern Ireland:

Seen through Protestant eyes, the years 1870–1940 were a succession of humiliations … They perceived that their dominance in national politics had been taken from them … and after the passing of the local authority act of 1898, they were no longer the people of power in local politics.[163]

Joseph O'Neill in his book, *Dark Blood Track*, compares the treatment of Protestants to the persecution of Armenians and Christians in Cilicia, Turkey, arguing:

> ... the migrant groups in Ireland and Turkey were remarkably similar. Both were minorities regarded as a fifth column of the foreign enemy; both suffered a demographic cataclysm unmentioned by dominant nationalist histories; and finally, both left a vestigial population in the new nation-state whose members instinctively understood that, whatever the political and constitutional affirmations to the contrary *their citizenship was a matter of indulgence and not of right* [my emphasis].

This is eloquently put, but the scale was different. Well over 1 million Armenians and Christians were murdered in Turkey, by no means comparable to the small number murdered in Ireland. Nevertheless, arguably O'Neill is right in one sense: the trauma was comparable.

Perhaps a more appropriate analogy is the exodus of United Empire Loyalists from the thirteen American colonies between 1775 and 1783. About 70,000 loyalists fled these colonies, with some 40,000 going to eastern Canada (Ontario, Quebec and Nova Scotia). They fled for reasons familiar to Southern unionists: intimidation, persecution, theft of goods and land and fear of changes to come and alienation on the basis of political principles.

Both communities were faithful to the Crown, with some dependent on the Crown for their livelihoods. Many were farmers and shopkeepers; some were clergymen, some labourers.

However, the Irish loyalists arguably suffered a comparatively harder fate. They had little compensation in the form of land grants given to Empire loyalists in Canada. They had to seek new lives with niggardly compensation. But they did share loss of home and country with Empire loyalists. To quote Ann MacKenzie:[164]

> Fleeing in panic and confusion, forced to leave behind most of their possessions and burdened with the prospect of building a new life in a new land, the Loyalists faced unpromising beginnings. The lands they were to settle were isolated, forbidding and wild.

There are two major differences between the United Empire Loyalists and Southern unionists. Firstly, the United Empire Loyalists went on to build one of the leading nations of the world: Canada, renowned for its liberal democracy based on pluralism, toleration and constitutional nationalism. The Southern unionists, meanwhile, suffered defeat at the hands of physical force nationalists who went on to build a country for one race and one religion, purportedly speaking Gaelic; a nation whose progeny was romantic nationalism and was demographically overwhelmingly Catholic. Canada, in contrast, was an inclusive, multi-faith, multi-race country. In the Free State, in contrast, 'This process of homogenization in turn had its own, very particular, consequences for social and cultural life in Ireland in the twentieth century.'[165] Southern loyalists did little to help to build this new nation but rather spread to the Anglosphere, to form a new life where their attitudes found new welcoming homes.

Secondly, the sharp decline in numbers of Southern Protestants caused by boycotting, murders and intimidation had a long-lasting effect on the 'vestigial population' which stayed on. It was a haemor-rhage that left the community anaemic. According to Kurt Bowen, the initial stance of Protestants was 'indignant marginality', which 'rapidly evolved into one of indifference, estrangement and apathy'. [166]

More than this, as mentioned earlier, the exodus 'shattered the confidence of those who remained and undermined their determina-tion to continue distinctive political activity … leaving Anglo-Ireland leaderless'.[167] A once-confident people were in effect laid low.

3

A Chain of Bonfires

Stephen Gwynn, the Irish National Party MP for Galway from 1906 to 1918, thought that the IRA campaign had been 'wrong on all the great things'. It failed to achieve a united Ireland. Instead, through violent terrorist actions motivated by the wish to separate from Britain, Ireland was deeply and lastingly divided. Protestantism is associated with loyalism and that tradition included the Irish landlord class. According to Terence Dooley's work *The Decline of the Big House*, between 1920 and 1923, the IRA burnt 276 of their houses,[1] most of them architectural treasures built and designed by Irishmen. More were destroyed later.

In Europe, and particularly in France, the castles and mansions of the aristocracy remained untouched during violent social upheavals and in revolutionary times. Some of their owners were guillotined, hanged or imprisoned, but their chateaux stand to this day, most of them lovingly restored. In the Loire valley, you can feast your eyes on countless Renaissance and classical period chateaux. Amboise, Azay-le-Rideau, Blois, Chambord, Chenonceux, Cheverny and Valency; all stand as tributes to the rich, varied architecture and rich social life of past eras. All are cared for by the State and most are open to the public all year round, with guided tours and nominal admission charges. The National Trust in Britain similarly maintains the architectural heritage of Britain, from smaller domestic buildings to the many vast castles and mansions of the former ruling class.

In Ireland the situation was different. The mansions of the Irish ascendancy were mostly owned and cared for by people separated from the native Irish by religion as well as class, unlike France, where class – not religion – was the main divisive factor. In addition, the ascendancy class (who became known as 'planters'), unlike previous invaders such as the Norse and the Normans, were not easily assimilated, nor allowed to assimilate, largely because the Reformation did not take root in Ireland. Essentially, the Protestant ascendancy were and are considered an alien people. Daniel O'Connell called Protestants 'alien', considering the true Irish to be Catholics. Protestantism profoundly divided the Irish 'planters' from the English Normans and the Gaelic Irish, who were Roman Catholics. Unlike in the neighbouring island, the 39 Articles of the Anglican Church were not enforced by an English government that was too remote and half-hearted to enforce them effectively. An unsustained approach was taken and there were a number of reasons for this. There was 'the question of whether effective power and resources existed … for the imposition of the Protestant faith in meaningful terms.'[2] Unlike Wales, where the Reformation took route, 'Ireland had not been thoroughly subjugated in the medieval period'.[3] The popular myth that Ireland was conquered and oppressed for 800 years was shown to be untrue in the sixteenth century. Had subjugation succeeded, the Reformation would have been enforced by Tudor monarchs. In reality, their hold on the island was confined to the east. Instead of courting the Catholic Irish chiefs, the Tudors antagonised them. A policy of compulsion was pursued, not awards of more power for supporting the Reformation. 'The Reformation came to be seen as an English, foreign imposition.'[4] Catholicism bound the old English and Gaelic Irish, hostile to an imposed Tudor Protestantism. 'Catholicism now came to be seen as essential to the definition of true Irishness, an emblem which was to last into the history of Irish nationalism.'[5] Lastly, the Irish language was not used in spreading the Reformation doctrines. The vernacular was not used in evangelism and the New Testament was not available in Irish until 1603.

The penal laws of the eighteenth century did little to reduce the power of Irish Catholicism, which by then was deep rooted. They denied political power and landlord status to Roman Catholics, as well as Protestant Dissenters such as Presbyterians, but we now know that laws preventing freedom of worship were more often breached than observed. Roman Catholics were free to pursue commercial careers, and many became highly prosperous merchants, as the historian James Lydon has made clear.[6]

Many large Roman Catholic landowners converted after the Reformation in order to retain their lands. By 1731 the 'convert rolls' listed 704, among them some leading gentry families. Their Roman

Catholic contemporaries did not condemn many of these turncoats. The O'Hara family of Cooperstown in Sligo was one of many such families that did not lose the support of their tenants when they became Anglicans, as they still are to this day. Some landlords, even large ones, remained Catholics and suffered.

Ireland was the home of these landlords who saw their Irish identity as being important, although ambiguous and multi-layered. They considered themselves to be Irish and intermarried with the Irish. It was religious affiliations that separated them from the majority of their neighbours, religion being the never-ending source of division in Ireland. But they were mostly conscientious and careful to fulfil their duties to their tenants, some even bankrupting themselves during the Famine.

Here is what Alexis FitzGerald wrote about their tradition in *University Review* 1958:

> There is nothing unchristian in the constructive Anglo-Irish tradition but much that was fine and much that was a stimulus to noble living – much that confirms the Christianity of the common people of Ireland.

By 1920, Irish landlords had sold most of their estates to their tenants under the terms of various land acts and particularly the Wyndham Act, which by 1920 had transferred almost 9 million acres to tenants on generous terms for both landlords and tenants. However, despite the loss of power and land, many in the IRA and Sinn Féin between 1920 and 1923 – and for years thereafter – thought that the hyphenated 'Anglo-Irish' were an alien people (the new, early twentieth-century descriptor 'Anglo-Irish' designed to exclude this class) and proceeded to burn down many of their mansions. Bruce Arnold, the author and columnist, wrote about these burnings:

> Three generations ago, we had a national field sport of burning down all the great houses and forcing their former owners to leave Ireland if we did not send them on their way to heaven or hell. Even as the country carried out this pyrotechnic dance of triumph there was some realisation that a symbiotic relationship existed, and always exists, between what was being assaulted and those who assaulted it.[7]

'Any idiot with petrol and a match can set fire to a house', commented Monk Gibbon. 'It needs trained architects, masons and carpenters to build a house. The latter class of technical competence is rare, the former are numerous.'

W.B. Yeats was unambiguous when writing about the destruction of the large Irish houses. One such place was Coole Park, the residence of the nationalist author and playwright and co-founder of the Abbey Theatre, Lady Gregory, whose husband was a pillar of the British Empire. It was demolished in 1941. Yeats wrote, 'To kill a house where great men grew up, married and died, I here declare a capital offence.'

As a class, the Irish landlords lacked the ability and the will to defend themselves, unlike the unionist community in Northern Ireland. They were too small in number, and the various security forces – whether British or Irish – were so stretched during this period of upheaval and anarchy that there was little they could do to protect them. In fact, actions of the Black and Tans and Auxiliary police forces too often led directly to tit-for-tat burnings of the big houses, which were seen to represent the British garrison in Ireland.

Much of the country's finest architecture went up in flames during the Troubles and the Civil War. From 1920 until 11 July 1921, when the truce was declared, 76 big houses were burned. Between January 1922 and April 1923, 192 more were burned. In all, some 500 mansions were burned, abandoned or damaged beyond repair during the twentieth century, including 37 houses belonging to senators in the new Free State parliament. There were approximately 2,000 big houses in the 26 counties, so some 25 per cent of the total were left in ruins. Of these, about 30 were rebuilt with the compensation that the owners received, either from the Free State or from the Irish Grants Committee in London. These burnings had the effect of enforcing the emigration of many Protestants. The County Inspector of Cork wrote in May 1921: 'Loyalists are being persecuted, their mansions and houses are being burned, and a huge number of them have cleared out of the country'.[8]

There were several reasons for burning the houses. Some were burned to prevent the British Army from occupying them. A famous example was the magnificent Summerhill in Co. Meath, where the Empress Elizabeth of Austria went to hunt in the summers of 1879 and 1880. It has been described as 'the most dramatic of the great Irish Paladian houses, probably designed by Sir Edward Lovett Pearce in collaboration with Richard Castle.'[9] (There is a picture of Summerhill in the Emperor of Austria's palace in Vienna.) It was burnt on 4 February 1920, when 30 gallons of petrol was poured all over the floors and windows were opened to ensure the flames would spread quickly. The owner, Lord Langford, was away and fortunately the servants escaped any harm. It was said that the house was burnt because Michael Collins' spies in Dublin had heard British forces were going to occupy it to commence a campaign of counter-insurgency in the area. However, according to Lady Fingall, author of the book *Seventy Years Young*, the owner of Summerhill had persuaded the British military authorities not to quarter soldiers there. Unfortunately the letter accepting this decision was not seen by the IRA spies in Dublin Castle in time. It was said that locals burned down the house and that paintings, silver and furniture were stolen and scattered among local houses. Lord Langford left Ireland, never to return. The spectacular ruins were demolished in around 1957, an act of erasure of magnificent Irish architecture – a mansion built by Irish craftsmen – destroyed by Ireland's new people, putting behind them its former people and stealing their furniture and silver.

Others were torched in retaliation for the burning of the houses of suspected IRA men, such as Moydrum Castle in Westmeath, the home of Lord Castlemaine, Dunboy Castle in Castletownbere, west Cork, and 7 houses in Innishannon, west Cork. But undoubtedly a major motive was agrarian greed, an example being the house of the popular landlord, Beaumont-Nesbitt, Tubberdaly, in Laois and Derrycastle in Co. Tipperary. Landlord Shawe Taylor was murdered because he refused to part with his estate in Portumna. According to Dr Terrence Dooley, who has researched the motivation behind the destruction of the Anglo-Irish mansions, 'by 1923, land grabbing was endemic'. Patrick Hogan informed President W.T. Cosgrave that 'the shooting of Land Commission officials [had] become widespread' and 'house burning [had] become a matter of course'. In Dooley's book *The Decline of the Big House in Ireland*, Hogan claimed that he had 'noted the cases throughout the country where houses have been burned and in more than 50 per cent of these cases the circumstances make it plain enough that the destruction was not for political but for agrarian motives'.[10]

Others were destroyed after their valuable contents had been removed, like the magnificent Mitchelstown Castle, Co. Cork, one of the largest and most sumptuous mansions in Ireland and the home of the King Harmans. In fact, over a third of the houses burnt were in Co. Cork. Mitchelstown Castle was burnt after the Irregulars had occupied it in August 1922 in order, so they said, to prevent the Free State army from occupying it when they left. Its many valuables were stolen and were destined to adorn houses around Mitchelstown. Pictures were desecrated: a large Rembrandt had broken glass thrown at it. Edith Somerville commented at the time that 'lavatories being considered useless institutions, the walls of the corridors were used instead'.

The Ponsonby family in Castle Mary, Cloyne, Co. Cork built and owned Castle Mary, which was the home of Rita Flower, a striking lady who had inherited it from her father, Colonel Longfield. They were the local landed gentry in the parish in which my father was Dean and where I lived from 1950 to 1963. Their family had come to Ireland from Wales after the English Civil War, the first owner being John Longfield, a Williamite. They held land around Mallow and around Cloyne, stretching to the picturesque fishing village of Ballycotton, which they once owned. The estate grew to 10,813 acres by 1873, including land in Louth and Kerry. When Longfield died, he left 670 acres to his eldest daughter, Rita, as various land acts had ensured that he sold most of his land to his tenants. Rita married a Ponsonby related to the aristocratic Bessboroughs in Co. Kilkenny. She had one son, Arthur, who inherited Castle Mary. Arthur's father Myles fell in the Great War in 1915 at Loos when Rita was only 24, and she remarried in 1918 to a Neville Flower.

Castle Mary house was added to the long list of mansions burnt by the IRA when in September 1920, two maids staying in the castle on their own were roused one night and given ten minutes to clear out. They placed a few paintings near the door and left in a hurry. The men then proceeded to help themselves to the contents of the house and burnt it to the ground. No one seems to know who was responsible; whether it was the official IRA or some local lads in the nearby village of Ballinacurra. Whatever, it had the desired effect: it broke the spirit of Rita's father, Mountifort Longfield. In the words of his relative Jane Hayter Hames:

> The burning of the castle broke Colonel Longfield. It was too bitter. He said he would never go back to Ireland. The Anglo-Irish had coped as best they could with their divided nationality. They had been deserted by the English politically, seen their estates sold away from them and the Union dissolved. Now the Irish, among whom they counted themselves, had burnt them out. It was not just the material loss (everything went up in flames), it was the brutal statement of feeling; the flames said, "this is what your past here means to us", and the emotional bolt, like a burning arrow went straight to Longfield's heart. The newspaper mentioned that Col. Longfield was popular in the neighbourhood;

he had allowed many tenants to buy their farms. But to him it felt as though Ireland had turned on him in a vicious, personal attack; his whole family history had gone up in the conflagration.

Apparently, during the Great Famine, Mountifort's father, a wealthy man, had evicted some of his tenants, and memories of this were still alive. Another ancestor had been responsible for hangings around the Cloyne area during the United Irishmen's uprising in 1798, when insurgents fought to establish an Irish republic inspired by the principles of the French revolution. At that time Irish landlords, such as the Longfields, were part of the British administration in Ireland, were charged with maintaining law and order. These deeds may have had some influence, as memories of past injustices are very long in Ireland. Perhaps there were local people waiting 'in the long grass'.

Longfield's English wife, Alice, was not to be easily defeated. Determined to go back and rebuild, she persuaded her husband not to follow in the footsteps of their relatives, the Bessboroughs in Kilkenny, who had suffered enough intimidation during this chaotic time and left for Sussex, never to return. Their castle had been burnt but was later restored and is now an agricultural college in Piltown, Co. Kilkenny.

Many other families the Longfields knew left after their houses were burnt and their estates encumbered. But the Longfields stayed on, and Alice supervised the rebuilding of the stables and coach house at a cost of £5,240. They were compensated by the new Irish Free State government for the loss of the Castle. Initially awarded a decree for £60,000, they only received half this amount.[11] Mountifort Longfield did not recover and his enthusiasm for his estate was gone forever. During the 1920s, his land withered away as land laws were passed by the new Irish Government.

A few other houses were burnt in the area around Castle Mary. The Penrose-FitzGerald's house, Careystown House, was burnt in the 1920s. Aghada Hall, owned by General Sir Joseph Thackwell, a Protestant, was burnt at this time, and the Goold-Adams family from Jamesbrook Hall were forced out in the 1920s and never returned, though the house was not burnt.

Since the Land War of the 1870s, relations between landowners and tenants were poisoned socially and politically. Landlords had been taken aback by the bitterness of the people around them, demonstrated in the series of outrages. Terence Dooley, in *The Decline of the Big House in Ireland*, tells of an incident that demonstrates the sad bewilderment of a landlord whose house had been burnt.

> Maurice Headlam related a story regarding an elderly landlord and his wife with whom he shared a train journey the night after their house had been burned. The old lady told him: 'When we went down the avenue into the village, every door was shut and barred. No one would take us in. I knew every one of them, their fathers and mothers, their grandparents, all their children, and I thought they were my friends.'[12]

Lord Lansdowne's house, Derreen, near Kenmare, Co. Kerry, was vandalised in September 1922, including the gardens that he had developed for over half a century. He served as Viceroy of India and Governor General of Canada; a pillar of the British Empire and its most loyal Irish servant. The trees were cut down and sold, the doors, windows and floors were wrecked, the staircase destroyed and furniture was stolen or smashed. The contents were taken away in carts. The gardener's house was burned to the ground and he and his wife lost everything. The housekeeper was robbed. Lord Lansdowne wrote a letter to *The Times* on 4 September 1922:

> What is happening, and has happened, is not a conflict in the open between enemies, but the relentless and persistent persecution of a helpless minority, which is obnoxious because it is regarded as of an alien origin, because it stands for law and order, because its possessions are coveted and because it is the settled policy of the conspirators to oust it from the country.

He was clear that the 'conspirators' were essentially partly motivated by a policy of ethnic cleansing, whether to gain more land or to 'oust' these aliens from Ireland. Lansdowne added in his application for compensation to the Irish Grants Committee that 'had the owner been a known sympathiser of Sinn Féin aspirations, Derreen would not have suffered'.[13] The once-Governor of Canada and Viceroy of India would hardly sympathise with the republican attitudes of Sinn Féin.

Later he received compensation from the Free State, and the local parish priest assisted in retrieving some of the stolen furniture that had found its way into local houses. Lansdowne loved Derreen. He planned to retire there, but died on the way back from England in 1927, aged 82.

My relative, Emily Howard Bury, whose son was Colonel Howard-Bury of Belvedere house in Mullingar, the leader of the first Everest expedition, was also the subject of various attacks at Charleville Forest, Tullamore in August, 1922. A house on the estate, Brookfield, was destroyed by fire. Mr and Mrs Brown, unionists, lived there, Mr Brown being the estate agent. Some of the walls of the estate were broken down and 80 deer were slaughtered. Charleville Forest Castle was occupied by the Irregulars for a considerable time and much damage was done. After that, the Free State troops took possession 'for a lengthy period'.[14] Emily obtained £3,480 in compensation from both the Free State and the Irish Grants Committee when she was 72, and restored Brookfield House. She wrote in her application for compensation:

> It is quite clear a conspiracy started in 1920 to drive all loyalists out of Ireland to make their places absolutely no use to them with the object of getting hold of their land as being aliens in the country.[15]

Some Bury descendents from the marriage of John Bury and Jane Palliser in 1704 lived in the Kilmacthomas area in Co. Waterford. One was Caroline Fairholme, whose Comeragh estate initially belonged to William Palliser, the Archbishop of Cashel. It had descended to Captain John Palliser, who did not marry, and because the estate was so encumbered, it was given to his sister, Grace Palliser, so that she and her husband William Fairholme could relieve it of its debts. The couple had 5 unmarried daughters, including Caroline. The IRA burnt part of it down in 1923, and with it 400 years of family history. The property then ended up in the hands of Pieter Menten, a Dutch Nazi who was hunted down, arrested and then spent much of his time in prison in the Netherlands. He had hidden there behind the gates, surrounded by the many valuables stolen from the Jews he had persecuted.

John, William and Grace were 3 of the many children of Wray Palliser and Grace Barton of the famous Barton and Guestier wine family. Sean Murphy, a local historian, commented on the Pallisers:

> The Pallisers were good religious people in this area, as were the Miss Fairholmes, neices of John Palliser. Comeragh house was burned not as any reflection against the Fairholmes but as an act against the Free State government who were carrying out a policy of executions in order to bring the Civil War to a close. You may be aware that the Civil War

finally petered out in the Comeragh mountains not far from Comeragh house when the IRA leaders then on the run agreed to dump arms. The house was rebuilt on a smaller scale but many of the artifacts of Palliser were lost including papers through burning or looting.

Nearby, the Hunts, other descendants of the Burys, lived in Rockmount house. The owner, Arthur Hunt, wrote poignantly to his wife after their house had been burnt:

Dungarvan, 16 February 1923

My dearest Old Girl,

You will have my wire with sad news about our house being burned could not save anything scarcely. I got my desk & papers out & your desk & just a few odds & ends, Nurse got the 2 kids away to John's room, & hope they have gone to Seafield by now. I sent Monahan (the groom) this morn fearing they might be burnt as Comeragh House also gone. I went last night to see them [the Fairholmes]. The fellows came at 9 o'clock & only gave us 5 minutes. All your things are gone- You better get measured for a habit at Perkins [Tailor at Porlock, Somerset, England].

Such luck Grace had gone as it would have been very bad for her. I came to see Jack Williams [solicitor] but he cannot take up claim so will go to Chapman.

I cannot write more - I will sleep in room next to John's for a night or two. I am bewildered but hope to hunt tomorrow & it will do me good.

Best love Yr. loving Arthur.

Arthur's son, Colonel Thomas Hunt, now lives in retirement in England. He recently wrote vividly about the events of that fateful night:

On the night of 15th Feb 1923, my father, Arthur Hunt, my brother Robin (two and a half) and myself (five and a half) were living in Rockmount. My mother was over in England staying with her parents in Somerset.

Earlier that day a delivery of some 50 gallons of paraffin had been delivered to the house and stored in the basement for use in the lamps. This was probably a coincidence, however the fire was started in the sitting-room which had been drenched in paraffin. I am convinced the house was destined to be burned, paraffin or no paraffin, but my father was doubtful.

My father had made no plans to safeguard any of the contents of the house because he believed that the IRA had given a promise that they would not burn the house down. We had an IRA company camped in one of our fields some quarter of a mile from Rockmount and each evening about 3 or 4 officers came into the kitchen for an evening meal. Before they left, when the IRA was disbanding they gave my father that assurance. Of course, we had no choice whether we fed them or not.

Although I can't be sure, I believe that the gang who burned the house were not the same men who were based on Rockmount. I was told that they were on their way home west to Cork & Kerry [IRA strongholds] and decided as a last act to burn several houses in County Waterford whose owners were believed to be unionists [i.e in favour of remaining inside the United Kingdom of Great Britain and Ireland]. Although my father was a unionist, he was not politically active; indeed it would not have been wise to adopt a strong political line with a considerable Republican force camped on your farm.

When the IRA arrived at Rockmount, around 9.00 pm, they told my father that he had 15 minutes to get out. Not having a pre-determined plan he must have been 'bewildered' (his term, not mine) so after calling out John, a groom, to rescue the two children, all he could think to do was to save his collection of cut-throat razors (one for each day of the week). I was asleep alone in the small front bed-room when John burst in, picked me out of my bed and carried me on his shoulders out to the farm-yard. I don't know who rescued Robin, but both of us were taken into a small unoccupied cottage in the yard which had been occupied until some months previously by Martin, the cow-man. The room was infested by swarms of hungry fleas which attacked my brother and myself so that I have seldom had a more uncomfortable night, even during my service in the War in Italy.

Next morning, my father took me over to see the still smoking shell of the house. All the walls were very strongly built of stone and remained standing; the centre of the house was a heap of rubble. Only two things remained intact – the iron safe built into an outside wall and just above it, a wooden cupboard also built into the wall, inside of which was a collection of old cylindrical phonograph records some of which had partly melted but others were almost intact. Many of the records were by the great Irish singer Count John McCormack, including one which I still remember 'When the fields were white with daisies.'

Not everything in the house was lost. As soon as the neighbours heard what was about to happen, they turned out and removed many pieces of furniture and other portable objects which they stacked up on the lawn. Perhaps the most valuable item to be lost was the very first Waterloo Cup for hare coursing by greyhounds. The event began in the early 19th century and was held annually until 2005 when hunting animals with dogs became illegal.

As I was quite young at the time, I cannot now remember how many houses were burned that same night in County Waterford. I think perhaps five or six. One was Comeragh House, about half a mile from Rockmount owned by three old ladies, the Fairholmes. Why these harmless old woman should have had their house destroyed is a mystery to me. Another house, Gardenmorris, not more than 6 or 7 miles away from Rockmount was also burned. It belonged to a Colonel O'Shea, a Roman Catholic who had served many years in the British Army. I mention his religion simply to explain that the destruction policy - if there was one - did not seem to be aimed exclusively at the Anglo-Irish Protestant community, although all the other houses which were burned did, I believe, belong to this group.[16]

The Langleys, also descended from the Limerick Burys, lived near Rockmount. The grandson of the 1923 owner of Tay Lodge, Peter Langley has his old home is only 2 miles from Comeragh House. It was also targeted by the IRA the fateful night of 18 February, 1923. Like his first cousin Arthur Hunt, Peter's grandfather had also just got in a fresh supply of paraffin oil for the lamps. In Peter's words:

> … I believe he had been warned that something like this might happen, so the previous Sunday, while everyone around was at mass, he had buried the drum in the garden and planted cabbages on top. Unable to get the fire going properly, the groom who lived in the yard rounded up a lot of the locals. The IRA departed eventually and the fire was put out without too much damage being done. I still have a dressing table one of the drawers of which is charred.[17]

In Monaghan, 7 big houses were burned, including Gola, Glenburne House and Ballybay, the home of Henry Leslie. Lord Lanesborough's house and furniture were burnt in Cavan in May 1921. In Co. Roscommon, Lord French's house was stripped and everything was carried away in carts. The contents of Glenfarne house in Co. Leitrim were stolen, and, as described in the previous chapter, Kilboy, owned by Lord Dunalley in Tipperary, was robbed of silver plate, jewellery and farm implements. The furniture was redistributed around local houses in the area.

Many houses were burned after the Civil War started; in fact, 199 big houses, which was about 3 times more than 'during the War of Independence'.[18] De Valera disapproved of the new senate and those who opposed the Treaty set about burning 16 of the senators' big houses. Many of the new senators were Protestants, and Sir Antony Esmonde was an example. He was a nationalist MP and a good landlord, yet his house, Ballynastragh, Co. Wexford, was set alight in 1923. His outstanding library went up in flames, which affected him more deeply than the loss of the house. Lord Carew's house was burned at Castleboro, Co. Wexford, as was Colonel Moore's mansion, Moore Hall, Claremorris, Co. Mayo. Palmerstown in Kildare, Lord Mayo's house, was burned in January 1923 as a reprisal for the execution of 6 anti-Treatyites, which had nothing to do with him.

Senator Horace Plunkett's home, Kilteragh, Co. Dublin, went up in smoke. The son of Lord Dunsany, he was a patriot and a practical visionary, who tirelessly worked to establish co-operative dairying and agricultural credit and experimental farming. He had played a major and controversial role in the 1917 Irish Convention but left for England afterwards, bitterly disillusioned. He had given his heart to Ireland, something John Redmond had in disillusionment advised Lady Fingleton never to do.

The Mayo home of Lord Killanin in Spiddal was burnt after the cook and maid had thrown out the linen and pots and pans. Roxborough House in Co. Galway, the childhood home of Lady Gregory, the ardent Protestant nationalist, was torched in 1922. Judith Hill in *An Irish Life* notes that 2 years later, Lady Gregory visited it and wrote: 'the house – the ruin – is very sad, just the walls standing, blackened, and all the long yards silent, the many buildings, dairy, laundry, cow-houses, coach-houses, stables, kennels, smithy, sawmill and carpenters' shop empty.' A whole way of life had gone.

In west Cork, Kilbrittain Castle was burnt in 1920. In *Head or Harp*, Lionel Fleming writes of 'a constant succession of events which were both shocking and mysterious. The house of some quite respectable man would be burnt down – nobody knew why.' Fleming's father wrote in his diary:

> Co. Cork was badly hit. On May 26th [1920], Kilbrittain Castle was burnt. On December 2nd, Timoleague House was burnt. In Cork in May 1921 Sir Alfred Dobbins' house in Montenotte, Cork was set on fire as was Maud Jacobs' in Blackrock. In the latter case, Maud Jacobs' crime was that her daughter was going out with a member of the Crown Forces. In Co. Cork in June Major Charles Coote's house and furniture, near Mallow, and the house and furniture of Mr Cooke-Collis in Kilworth were burnt. On June 30th (1921) Castle Bernard was burnt (Lord Bandon's home) and Lord Bandon kidnapped. On June 24th, the Hawkes left Barry's Hall, and on the 28th, Mayfield was burnt … on 26th March (1923) Richmond and Brookfield were burnt … On April 13th Gortnahorna and Hare Hill were burnt.[19]

In Donegal, *The Irish Times* reported on 27 May 1921 that Culduff House in Inishboffin, the home of George Young and 'one of the finest in the country' was burnt down, and a week earlier Lord O'Neill's castle near Randalstown met the same fate.

Molly Keane's father's house in Ballyrankin, Co. Carlow, was torched, along with three others, as a reprisal for Black and Tan activities. A splendid new mansion, Dunboy near Castletownbere, Co. Cork, was also burnt. The English butler, Albert Thomas, wrote on the night it went up in flames:

> Tonight I was called up and shown a large glow in the sky overlooking the castle about a mile away. The rebels had burnt the castle down as they said they would. I was very, very sorry for all that lovely silver, the beautiful glass and splendid linen all being burnt, and all those gorgeous statutes and pictures, the wonderful drawing room all burning, for what?[20]

This house had an interesting history. It was owned by the Puxley family, friends of Daphne du Maurier, who wrote the book *Hunger Hill* based on the house and area. The Puxleys were originally from Galway, going back to 1685, and one of their number married a Sarah Lavallin from Castletownbere. Their son 'Copper John' started the copper mines at Allahies hills in 1812, employing local men. His son Henry started work on the Gothic mansion, Dunboy, in 1866. They were burnt out, it seems, because some houses of local IRA families had been burnt by the Auxiliaries. The family was Protestant, supporters of the enemy, England, which also made them an enemy. One night 10 IRA men called, saying that they were going to burn the castle down on the grounds that local soldiers stationed on Bere Island were to take it over as their headquarters. Albert Thomas, who knew the soldiers, told them this was untrue.

> I asked them quietly if, being local men, it had struck them that without the castle and its grounds there would be no work for six of them; no rates and taxes could be collected, and between £800 and £1,000 a year less would be spent in the town if the castle were no more. They listened for at least 6 of them could see my point. The head one was, no doubt, on the run and appeared to be domineering the others, so I suggested putting it to the vote. At this point it was almost twelve o'clock, and just on the stroke a most awful, gurgling noise came from the passage, and a hollow rattling of chains. As the wife was with me, the men could see they were not responsible for this, and, as the noise drew nearer, they up and ran from the castle as one man, just as if 'Old Nick' had spoken to them.[21]

It was the dying sounds of a hen Albert had not killed properly. It was upside-down, having been hung by the legs to bleed in the armoury when it suddenly started making gurgling noises and flapped its wings, terrifying the supposedly tough IRA men.

A few weeks later, the colonel called to tell Albert and his wife, who was half Irish, that their lives were in danger as 'he knew from information he had received that they were going to burn down the castle'.[22] They left with the army. Soon afterwards, they saw the glow of the burning castle at night, described above by Albert. He was convinced that the 'rebels were under the impression that the soldiers were going to take the Castle over'.[23] Three houses of the IRA were later burnt down as punishment for burning the castle, while the Thomases left Ireland to take up employment in England.

The Puxleys were awarded £17,900 as compensation by the Free State government. Today, a huge new hotel stands on the site of the old castle, using the shell of the old mansion. It appears that the hotel was built to take advantage of the tax incentive scheme to encourage more hotels to be built in Ireland. Although the Puxleys had lived in Ireland for over 250 years, they are described on the poster outside the tourist board office in Castletownbere as 'The English Puxley family'.

In Tipperary, some 20 houses of Anglo-Irish occupants were burnt during 1923, including a dwelling belonging to writer Hubert Butler's mother. A large early Victorian building, it was called Graiguenoe Park in Holycross. A revealing and touching letter was sent by the house-keeper to Mrs Clarke, Butler's mother-in-law.

Madam,

By now you know the bad news how Graiguenoe Park is burnt down. Oh it was terrible to see it blazing away.

Just at 5 past 12 on Wednesday night the bell was rung. I was only just in bed, so I jumped up and called the girls and went to Nolan; but he was up. They never stopped ringing till Nolan and I went to the hall door; and there were two men with revolvers and demanded to know why we did not open before and come out; so I said, "Surely you will give us time to get our things out." He said, "Yes, if we were not too long." He wanted to know who were all those inside the house. I said "Three girls more." He wanted to know who were all those inside there. I said, "That is yourself in the mirror". He thought (when he saw our reflections in the glass) that a lot of people were there. So we all got our things put together as quickly as we could, but all of us had to leave a lot of things as they kept asking, "Are you ready, as we are in a hurry", so we got out. Nolan saved three pictures out of the dining room and your dressing case and a small case under the bed and Mr Clarke's dressing bag, but they did not want him to take anything only his own things. He also saved the harness; he worked like a nigger but he could do nothing more. He also tried to save the harness room by throwing buckets of water on the inside and the roof; but no use. The fire got too firm a hold on everything before those demons left. They had petrol, straw and hay so they made a good job of it. The only place not burnt out is the scullery and Mrs Curtun's room. We were in the coach house watching it blazing. The flames were very high but the wind was in our favour or the outhouses would also be in flames.

It was heartbreaking to see the house burning where we were living so long. But we were thankful Mr Clarke was not there for the story was bad enough and he may be shot. They asked several times where was the Boss. We all came up to Mrs Hilton's at 7 o'clock in the morning . Bridget has gone home, also Maggie and Josie. I am staying here with Mrs Hilton for the present. I will never forget the sight and experiences of Wednesday night. I feel sorry for you and Mr Clarke, but I'm thinking there will be no gentlemen's places soon.

She was right. Not many of the gentry stayed on. Hubert Butler, descended from a Norman family that settled in Kilkenny, the Ormondes, believes the Anglo-Irish could have prevented their fate if their interest and involvement in Ireland had been deeper. If they had been Roman Catholics, I question whether they would have been intimidated. Butler notes:

> ... they largely did recognise a duty to their neighbourhood and this duty was usually intelligently fulfilled, but only rarely happened that, like Plunkett and a few of their contemporaries, they could give their first love to their country. I believe that in a generation or two, had there been no 1914 war, no rebellion and no civil war, this duty might have turned itself into love as it often had in the eighteenth century.
>
> Then, for a brief period, they had been able to represent something very precious. Only they could give Irishmen a sense of historical continuity and of identity. It was to be found in their bookshelves, when those who remained no longer read books, in their estate maps when they no longer had estates, in their memories when they no longer had the leisure or literary skill to write them down. The Irishmen who burnt down those Tipperary houses were sawing away the branch on which they were sitting. Clamouring that they were a distinctive people, they obliterated much of the heritage that distinguished them. The burning of the Four Courts, which swept away the records of eight centuries, was only a single instance in this tale of self-destruction.
>
> A new and more suffocating ascendancy, that of international commerce, was on the way; many of those ruined houses would have been strongholds of resistance to it, and the Anglo-Irish, with their easy-going pragmatic Christianity, would certainly have tempered the religious and political passions of our northern countrymen.

Butler perhaps protests too much, and the 'international commerce' he refers to so disparagingly became an unstoppable wave after the Second World War. The protectionist Ireland inspired by Arthur Griffith held out for far too long against it, leading to a stagnant economy and mass emigration. It was only when Ireland embraced it, perhaps too whole-heartedly, that it became a prosperous and vibrant country. It educated its young, providing free secondary education in 1967, at last catching up with the North, which had provided free secondary education since shortly after the war. It did not need the Ascendancy to achieve this. But what if the Irish Parliamentary party had led Ireland after the First World War within the United Kingdom under Home Rule, along the lines of devolved government at Stormont? That would have secured a better-educated, more egalitarian South drawing down funds from the British exchequer. Roman Catholics in the North fared better than their fellow Catholics in the South in terms of both educational support and a superior universal health care system.

No, the Ascendancy was not going to provide leadership for a new Ireland, and in any case, by 1914 it was a spent force. But their houses are another matter.

Lady Fingall wrote:

> The country houses lit a chain of bonfires throughout the nights of late summer and autumn and winter and early Spring … People whose families had lived in the country for three or four hundred years, realised suddenly that they were still strangers and that the mystery of it was not to be revealed to them – the secret lying as deep as the valleys in the Irish hills, the barrier they had tried to break down standing as strong and immovable as those hills, brooding over an age-long wrong.
>
> It was those who tried to atone for that wrong and to break down this barrier that did most of the paying.[24]

'Brooding over an age-long wrong'. Perhaps that is part of why so many mansions were burnt. It certainly seems to be the case at Castle Mary in Cloyne. Rebels hanged by the Ponsonbys in 1798, and later evictions of some tenants in the nineteenth century, were long remembered for a variety of reasons. Undoubtedly one was a military response, such as at Summerhill. Other mansions were burnt as reprisals. Some of the houses of senators – such as the house of the patriot Horace Plunkett, who worked tirelessly and at some personal expense to establish co-operatives in Ireland – were burnt by Irregulars opposed to Senators post the Treaty. Plunkett left for England, never to return.

Many houses, especially in Co. Cork, were destroyed in retaliation for actions taken by the Black and Tans, such as the Peacocke residence. These houses were the precious possessions of Protestants, politically and economically humbled prior to the burnings, knocked from their pedestals. Their mansions were burnt in part because they were no longer considered to be Irish, or to be supportive of the drive for separation.

I doubt they were considered 'strangers', despite Lady Fingall's account. They were deeply involved in Ireland, some for hundreds of years. They knew their Irish neighbours well, and their 'fathers and mothers, their grandparents, all their children', as Maurice Headlam wrote in *Irish Reminiscences*. No, they were no strangers, nor were they any longer a political threat.

The owners of the burnt houses were understandably shocked by the harshness with which they were treated. Ireland was left the poorer, with much of its rich architectural heritage destroyed. The IRA destroyed buildings, furnishings, paintings and plate. The message was clear: their owners were made to feel homeless at home.

John Pentland Mahaffy argued that the landlord class did little or nothing to defend itself, as noted in Dooley's *The Decline of the Big House in Ireland*. But with the Land League vigorously attacking it and the Home Rule movement alienating it, the onus was on London to protect its own people, people who had unstintingly given generations of their offspring to serve in the Empire.

They were much too small and scattered to organise an effective political opposition against leaders like Parnell and Redmond, who had the mass of the Irish people behind them. They were, in effect, doomed once Westminster decided to give way to the Land League and the demand for Home Rule. Their own let them down, people like Parnell, perhaps inheriting anglophobia from his American mother. The Irish nationalism that triumphed through political organisation at Westminster and violence in Ireland saw them branded as mongrels and hyphenated as Anglo-Irish, a label that sticks to this day: neither fish nor fowl. Their houses were seen as monuments to an oppressive class, an affront to the nation. Up to recently, schoolchildren were taught that landlords in general were tyrannical, rackrenting and responsible for heartless evictions. Historical reassessment has changed this picture, however. We now know that many were helpful and generous to their tenants, men such as Lord Fingall, Lord Meath, and Horace Plunkett. In any case, it was their agents who managed their estates, the landlords giving them responsibility for collecting rents and for evictions when rents were well in arrears.

Nevertheless, a harsh impression of landlords largely remains. Sean Moylan T.D. said of their houses that remained post-1922:

Not structurally sound, they have no artistic value and no historic interest. From my unregenerate point of view, I choose to regard them as tombstones of a departed ascendancy and the sooner they go down the better. They are no use.

Some of the owners left for England and the colonies, fearful for their future in a country that was not to welcome Protestant ex-loyalists. The destruction of their homes was a personal assault on the owners. The message was in the flames, as James Hayter-Hames wrote about the burning of Castle Mary (p. 83): you have outlived your welcome. This class was the detritus left behind on the spring tide of Irish nationalism and became, scapegoats for British rule in Ireland. The new nation was built on the embers of their destroyed houses, embers that may have heralded the beginning of the end of the British Empire everywhere.

After the end of the civil war, the expense of maintaining the big houses became prohibitive and many were abandoned and some – such as Island House, a large Georgian mansion built by my family on Little Island in Co. Cork – were demolished. Tarquin Blake's two books are an eloquent testament to the decay and abandonment of Ireland's mansions.[25] Recently, attitudes have changed and some of the finest big houses have been restored, both by the Office of Public Works and by their wealthy new owners. The Irish Georgian Society has played a crucial role in preserving some of the architectural treasures of the nation, particularly under the leadership of the late Desmond FitzGerald, the Knight of Glin, Desmond Guinness and the late Kevin B. Nolan. Castletown was saved by Guinness and is now cared for by the Office of Public Works. Malahide Castle and Newbridge house were bought by Dublin County Council and restored and the parklands are maintained. Killkenny Castle and Belvedere house in Mullingar, once owned by Colonel Howard-Bury, are now in the hands of the Office of Public Works.

Some of Ireland's finest mansions have been restored, often at great expense. Castle Hyde in Fermoy was bought by Michael Flatley and lavishly restored. David Davies bought Abbeyleix, Martin Naughton restored Stackallan in County Meath and Killeen Castle is a conference centre and golf course, as is Carton House and demesne. Powerscourt in Enniskerry has been restored and has magnificent gardens, an exhibition hall, restaurant and golf course. Some of Ireland's big houses and rich architectural heritage has been saved, but alas, all too much of it has vanished.

4

Low-Intensity Unhappiness

What sort of Ireland emerged after the establishment of the Free State in 1921? The American poet Richard Tillinghast was unequivocal when he wrote: '... the new nation, defining itself as Gaelic, Catholic, and nationalist, became anti-intellectual and inward-looking to a pathological degree.'[1] It was an agricultural country with few industries; a frugal country, profoundly influenced at political and personal levels by the Roman Catholic Church. People were rooted in their local communities, with social life centering on market days, daily visits to the local creameries, the local pub and parish halls. Sunday Mass was the focal point of the week; almost all Catholics attended, the parish priest being accorded unquestioned allegiance and deference well beyond his spiritual duties. It was an Ireland that 'placed great emphasis on the appearance of things. That culture was increasingly authoritarian in its approach to the ordering of the nation, and a preference for autarchy in not only economic but cultural affairs emerged as the dominant mode of the de Valera years.'[2]

The small number of Protestants who stayed on after independence lived in separate communities from their Roman Catholic neighbours. A form of apartheid came into being, accepted by both Catholic and Protestant communities. The cliché has it that Protestants 'kept their heads down' and only spoke openly to each other behind closed doors. Few Protestants subscribed to de Valera's vision of a Catholic, Gaelic, Irish-speaking rural republic. Most resented the imposition of compulsory Irish language learning in their primary and secondary schools. As the Canadian Kurt Bowen wrote, perhaps somewhat harshly, that the Department of Education used schools:

... as the chief means of restoring Irish to the status of the national language...No other government policy provoked such widespread and sustained criticism from Protestants. For forty years, the annual reports of the Church of Ireland's Board of Education repeatedly condemned the compulsory and restrictive character of the regulations...the minority regarded Irish as an alien, primitive, and anachronistic language with no roots in their own English-speaking tradition ... In the main, they argued on the pragmatic ground that the heavy emphasis on Irish reduced the amount of time available for other more important subjects, had no practical value, and was doing little to further a true revival in the everyday use of Irish ... In 1966 an independent and quite sophisticated piece of research vindicated many of their claims when it found that the great amount of time devoted to Irish was responsible for the lower standard of education among Irish primary school children compared with their counterparts in England. But arguments of this sort when they came from Protestants, has no appreciable influence on the government before 1945.[3]

Brian Walker tells us: '... many in that community (Protestant) objected strongly to how the Irish language was made compulsory in schools and for all government positions, public appointments, such as law, and cultural bodies.'[4]

Walker goes on to quote the bishop of Limerick, Dr H.V.White, who said at the 1926 General Synod of the Church of Ireland: 'We have no wish to discourage the teaching of Irish, but we have every wish to discourage the compulsion placed upon our people.' A little later, on 9 June 1929, an editorial in *The Irish Times* 'described how many Protestants regarded the State policy of compulsory Irish as not only a substantial material burden, but also a "denial of intellectual freedom".'[5] Not all Church of Ireland parishioners thought like this; however, two archbishops of Dublin, George Otto Simms and Donald Caird, spoke Irish fluently and 'were enthusiastic supporters of the Irish language'.[6]

English had become the native tongue of the Irish several centuries before independence, especially in the main cities of Dublin, Limerick, Galway and Cork. Some 14 per cent spoke Irish as their first language in the new Free State in 1921, and were mostly situated in the remoter parts of the south (Kerry), west (Connemara), and in Donegal. By 1891 only 3.5 per cent of children under 10 were able to speak Irish.[7] As early as 1700, many Catholics had abandoned the Irish language.

There were at most 21,000 native monoglot speakers in 1901, and by 1891, only 17.6 per cent of the population spoke the language, and many of these did not speak it regularly. By the time the Gaelic League was founded in 1893 to promote Irish, 'The Irish language had been substantially abandoned by the mass of the population and all main towns.'[8] Hindley went on: 'By the late eighteenth century Irish was an interest for scholars and occasional Protestant activists as a medium for conversions.'[9]

It had become the dying language of a rural peasantry. Galvin wrote: '… it (Irish) had not even survived that century (seventeenth) as the first language of Irish Catholicism … By the early nineteenth century Irish was already a minority language, spoken outside the towns and in areas far away from commercial penetration.'[10]

So why revive it? One theory is that it was to give the new Irish State a distinct identity. The Free State was based on a romantic brand of nineteenth-century nationalism, which intimately linked language, blood and soil. Irish became a sacred cow and the 'prosecution of the Irish language became the necessary bench-mark of an independent ethos': part of 'a national philosophy', as Roy Foster explains.[11]

The Protestant community found this ideology alien. An irony is that Ireland's current success in the global economy is partly derived from the ascendancy of the English language. It can be argued that the language became a fig leaf for narcissistic nationalism. As Jack White wrote in *Minority Report*, 'W.P. Ryan expressed the confrontation in a single sentence: "We are working for a new Irish civilisation, quite distinct from the English".' White went on: 'Gaelic society had been shattered before 1700. The new civilisation would have to be built, presumably from the fragments that survived in the peasant cottages of the south and west … It would have to express itself in a language unknown to a majority of the nation…'[12]

Those who opposed the imposition of Gaelic 'were up against lingo-fanatics who 'through ignorance, lack of perceptiveness, closed minds, excess of idealism, refuse to accommodate the reality of an English-speaking Ireland'. Hindley also concluded that compulsory Irish was 'a fundamental error in social psychology by making a language "essential" or "required" by what the public sees as artificial means. It is not natural and the outcome was that the Irish rejected it. "Loyal lies" are told about it for patriotic reasons. They "honour it as a symbol but have no practical use for it".'[13]

Today, idealistic nationalists who associate language with nation have acted as a parasite on a dying host of native speakers. These people are mostly middle-class, speaking a version of Irish that is designed to make it easier to learn but that is 'excruciatingly embarrassing to any natural Gaeilgeoir'.[14] These mostly middle-class professionals and intellectuals, such as Douglas Hyde and later Church of Ireland bishops – together with advanced nationalists like Gerry Adams – speak, or try to speak, a language their great grandparents had rejected for sensible pragmatic reasons. This they do in the face of the willingness of native speakers in the Gaeltacht 'to allow the language to die now it has ceased to serve any practical purpose.'[15]

It was 'an ideological weapon for nationalist and fundamentalist Catholics, feared by Protestants' and used for 'moral superiority', according to Tom Garvin in *Nationalist Revolutionaries in Ireland*.[16] Garvin concludes: 'The extremists confiscated the language much as they had confiscated Gaelic games, they identified the language and games with a particular political ideology – *Protestants naturally excluded themselves* [my emphasis] but so did most of the Catholic middle class.'[17]

Irish was not only compulsory; it was discriminatory, as Myles Dillon pointed out.[18] Dillon believed that the compulsory language was alienating to Protestants in independent Ireland. He argues that it was used as 'a means of transferring power, or rather authority'. He explained that after 1922:

> All the cultural institutions of the country were in the hands of the Protestants: the Royal Irish Academy, the National Library, the National Gallery, the Royal Irish Academy of Music, the Royal Dublin Society, the Museum, the College of Science, the Botanical Gardens, even the Society of Antiquaries. All that must now be changed: a new administrative class was to be established, and the language was one of the means to be used. Lyster, Eglington, Praeger, Best, Armstrong, Westropp, Sir Frederick Moore, none of these men could have passed the test. None of them could stand a chance of civil service appointment now. I shall not dwell upon that painful subject: I believe that far from helping the language movement, this turning of the screws has destroyed its value as a form of allegiance.[19]

The policy was also criticised by Archbishop McQuaid of Dublin in the 1950s when he told de Valera that he should give up on compulsion as when school children went home, their parents spoke to them in English.

De Valera replied 'the experiment is not over'. Although there have been important changes since then, Irish is still a compulsory subject in national schools and is taught as a compulsory subject in secondary schools to leaving certificate level today. A pass in Irish is a requirement for entrance to the National Universities of Ireland (NUI) situated in Dublin, Galway and Cork and to the Recognised Colleges and Constituent Universities of the NUI. For example, the Royal College of Surgeons in Dublin requires a pass for Irish students who would not require a knowledge of Irish to study medicine. Textbooks and lectures are in English. The total cost of promoting the Irish language is some 1.2 billion euro a year, at a time when the Irish Government is deeply in debt. Irish has become a school language changed and re-changed to make it more acceptable, but the policy has not worked in attracting children to speak it as a second language. Hindley believes:

> The demoralizing efforts of long continued language decline leave little to be proud of, and the failure of almost all efforts at preserving or reviving Irish causes general pessimism, defeatism, and cynicism about the motives, intelligence and possible success of continued efforts by those who refuse to be discouraged. At best apathy and indifference ensue.[20]

Irish Protestants tended to live quiet lives after the foundation of the Irish Free State, meeting in church on Sundays and socialising in their many parish halls during the week where badminton, whist drives and indoor bowling were usually provided, followed by tea and cakes. These social events kept a sense of identity and difference alive in what many regarded as an alien environment. Kurt Bowen summarizes the situation thus:

> Prior to the 1960s, when tensions between the two communities were much stronger, rural Protestants maintained polite but very distant relations with most Catholics. While they knew their Catholic neighbours far better than did urban Protestants, to mix socially at this time was quite another matter. Their overall superiority in class terms must have strengthened their sense of separateness and solidarity … For the most part, their sense of identity and communal life revolved around religion and parish.[21]

Protestant numbers continued to decline sharply, for reasons to be explained later, and by 1947 they had been sidelined – even beached – in the newly independent Ireland. They had lost power and influence in a State that dumped Catholic-inspired legislation on them. The sort of Ireland that Thomas Davis had advocated, where all religions and traditions would be respected, was not to be. Ireland had become a Roman Catholic, Gaelic, nationalist country where a succession of governments promoted a homogenous culture. De Valera's vision of Ireland was similar to the vision Gandhi had for an independent India: a frugal, self-sufficient country, pious and simple. He summed it up when he said:

> Whenever men have tried to imagine a perfect life, they have imagined a place where men plough and sow and reap, not a place where there are great wheels turning and great chimneys vomiting smoke. Ireland will always be a place where men plough and sow and reap.[22]

Fianna Fáil espoused 'a self-sufficient rural republic, Catholic in religion and Irish-speaking – the vision at the heart of earlier Sinn Féin rhetoric'.[23] Wills further argues:

> … de Valera's vision of a rural republic was undoubtedly idealistic, but it expressed a genuine respect for the life of the small farmer, so numerous in the Irish countryside. His dream reflected a widespread belief that the integrity of Irish existence should be defended against the commercial, industrial, cosmopolitan life of modern society.[24]

From the 1920s until recent times, there was an unquestioning deference towards the Roman Catholic Church and State nationalism, an acceptance of 'a sincere attempt to develop practical ways to organize Irish society on Catholic social principles'.[25] In such a society, Protestants had become almost irrelevant. The cliché used when referring to Northern Ireland is that post-separation from the South, it had become unashamedly a Protestant place for a Protestant people. In the South, the cliché was 'Home rule is Rome rule'. There is much truth in both; a legacy of partition.

The Protestant minority had lost confidence. Once British in identity and unionist in sympathy, it was left on the margins of Irish society. Brian Inglis wrote about the so-called 'West Brit' community in 1962, in his memoir *West Briton*.

> This class, opposed to the Anglophobia of the new State with its emphasis on Celtophilia, minded its manners and kept quiet. It played

cricket and tennis, games considered 'foreign' by many. It was moneyed and snobbish, sending children to English public schools or as second best, to St Columba's College in Dublin. By definition, it did not fit in, no more than British people did in post-independence India and in African countries like Kenya and Zimbabwe. The middle-class Protestants who were in trade were looked down on in rural and urban Ireland by the ex-Ascendancy Protestants. Class distinctions prevailed. However, there were binding factors. Almost all southern Irish Protestants were ex-unionists; many had served in the British forces and in the now-defunct Empire. Those who had not served had relatives who had; the links with Britain were long-standing. For generations, they had intermarried with their own people.

Protestants had largely lost their old arrogance, though most considered themselves straighter, more conscientious in their financial dealings, and possessing a more disciplined, careful temperament than their Catholic neighbours. They believed that their word was their bond. They were thriftier, more punctilious and looked after their own tribe in the businesses they ran, from Guinness and W&R Jacobs, Lamb's Jams, Lemons, and Goodalls in Dublin to R.H. Hall in Waterford and Shaw's department stores around the country. They had their own hospitals – the Adelaide in Dublin and Victoria in Cork. They ran most of the banks, particularly the Bank of Ireland, where they ensured the directors came from their own ranks. By and large, these Protestant-run banks adhered to the principles of integrity essential to bank management, unlike the recent behaviour of most Irish banks, which ended in having to be bailed out by the State with huge loans from the Troika.

Most Protestants, privileged as they had been, believed that they had administered Ireland with an even hand. Many of the country's leading patriots came from their ranks – Henry Grattan, Theobald Wolfe Tone, Lord Edward FitzGerald, Thomas Davis, Charles Stewart Parnell. The Protestant community also produced literary giants: Jonathan Swift, Oliver Goldsmith, Richard Brinsley Sheridan, Bram Stoker, Oscar Wilde, Bernard Shaw, William Butler Yeats, Sean O'Casey, John Millington Synge, Elizabeth Bowen and Samuel Beckett. But by the 1930s, they had become the opposite of what W.B. Yeats once called them: 'no petty people'. They had become a petty people, arguably one that had lost its way. Without the support of Protestant numbers in Northern Ireland after partition, they became an insignificant minority.

The 1st Earl of Midleton, St John Brodrick (1852–1942), was the last leader of southern unionists. He worked tirelessly to prevent partition along with Lord Barrymore, Lord Desart, Lord Iveagh and Archbishop of Dublin, John Henry Bernard, all members of the Unionist Anti-Partition League. As Lord Midleton wrote:

> The Southern Unionists had a still wider aim and an equal nemesis to face in case of failure. They recognized, as Redmond did, that the aspirations of an island of 4,000,000 people, situated as Ireland is, could only be realized if the whole country remained together, and that the penalty of detachment from Great Britain would be that Ireland would subside into the rank of a third-rate power. Past injuries must be forgotten and past differences buried, if a solvent and prosperous State was to be built at this crisis of the national history.[26]

His counsel was ignored and 'past injuries ... and past differences' were to become centerfold in the teaching of Irish history for generations of school children in an independent Ireland.

There can be little doubt that by 1947, Ireland had indeed become 'a third-rate power'. Clair Wills, writing of Ireland in the Second World War concluded that:

> Far from achieving self-sufficiency, rural Ireland's failure to thrive questioned the very economic survival of the state. In large measure Ireland had remained a backward part of the British Isles, and this dependency seemed only to be getting worse. The departure of young men and women, with no prospects of a livelihood from the family farm or in local industries, led to a further contraction of rural life for those who stayed. Depopulation produced its own vicious circle. As the numbers dwindled, there was less and less work for those who stayed behind. With farms abandoned, small businesses closed down, school teachers in outlying areas laid off, there were fewer and fewer opportunities for socializing, and so diminishing prospects of marriage and family. The choice was either to board the emigrant boat or be buried alive at home, in a world with no future.[27]

Most southern unionists who stayed on in this 'world with no future' played down their British sympathies. They were conscious of discrimination against Catholics during the penal laws, though these laws also applied to Catholics in England, and non-Anglicans such as Presbyterians and Methodists in Ireland. Modern historiography accepts that the penal laws were largely unenforced and unenforceable.[28] Had they been enforced, the Roman Catholic Church would have been completely suppressed and forced out of Ireland. Instead, it enjoyed the widespread allegiance of Irish Catholics and Thomas Bartlett argues in his book *Ireland: A History* that the penal laws strengthened the Catholic Church and a strong network of Catholic parishes were laid down during penal times.

Whether guilty, timid or both, in the words of Hubert Butler, '[a] once voluble people seems now to be stricken with aphasia'.[29] They played an insignificant part in the public life of the new State, particularly after the 1937 constitution changed Protestant representation in the Senate. In 1930, there were over a dozen Protestant senators and in 1927 there were 14 TDs in Dáil Éireann. By 1948, there were only 3. As Brian Walker has pointed out, the 'electoral act of 1935 ... reduced the size and redrew the boundaries of a numbers of constituencies. Probably more important was the fall in numbers of Protestant electors and a paucity of Protestants among the membership of the main parties.'[30]

There were a few notable exceptions of Protestants who had high office, such as Presidents Douglas Hyde and Erskine Childers. The co-founder of the Gaelic League in 1893, Douglas Hyde sought to revive the dying Gaelic language as the main platform of the pre-independence cultural nationalist movement. Hyde's dream was to replace what he considered a debased English language with a pure Gaelic one. English was the language of the 'penny dreadfuls', of vulgarity and immorality. But Hyde did not want the language to be politicised, and he withdrew his support from the Gaelic League when it came under the control of Sinn Féin.

Hyde was atypical of the general run of Protestants, who had little or no time for Gaelic revivalism. He had become 'the archetype of the Catholic Protestant, cunning, subtle, cajoling, superficial and affable'.[31] Edward Carson referred to these 'Catholic Protestants' as 'those rare birds'. Hyde and Childers, Protestant Irish presidents, are regularly held up as examples of generous treatment of Protestants in independent Ireland. But as Conor Cruise O'Brien has pointed out, they were token Protestants, paraded as examples of the pluralism of the new State. Like Martin Mansergh, the speech-writer for Charles Haughey, a Senator and former Fianna Fáil TD and major player in the peace talks in Northern Ireland, they were unrepresentative of their tribe.

Protestants had no political party with which they could easily identify. It was a question of choosing between various shades of green: Fine Gael, Fianna Fáil and Labour, who shared a common 1916 genesis. (Though Labour was founded in 1912, it provided the Citizen Army in 1916 under the leadership of socialist James Connolly. They were largely absent from the civil service, partly because a knowledge of spoken Irish was required up until 1974, partly because it was not their preferred career choice, with prospects of promotion to the highest grades.

The Protestant community was a victim of history, as R.B. McDowell wrote in *Crisis and Decline,* a thoroughly researched record of southern unionists during the early twentieth century. They had for centuries upheld the authority of the British Empire and 'flourished under its aegis', like 'Germans in Bohemia, Swedes in Finland … Greeks in Asia Minor, Muslims in the Balkans. Among those who abandoned adherents of a lost cause were the unionists in the south and west of Ireland' who were left behind, or chose to emigrate.[32] As Conor Cruise O'Brien wrote in *Ancestral Voices,* the past 300 years of Irish history 'has been the recovery of the Irish Catholics: the Catholics getting their own back, in more senses than one'.

In 1935, there was an outbreak of widespread sectarian outrages against the southern Protestant community, as reported in considerable detail in the National Archives of Ireland.[33] The trigger was an outbreak of violence in Belfast. Catholic frustration with their exclusion from power and their disadvantaged position led to violence at the end of an Orange parade on 12 July, when rioting broke out and continued to the end of August. Reportedly, 8 Protestants were killed and 5 Catholics and up to 2,000 Catholics were driven from their homes.

However, an outrage occurred in Cork that was not motivated by these riots.[34] The Masonic Lodge in Tuckey Street, Cork was raided by some 10 men who clearly had inside information, as they arrived just as the 72 Masons were sitting down to dinner at their annual meeting. These men lined the Masons up against the wall of the dining room and proceeded to fire shots in the air (later discovered to be blanks). They smashed the china and some tables and chairs, using two sledgehammers. An unsuccessful attempt was made to force open the safe.

The Gardaí undertook a thorough investigation but were severely hampered by the refusal of all Masons present to co-operate with an identity parade. 'Not one of those men who were present will make any attempt to identity anyone on the parade as being one of the raiders.'[35]

Clearly the Protestant professionals and businessmen present feared consequences and adopted the wise approach of keeping their heads down. The American Consul was present and agreed to attend an identity parade but refused to identify suspects. He complained to his superiors in America, who brought the incident to the attention of the Taoiseach, de Valera.

The Gardaí suspected prominent IRA men were involved but were unable to arrest anyone, lacking evidence. They reported that the 'object appears to be an attempt to break up the Masonic Society in Cork'.[36]

Following the Belfast riots in July 1935, there were widespread outrages against Protestants in 19 of the 26 counties of the Free State. A Church of Ireland church was burnt to the ground in Co. Limerick and attempts were made to burn others as well as a Masonic Lodge and Protestant halls. There were anti-Protestant riots in Limerick and Galway and some individual Protestants were targeted elsewhere. The police reported that these outrages were not 'organized by particular or central organization', though in Galway a trade union was involved.

Very early on Monday 22 July, some men broke down the door of the Church of Ireland in Killmallock, Co. Limerick. They poured petrol on the wood inside and burnt the building to the ground. The rectory nearby where Canon Taylor lived was attacked and the windows were broken. The Circuit Judge awarded £4,555 to the Representative Church Body (Church of Ireland). Apparently 4 men were arrested but never tried, as the jurors 'were canvassed with a view to an acquittal of accused in this case'[37] and 11 refused to convict. A Garda report recommended that the trial be referred to the Central Criminal Court.[38]

In Limerick and Galway, large mobs assembled and targeted Protestant premises and individuals. The plate glass window of a Protestant shop owner was broken on 20 July at 10.30 p.m. in Limerick. A large crowd gathered of some 600 young men. They attacked the Mission Hall, the Diocesan Hall, Archdeacon Waller's house, the Masonic Lodge, the Baptist and Presbyterian churches and tried to burn down the Church of Ireland church in Henry Street. The mob shouted, 'We won't let a Protestant house standing'. The Gardaí decided to bring in military aid and it was reported that 14 cases of malicious damage and attempted arson were brought. However the Lord Mayor, District Justice and Catholic clergy sought to interfere, in an attempt to stop the police making further investigations. A police report from the superintendent stated that 'further proceedings would tend to revive the bitterness and ill-feeling which have died down.'[39]

On 23 July in Galway, dockers refused to unload a coal boat owned by a Belfast man by the name of Mr Kelly. Later the SS *Dun Aengus*, which sailed to the Aran Islands, was not allowed to leave until the Protestant chief engineer disembarked. A crowd of about 500 assembled and marched with a band, demanding Catholic workers down tools in the Galway Foundry, Connaught Laundry and ESB centre, where the workers refused to leave and a police baton charged the mob. They dispersed to Eyre Square, where they visited Protestant houses in the area with the band playing. The ATGWU union and two councillors led the way; a police report noted that 'all are of a poor type'.

Two Protestant men were targeted in Marlow, Co. Tipperary. Richard Pennefather, related to the author, was a 70-year-old farmer with over 300 acres of land. He 'lived on very good terms with his immediate members [sic] and had 'a quiet and very honest disposition', according to the police report, and this was borne out by the fact that his two sons assisted in the farming. He had been attacked during the civil war, when his car was commandeered and attempts were made to make him leave the area so that his farm could be taken.

Joseph Abercrombie was Pennefather's secretary, aged 75. He was a retired RIC sergeant who did not take part in politics. He and Pennefather lived very near to each other and both suffered their houses being shot at by a rifle or rifles on 26 July. Approximately 12 shots were fired at Pennefather's house and 18 at Abercrombie's, but no damage was done. Police had suspicions of who the attackers were but, despite many attempts to find incriminating evidence, could not make any arrests. They believed that 'the real motive for underlying the attacks is agrarianism and that the conditions now prevailing in the North together with some incidents in An Staorstát (the Free State) are merely a cover up for restarting attacks – especially on Mr Pennefather'.[40]

Masonic Halls were targeted in Kells, Co. Meath, and in Athlone, Co. Galway. In Clones, Co. Monaghan, the Masonic Hall was destroyed and the Pringle Memorial Hall and Plymouth Brethren Gospel Hall were 'badly damaged'.[41] An attempt was made to burn the Methodist church in Boyle, Co. Roscommon, in which petrol was poured at the end of pews and set on fire, but little damage was done. The Garda report stated: 'the general public in Boyle are [sic] not in sympathy with any demonstrations by way of retaliation for North of Ireland incidents.'[42]

There were a number of other incidents in which individual Protestants were targeted in Listowel, Co. Kerry, and in Castlepollard, Co. Meath, where the Church of Ireland church had a notice put up on 21 July warning 'people that attend this church – if this trouble in Belfast goes on much longer we will be compelled to make it hot for you and your friends. To hell with King William'. In Clones, Co. Monaghan, the plate-glass windows of W.M. Meighan, a Protestant shop owner, were broken. Furthermore, a letter was sent to T. McDonagh's furniture factory, which read:

> God bless our Pope.
> Remember Belfast.
> Up de Valera.
> To hell with the King.
>
> We don't want you or your Orange Bastards in the Free State. We want revenge take a kindly warning you and your orange employees clear out.
>
> Beware the IRA.

In Feint, Co. Kerry, 50 dockers refused to unload a boat containing coal owned by a Belfast man.

The Taoiseach, Eamon de Valera, had no doubt that the riots in Belfast gave rise to these sectarian outrages. Yet clearly the Gardaí who so thoroughly investigated all these outrages laid no blame at the feet of any of the Protestants who were attacked in the South. They had provoked no one but had been provoked themselves. It is hard to avoid the conclusion that the Irish Catholic people who were responsible for the attacks were motivated by a desire to remove Protestants from 'their' nation, to drive home the message they were unwanted.

Some did leave. According to the *Belfast News-Letter*, a unionist paper, in 1936, '… Loyalists were finding it more and more difficult to live in the Free State. During the past two or three years scores of Cavan and Monaghan families had crossed the border.'[43] Dennis Kennedy adds: 'the conclusive proof that Protestants were being "squeezed out" was that they were undeniably leaving the Free State. Between 1926 and 1936 another drop of roughly 12 per cent, or 25,000, had been recorded in the Protestant population.'[44] The drop cannot be attributed to natural decline and little of it to mixed religion marriages and the dreaded *ne temere* decree which took effect later on. By the early 1960s it was reckoned that at least 16 per cent of Protestant marriages were to Catholics and most of the offspring were brought up as Catholics.

Protestants targeted during these outrages were unsympathetic to the behaviour of the Belfast Orangemen. They had to live in a country where they suffered cultural and constitutional discrimination. Catholic social principles were enshrined in law. Contraceptives could not be sold (though many ordered them through the post) and the 1929 Censorship of Publications Bill banned all books that 'advocate the unnatural prevention of conception or the procurement of abortion or miscarriage'. Some of the works of the best Irish writers – indeed the best international writers – were banned, regardless of religious denomination, including Brendan Behan, Samuel Beckett, Edna O'Brien, Sean O'Casey, George Bernard Shaw, Seán Ó Faoláin, and Liam O'Flaherty. Added to that were Graham Greene, J.P. Dunleavy, Muriel Spark, Morris West and Compton MacKenzie: all Catholic writers. The films *Girl with Green Eyes* and *August is a Wicked Month,* based on the novels of Edna O'Brien, were also banned.

In 1937, de Valera, working with the conservative Archbishop John Charles McQuaid, introduced a constitution that gave the Roman Catholic Church a special position. Divorce was outlawed. De Valera also did away with the provisions in the 1922 constitution, which were designed to protect the minority Protestant interests, such as executive appointments to the Senate and appeal to the British Privy Council. In its preamble, this constitution defined Irishness as being Roman Catholic, Gaelic and nationalist. There were, however, legal provisions for the protection of all citizens, regardless of religion, and 'practice of religion' was 'guaranteed to every citizen'. However, there can be little doubt that the State's legislation was Roman Catholic in social and moral terms.

The first Irish constitution, written by the British and Irish, sought to avoid the imposition of Roman Catholic dogma in matters of civil rights such as divorce, birth control and censorship. Pressure by the southern unionists saw to it that their religion and culture would be recognised and protected, and Kevin O'Higgins and Arthur Griffith made this clear from the days of the first Dáil. But de Valera's constitution changed that. The introduction to the 1937 Constitution stated:

> In the name of the Most Holy Trinity, from Whom is all authority and
> to Whom, as our final end, all actions of both men and States must

be referred, We, the people of Eire, humbly acknowledge all our obli-
gations to our Divine Lord Jesus Christ, Who sustained our fathers
through centuries of trial …

This is in keeping with Pope Leo XIII's teaching that all sovereignty
comes from God, with the Roman Catholic Church serving as divine
arbiter. The people allowed the creation of a State that looked to
Rome for its civic values, though there were many who believed that
de Valera had betrayed true republican principles.

As indicated, the majority of Protestants had little interest in getting
actively involved with this State. The young mostly emigrated and
rarely returned, Samuel Beckett being a famous example. He considered himself to be Irish but disliked Irish nationalism. In the words of
Terry Eagleton, Beckett and most Protestants after 1922 felt 'homeless
at home'.

Those who stayed on mostly worked in farming and Protestants
ran manufacturing industries, motor car distributorships and businesses like Guiness, Jacobs, Lambs, Lemons, Dockrells, Brooks Thomas
and Switzers. These companies and retail outlets employed fellow
Protestants to support their small community. This caused concern:

> [in] some Catholic circles, which led to action by a number of organisa-
> tions to restrict the Protestant presence in these areas. By the 1960s,
> however, there was less concern about this Protestant role, partly
> because of the fall in Protestant numbers and partly, as Kurt Bowen
> has pointed out, because of the many new opportunities for Catholics,
> not only in the expanding professions, but also in the businesses and
> semi-state bodies established from the 1920s onwards.[45]

Inter-church relations were poor, if not openly hostile. Something
that added to the suspicion and bad feeling was the Roman Catholic
Church's refusal to allow its followers to attend Protestant funerals. A
high-profile example was when the Protestant ex-President, Douglas
Hyde, died in 1949. The Taoiseach, John A. Costello, his cabinet, and
the then President, Mr Sean T. O'Kelly, would not enter St Patrick's
Cathedral for the funeral service and instead sat outside.

Patsy McGarry, the Religious Affairs correspondent of *The Irish
Times*, wrote in *Magill* in February 1989: 'Being Catholics, Costello
and his cabinet were banned, under pain of mortal sin and eternal

damnation, from entering Protestant Church grounds or partaking in Protestant services.'

Henry Patterson sums up the situation in *Ireland: Since 1939*, when he wrote:

> ... the Interim Report of the Irish Census of 1946 ... showed a sharp decline of 13 per cent in the state's Protestant population during the previous decade. Speeches by Unionist politicians increasingly focused on what one referred to as an inexorable tendency to 'the complete and utter extinction of the Protestant population south of the border.

Perhaps this language was rather shrill, but Protestants were leaving the South and a large part of the reason was that they felt 'homeless at home'. In the North, by way of contrast, Catholic numbers were growing.

The government was quick to point out how well Protestants were doing in the Free State. They were, in proportion to their numbers, still strong in ownership of large farms, in banking and insurance. But this had been the case before partition. Was the government congratulating itself on leaving Protestants in situ, for not replacing them? Might they have expelled them, *in extremis*, as Idi Amin expelled the Asians in Uganda? This was unthinkable, partly because it was important for northern Protestants to see that their fellow Protestants in the South were being treated fairly well, but also because southern Protestants were patriots, providing services and jobs that were much needed, whether in the banks or in manufacturing industries.

Henry Patterson tells us that:

> [as] a leading government statistician pointed out, the figures for the decline reflected the fact that non-Catholics had emigrated at a markedly higher rate than Catholics in the decade. This was due to 'pull' factors: 'this class, relatively well-educated…could make a living here but they could do much better for themselves in an environment that suits them.' (Letter from R.C. Geary, Central Statistics Office, to the Secretary, Department of External Affairs, 23 October 1951, in 'Position of the Minority in the 26 Counties'.) While the pull of higher wages and salaries in Britain was one dimension of the problem, the fact remained that many had gone to serve in the Forces and 'an environment that suits them' was an oblique reference to the reality of *low intensity unhappiness* [my emphasis] with what many southern Protestants saw as the anti-British and confessional

nature of the Irish state, while compulsory Irish in schools aroused much
Protestant resentment. The claim was made that in government service
and the judiciary Protestants were well represented, although the only
example given was that they were two of the eleven members of the
Supreme and High Courts. There was no response to the Unionists who
pointed out that in the three border counties of Donegal, Cavan, and
Monaghan with a Protestant population of nearly 15 per cent, there were
virtually no Protestants on the public payroll.[46]

As Marianne Elliott has written, Protestants and ex-loyalists in the Irish
Free State 'felt isolated in a country whose ethos was now so demon-
strably Catholic and whose national narrative bore so little relationship
to their own'.[47] They retreated into a ghetto of the mind or 'parallel
universe'.[48] Their churches gave them social and sports facilities (for
activities such as badminton and indoor bowls) and they had their own
schools. They regarded themselves as Irish, as Brian Walker has pointed
out,[49] rejecting the descriptor 'Anglo-Irish', so commonly used today
in the media and by some historians. In 1939, the 'Archbishop John
Gregg described how the Protestant and Catholic communities were
'outside one another', and how 'we are outside the close knit spiritual
entity which the majority constitutes'. Nonetheless, he insisted that
'our smaller community … is yet conscious of an identity genuinely
Irish, which is more natural to it than the identity it recognizes in the
majority', and stated that it was 'not necessary to be Gaelic in order
to be Irish'. He warned particularly of the danger of 'Gaelicisation'
which, 'added to other factors in our environment, would involve our
absorption …'[50]

Writing in 1946, Professor W.B. Stanford maintained that an
exclusive form of nationalism had become prevalent, which took
the view that it was 'we against you, our gang against yours, and may
the astute intriguer win.'[51] He argued that there was discrimination
in 'some local government bodies and semi-public firms', giving
examples with which he was familiar.[52] A young skilled worker in
Dublin was offered better-paid work in another firm. He gave notice,
and in due time went to the new firm. Within a few days of his arrival,
the manager called him for a private interview. He explained that
pressure had been put on him by customers and others not to employ
a Protestant worker. He offered the man some money as compensation if he would resign and the man found that he had to take it.

His former post had been filled and he was forced to take another at a lower salary than he had before. Some other typical cases ran as follows: a factory manager made it clear that unless a Protestant in his employ became a Roman Catholic, he could not hope for any promotion, but the reverse: a bank manager whose maid, formerly a Roman Catholic, had become a Protestant, was threatened and boycotted by a clerically incited public conspiracy; when another Protestant bank manager was about to retire in a provincial town and the directors had appointed another of the same faith, a long list of signatures was locally collected to petition for a reversal of the decision and the appointment of a Roman Catholic; a Protestant institution was refused a lease by the local government officials on the grounds that it was given to pros-elytizing, though a Roman Catholic organization of a similar kind had been granted land without question; applicants had been refused houses built by public funds because they were Protestants; a charitable organisation for non-sectarian benefits was skillfully manoeuvred out of existence.

Ireland had become poor and backward. In 1912, it was the 11th richest country in the world, but by 1947, the dreams of the Irish founding fathers lay in ruins. They had predicted that once Ireland cast off the yoke of British rule, it would become more prosperous. Arthur Griffith envisaged strong, protected local industries giving employ-ment to their communities. He wanted an industrialised Ireland, which would give economic support to a greatly increased population of perhaps 20 million people. He also believed there were rich mineral reserves that the British administrations had left untouched. Instead there was widespread poverty.

In contrast, in Northern Ireland, Atlee's welfare state was introduced in 1947, giving children of low-income families the opportunity to have free secondary education. They could go on to university by availing of the new grants. Children in the Free State, however, had to wait almost 2 decades before free secondary education was provided. The Northern Irish welfare state also introduced family allowances, which provided twice the amount of money for the child after the firstborn as was granted in the Republic. There were equally signifi-cant differences in unemployment benefits, pensions and sickness benefits. Professor F.S.L. Lyons of Trinity College, Dublin pointed out that 'between the health services the differences were so great that little comparison was possible.[53]

The Inter-Party government of Fine Gael and Clann na Poblachta
came to power in 1948, and in the words of the historian Ronan
Fanning, it 'was to conduct the most cringingly servile and sickening
obsequious Catholic foreign policy in the history of the State'.[54] One
of the first acts of this government was to send a message of 'filial
devotion' to Pope Pius XII, signed by Costello, which read:

> On the occasion of our assumption of office and our first Cabinet meeting,
> my colleagues and myself desire to repose at the feet of Your Holiness the
> assurance of our filial loyalty and devotion as well as of our firm resolve to
> be guided in all our work by the teaching of Christ and to strive for the
> attainment of social order in Ireland based on Christian principles.'[55]

The inspiration behind this government initiative was Joe Walshe,
the Irish Ambassador to the Holy See. He was, according to Ronan
Fanning, 'as notoriously misogynistic as he was polemically Catholic'[56]
and wrote in March 1950 to the Archbishop of Dublin, John Charles
McQuaid, following a visit to Rome by Costello, 'T(hank) G(od) we
have such a wonderful Catholic at the head of Govt.'[57] Home Rule
had become Rome Rule to an extent even hardline Ulster unionists
would have hardly imagined possible in 1914. This message to the
Pope was 'the most abject statement of Catholic piety since independence'.[58] It sent an unambiguous message to the Protestant minority,
and all minorities which were not Catholic: the state you live in is a
Catholic one for a Catholic people.

In 1949, the coalition government – under the influence of Sean
McBride and leadership of Fine Gael's John A. Costello – took the
country out of the British Commonwealth in a hurried and clumsy
manner, declaring a republic. De Valera would not have left the
Commonwealth, as he believed that it provided a bridge to Northern
Ireland and his dream of unification. In fact, there was no need to
leave the Commonwealth to achieve a republic, as India, which left the
British Empire a few days later to also become a republic, remained in
the Commonwealth and is today an advocate for Ireland to return. In
the words of the historian Richard Davis:

> … by that time the action was both otiose and impolitic. India with a
> history more venerable than that of Ireland, was demonstrating that a
> republic without loss of dignity could maintain its association with the

British community; the problem of reconciling Ulster Protestants to a united Ireland was increased rather than lessoned by the withdrawal of the Irish Republic.[59]

Before turning to some Protestant views of modern Ireland and to the failure of the Orange Order to celebrate the centenary of its' foundation, perhaps it is worth giving a picture of the Irish Protestants seen from the eyes of a distinguished English politician, Lord Hailsham, who married Mary Martin of the old Norman family of Martins of Ross in Lough Corrib, related to Violet Martin of Somerville and Ross fame. He wrote:

> Mary and her family had all the best qualities of Southern Irish Protestants: a steely loyalty to one another and to the Crown, an unshakeable personal courage, a nice sense of fun, and great personal courage. They lack the fierce Calvinism and garrison mentality of the Protestants of the North. They are wholly without fanaticism. They take their own Protestant Christianity for granted without flaunting their faith in the face of different persuasions. They treat the English with amused affection, but are as different from them as the Scots and the Welsh. They bitterly resent Sinn Féin, who have exiled them from their old homes.[60]

5

Grabbing their Children

In 1907 a stronger, more militant Roman Catholic Church introduced the decree *Ne Temere*, under which dispensation for a mixed-religion marriage would not be granted unless both the Protestant and Roman Catholic partners gave a written guarantee that the children would be brought up in the Roman Catholic faith. The *Ne Temere* decree played a major role in reducing Protestant numbers for a large part of the twentieth century. In fact, it was the most important factor in reducing Protestant numbers post-independence in 1922. The decree remained in effect until 1970, when local bishops were allowed to relax the rules on mixed-religion marriages. However, as Brian Walker has made clear, in Ireland the bishops in general did not step back and let parents 'decide on the upbringing of children' and 'the Protestant community continued to decline'.[1]

What was the *Ne Temere*? Pope Pius X issued it to replace the Dutch Precedent, a mid-eighteenth century ruling which stated that Catholic-Protestant marriages were valid under Catholic canon law. This was valid in countries where Catholics were under penal laws, long since gone in Ireland. To quote Don Akenson:

> Henceforth, no mixed-marriage would be valid under Catholic canon law (even if valid in civil law) unless a Catholic priest presided and the non-Catholic partner signed a legal form that was imperious in tone and humbling in detail. The non-Catholic affirmed that he or she would not intervene of the religion of the Catholic partner; the Catholic partner affirmed that he or she would endeavor in every way to bring the non-Catholic to the True Faith. They both swore and signed that all children of the marriage would be baptized Catholic and

educated in Catholic schools. And they both swore that they would not engage in any parallel marriage ceremony – either civil or Protestant. The only marital bond was the Church's.

Then, and only then, the mixed-religion couple could be married in a side chapel and without a nuptial mass.

The *Ne Temere* pledge reads like some jog-trot insurance document or commercial bill-of-sale and would be easy to ignore. But that would be a mistake: it is in fact one of the most inflammatory pieces of prose in twentieth-century Irish history. Protestants are not keen on mixed marriages any more than their Catholic counterparts. But what they hear – accurately – is that any marriage that includes a Protestant is necessarily second-rate. And, crucially, they understand that the children of any mixed marriage will be 'grabbed' – that is the most common term – by the Roman Catholics.[2]

It has been emphasised in correspondence in *The Irish Times* that there was 'no reference in the decree in any shape or form to the religious upbringing of the children'.[3] Be that as it may, the practical reality was that before the *Ne Temere*, Catholic clergymen advised the Catholic partner that the children should be brought up as Catholics, although they did not insist on it. In practice, before the coming of the *Ne Temere* in Ireland there was flexibility over mixed marriages and the religious upbringing of children from such marriages.

The *Ne Temere* 'made the presence of a priest and two witnesses a necessary condition of the validity of any marriage involving a Catholic.'[4] Crucially, priests 'would not perform such a marriage until a dispensation had been granted, and this a bishop would not do until the promises had been given.'[5] Ultimately this meant that 'in practice the promises became necessary for validity'.[6]

Due to the social and cultural apartheid-style lives operated by Protestant and Catholics, an apartheid I experienced as a child growing up in Co. Cork, it has been argued that the *Ne Temere* was rarely an issue before the Second World War. But with increased social mobility and the erosion of old prejudices, mixed religion marriages became more frequent after the war was over. Arguably no other country applied it more harshly than Ireland. It is difficult to get reliable statistics, not least because the Church of Ireland did not keep them, believing that one's faith and not numbers was what mattered, but Dr Brendan Walsh of University College Dublin estimated that by 1961 around 25 per cent of Protestants were in mixed-religion marriages; and 30 per cent of Protestant men and 20 per cent of Protestant women were in mixed marriages in 1961. Almost all of the resulting children were raised as Roman Catholics.[7]

In a detailed analysis of numbers of Protestants entering mixed-religion marriages, Richard O'Leary concluded that Protestant brides were marrying Catholic partners in small numbers pre-1926, only 6.1 per cent, but by 1962–66, that had increased to 33.5 per cent.[8]

By 1971, some 30 per cent of Protestants were marrying Roman Catholics. Today the figure is closer to 50 per cent. Few Protestant leaders spoke up to defend their faith and the effect on the arrogant rapaciousness of the Roman Catholic Church on Protestant numbers over generations. Dr Kenneth Milne of the Church of Ireland wrote:

> The regulations of the Catholic Church governing mixed marriages, particularly as expressed in the *Ne Temere* of 1908, played a key role in the Church of Ireland's demographic decline. In an environment such as that of the twenty-six counties, where mixed marriages are common, the obligation imposed on both partners to bring their children up in the faith and practice of the Catholic Church has had considerable demographic impact.[9]

Many marriages were deeply influenced by the decree and one such marriage broke down very publicly. A Church of Ireland husband, Mr Tilson, took custody of his children and placed them in a Protestant home so that they would be raised as Protestants. The marriage must have been under considerable strain as the Catholic mother took a case to the High Court in 1950 where the President of the Court, Justice Gavan Duffy, ruled that as Mr Tilson had given a written promise under the *Ne Temere* to raise the children as Roman Catholics, he was legally bound to do so. As justification for his decision, the judge referred to Article 44 of the Constitution, which recognised 'the special position' of the Roman Catholic Church. The children were therefore ordered to be returned to their mother. Their father appealed to the Supreme Court and lost his case, but not on the grounds of article 44. Of the 4 judges, 3 were Roman Catholics and voted against him. The dissenting judge, Justice Black, was a Protestant.

Garret FitzGerald wrote in *Towards a New Ireland* that the *Ne Temere* decree 'has been responsible for a significant part of the decline in the Protestant population of the Republic'. He tried to bring this to the attention of the Pope when paying an official visit to the Vatican, but was brushed off. FitzGerald said in an RTÉ interview on 27 September 1981:

> If I were a northern Protestant today, I cannot see how I would be attracted to getting involved with a state that is itself sectarian … the fact is our laws and our Constitution, our practices, our attitudes reflect those of a majority ethos and are not acceptable to Protestants in Northern Ireland.

However, FitzGerald failed to mention Protestants in the South. Were they happy living in the sort of State he described? He seemed to be unaware, whether through innocence or doublethink, that Irish Protestants who had lived in a 'sectarian' State for 60 years, a State that was institutionally and emotionally anti-Protestant, were not likely to be contented. Like Conor Cruise O'Brien, while seeing the serious shortcomings of the Irish State for northern unionists, he failed to see how southern Protestants might also have been alienated by a puritanical, ethno-nationalist Roman Catholic, Gaelic Irish State. When I mentioned this to him in email correspondence, he told me that Protestants had not complained to him, to which I responded that I could introduce him to some who would if he so wished! He did not take up my offer and the correspondence ended. Victor Griffin, the brave ex-Dean of St. Patrick's cathedral, might have told him that 'Protestants were scared … I can hear my mother's warning: "For goodness sake, keep quiet, Victor, or you'll get us all burnt out".'[10]

One writer put it thus: 'The Church has been the guiding influence on the politics of the nation since the fall of Parnell. It determined the inner life of the nation, and later it determined the inner life of the State. All parties and all Governments have functioned within its ambience.'[11]

Protestants were living in a State, under a Constitution, and under laws that were 'appropriate only for those who subscribed to the authority of the Catholic Church.'[12]

Dr Martin Mansergh, the nationalist Protestant Fianna Fáil TD, wrote that 'post independence … notwithstanding vestiges of a more idealistic and inclusive republicanism, there was a concerted effort to create a homogeneous 26-county society, in which there would be no challenge to the hegemony of the Church'.[13]

Another mixed-religion marriage was to hit the headlines more sensationally in 1957. My father was Dean of Cloyne at that time and although I cannot remember him talking about it, he must have been shaken by the stand taken by the Roman Catholic Church. This mixed-religion marriage was in Fethard-on-Sea, a small holiday coastal village in Co. Wexford, where a boycott of Church of Ireland traders started in May 1957, initiated and strenuously encouraged by the local parish curate, Father James Stafford. The boycott was supported by Father Allen, the parish priest; by the Bishop of Galway, by Cardinal D'Alton in Armagh; and by the local bishop, James Staunton of Ferns. Irish politicians, with two exceptions – namely Senators William Bedell Stanford and Owen Sheehy-Skeffington of the Protestant Trinity College, Dublin – failed to speak up, showing the control the Roman Catholic Church exercised over elected representatives of the Irish State.

Inevitably, the boycott drew the attention of the international press, notably *Time* magazine. Eamon de Valera, the Taoiseach, did intervene eventually on 5 July 1957, some 2 months after the boycott started. He said in the Dáil that the boycott was 'ill-conceived, ill-considered and futile for the achievement of the purpose for which it seems to have been intended'. By then the incident was causing international embarrassment. De Valera described the events as 'this deplorable affair', but he did not oppose the *Ne Temere* decree itself. Senator Owen Sheehy-Skeffington, however, was outraged. He was concerned that 11 Protestant children were getting no primary education, the 22-year-old Roman Catholic teacher, Anna Walsh, having withdrawn her services as soon as the boycott started. He raised the issue in the Senate on 5 June 1957, calling the boycott 'cowardly and disgusting', pointing out that 'small children are deprived – I might use the word victimised – in relation to the educational facilities.' The Minister for Education at the time, Jack Lynch, did not turn up in the Senate to debate the boycott, despite Senator Sheehy-Skeffington having been assured that he would, or that he would send a representative. Professor Stanford supported Sheehy-Skeffington, saying that the incident 'may do grave harm to the good name of the country at home and abroad'. Sheehy-Skeffington separately wrote to Revd Adrian Fisher on 10 August, enclosing a small cheque for the relief fund that had been set up.

What happened to bring all this on? I interviewed a number of people in the summer of 2007, among them Gerry Gregg, who produced a gripping film called *A Love Divided*; the clergyman in Fethard-on-Sea at the time, the Revd Adrian Fisher, who had to look after his tiny number of parishioners through this ugly time, and Eileen Kehoe, the daughter of the woman who brought on the boycott.

Sheila Kelly was the daughter of Thomas Kelly, a Church of Ireland farmer and cattle dealer. Her mother, meanwhile, came from a Palatine background. The Palatines came to Ireland from the Rhineland Palatinate in the early eighteenth century to escape Roman Catholic persecution, only to find it in Co. Wexford during the 1798 rebellion and again later. About 5,000 Palatines were settled in Ireland with tiny holdings of between 8 and 10 acres in counties Limerick, Kerry, Tipperary, Carlow and Wexford. They spoke German initially and had a reputation for working hard and being self-sufficient. They sowed wheat, barley, oats and potatoes in rotation; they even grew flax. During the Great Famine of 1845–49, no Palatines died of starvation or disease, because their mixed-crop methods of farming gave them an alternative food to the potato. They had another major advantage over the Irish: being Protestants, they enjoyed security of tenure; they were given 50-year leases on arrival. No doubt if the Irish had been encouraged to rotate crops and given security of tenure, there would have been far fewer deaths from disease associated with starvation during the Famine.

It seems that Sheila inherited this tradition of hard work, self-reliance and independence of mind. She was a driven woman and not one to spend money on herself. She was a dedicated member of the Church of Ireland, deeply involved in the local parish. It was Sheila who proved to be the farmer, not her husband, Sean Cloney, who inherited his farm of 120 acres. He came from a Roman Catholic family, which had managed to keep its land throughout the time of the plantations and the penal laws. His ancestors had been prominently involved in the 1798 rebellion and fought with Wolfe Tone's insurgents in the Enniscorthy area. Cloney was aware of the burning of innocent Protestants in a barn in Scullabogue near Wexford at that time and would have been horrified by it. Some 100 men, women and children had been burnt to death in reprisal for the deaths of United Irishmen in New Ross, 6 miles to the west. Cloney became a member of the Scullabogue memorial committee, as he was a man without religious bigotry. Why otherwise would he marry a Protestant of Palatine descent?

Sean and Sheila met at the local national school in Fethard-on-Sea. Sheila then moved to London, but Sean visited her when in town on business. They married in a registry office in 1949, as well as in both an Anglican and a Roman Catholic church. They later returned to Wexford to farm Sean's land and had 3 children: Mary, Eileen and Hazel.

Sheila signed the *Ne Temere* decree in London in order to get married in a Roman Catholic church, clearly to please her husband. But later she decided not to comply, just before her eldest daughter, Eileen, was due to go to the local Catholic national school. She decided instead that she wanted to send Eileen to the local primary Church of Ireland school, which ironically had a Roman Catholic teacher, Anna Walsh. There were only 11 pupils. However, the curate, Father William Stafford, insisted that Eileen went to the Roman Catholic school. He had been allegedly bullying Sheila Cloney; it became apparent that he had been dogmatic about the subject for some time, and made it clear that it was Sheila's duty. Even her husband, a gentle person, took it for granted that Eileen was to go to the local Catholic school.

Rather than conform, Sheila took her two children away from Fethard-on Sea on 27 April 1957. She packed suitcases while Sean was working on the farm, banged the car while exiting the yard, and drove to Wexford, where she caught the train to Belfast. Her father, Tom Kelly, had given her £30. He did not support her actions, but saw he would not be able to change her mind, so thought it best to make things easier for her.

After Sheila had disappeared, Father Stafford went to Tom Kelly's bank, the National Bank in nearby Taghmon, to ask the manager if Tom had made money available to Sheila. Quite properly, the manager said that this was a confidential matter. Not discouraged, however, Stafford returned soon afterwards and bullied a young bank clerk into revealing that Kelly had given £30 to Sheila. This was the evidence he considered he needed to declare a boycott of Protestants in his parish.

A writ of *habeas corpus* was issued on behalf of Sean Cloney to produce the 2 children (the youngest, Hazel, was not born until after the boycott). Belfast-based barrister Desmond Boal, a friend of Ian Paisley's, visited Sean, completely unknown to Sheila, some 3 days after Sheila arrived in Belfast. It has been consistently said, and said by Sean Cloney, that Sheila's terms were that Sean must sell his farm and emigrate to Australia or Canada where the 2 children were to be raised as Anglicans. But Sheila's daughter, Eileen, told me that this was never the case. In any case, Mr Boal advised Sheila on his return that she should leave Ireland immediately with her 2 daughters.

After Mass from the altar of Poulfur chapel on 12 May 1957, Father

Stafford instructed his flock to boycott the tiny Church of Ireland community, which he held responsible for financially assisting Sheila Cloney. But his action was in vain. How could her fellow parishioners have influenced Sheila? And how could they bring her back? They did not know where she was. Sheila had acted as a Protestant. She had her own relationship with God and no priest nor bishop of her husband's church would tell her what to do.

The boycott commenced on 13 May and lasted about 9 months. Roman Catholics were told not to go to Church of Ireland shops, not to work on Protestant farms, not to purchase milk nor cattle from Protestants, nor to support them. The local delivery of milk had, until that point, been carried out by a Church of Ireland man, Alex Auld, who lost 95 per cent of his orders for milk. J.W. Clarke lost the school transport at 16s a day for 33 days. The Roman Catholic teacher in the Church of Ireland primary school, Anna Walsh, withdrew her services. The local owner of the newsagents' shop, Betty Cooper, even declared that Protestant children were forbidden to buy sweets in her shop and promptly lost 58 customers. By June, all Roman Catholics had withdrawn their labour from Protestant farms. One farmer, William Cruise, grew corn. A Catholic woman and her son left him to fend on his own and the results were dramatic: he had sold between £50 and £100 worth of corn in previous years, but only £15 worth in 1957. The local music teacher, Lucie Knipe, lost 12 of her pupils. Leslie Gardiner, the owner of a seed and hardware shop in the main street, found himself without customers. A boycott vigilance committee was formed and the boycott was extended to Catholics who defied it.

Attempts were made to extend the boycott to Wexford town, 25 miles away. There was a large Protestant drapery shop – Jenkins – and customers were encouraged to boycott it. Father Stafford personally visited a bank in nearby New Ross, where he asked the manager to refuse to give credit to his Protestant customers. He was ignored.

Bishop Browne of Galway stirred matters further on 30 June at the Annual Congress of the Catholic Truth Society by stating that all the local Protestants were guilty of the 'crime of conspiring to steal the children of a Catholic father. But they try to make political capital when a Catholic people make a peaceful and moderate protest'. Dr Browne, however, defended the boycott in front of Cardinal D'Alton and 6 other bishops, calling it a 'peaceful and moderate protest'.[14] Hubert Butler, the courageous Church of Ireland writer, unlike almost all the leaders of his timid church, argued in his essay on Fethard-on Sea that the motivation for taking such a hard line was to demonstrate to Northern Protestants that the Roman Catholic church was in charge of such matters in the Republic and did not intend to make concessions to appease them in the event of a united Ireland.[15]

Mr Boal arranged for Sheila to go to Edinburgh through Dun Laoghaire, as he knew Larne was being watched. She went to one of the Orkney Islands in Scotland, where she worked for a missionary society. A Mr Long in Edinburgh found a home for Sheila and her daughters in the Orkney Islands, where Sheila worked hard to earn her keep, milking cows and doing general farm work. She found herself in a tolerant, liberal environment, unlike home. Eventually, she read in *Time* magazine that there was a now internationally reported boycott in Fethard. Alarmed and upset, she contacted her husband and secretly they arranged to meet in Orkney. He persuaded her to return on condition the children were educated at home, a provision allowed for in de Valera's constitution. She returned, but she was never the same again, nor were her children. They were homeless at home, living in isolation, a sort of exile. It affected them deeply all their lives.

Revd Adrian Fisher, the clergyman who had arrived just before the boycott started, tried his best to cope. He was only 33 and this was his first parish. He had been a military chaplain with the British Army in Cyprus, and his father had been a clergyman in Newbridge, Co. Kildare. He remembers the archdeacon saying to his bishop, Percy Phair, right after his installation, that 'there is going to be trouble in this village'. He had no inkling how bad the 'trouble' would be.

Fisher believes Sheila left because she knew that her husband was not going to support her. He told me: 'He broke his promise to Sheila that they would agree on which school the children would attend. They could not agree on the education of their child. The husband wanted to follow the priest'. He added, 'I feel strongly that the *Ne Temere* is a curse on our nation. Brought forward in the early twentieth century, it is so very wrong to be so totalitarian, as if the church of Rome was the only church, that all other churches and denominations were outside the love of God.'[16] But during the boycott, Fisher did condemn the action of Sheila in a letter to *The Irish Times* on 7 June 1957: stating, 'I have already condemned the action of Mrs Cloney. We all deplore the break-up of a family home.'

Fisher took action to negotiate an end to the boycott a few months after Sheila had gone. He phoned Father Stafford and asked to see him, as there was no question of Stafford making a gesture towards him. Stafford agreed to talk to him, but in his house, on his terms: 'He opened the door and I was told to sit down at the table and in a flash of lightning his fist came down on the table in front of my nose with force. He said, 'You are to go to Belfast, see a solicitor and do all you can to bring back Mrs Cloney'.

Fisher was dumbfounded. He politely explained this was out of the question. He could take no such action, as the matter was a legal one for the Cloneys to sort out, and suggested that Father Stafford should know his law before making such demands. Furthermore, Fisher had no idea where Sheila was and his first duty was to care for his flock.

The Church of Ireland, marginalised and passive, encouraged Fisher to keep quiet:

> Just to have a smile on my face. Extraordinary! If I were free, I would have spoken up. There was no lead from the Theology department in Trinity College. Dr Luce, a godly man, wrote to me to tell me to keep quiet. The Dean of Christ Church silenced me, told me not to say a word. My bishop was the same. I do not think he ever visited the parish during the boycott. But we need to remember my hierarchy was afraid of tremendous repercussions at the time.

Dr Luce wrote to Fisher to tell him the following:

1. Do nothing provocative;
2. Don't exaggerate the dangers
3. Be careful what statements you give to the press;
4. Do not try to work up an agitation, unless things get worse
5. Do what you can to improve relations locally, and respond to any olive branch.

This was hardly a brave and forceful reaction to the behaviour of the Catholic Church. But Luce did say in a letter to *The Irish Times*, 'These poor suffering Protestants are being persecuted for their religion. It is petty and mean at a distance but it is a terrible experience for those who are in it.'[17] The Dean of Christ Church cathedral, E.H. Lewis-Crosby, sent Fisher a cheque 'to assist your people in the evil boycott to which they are being subjected'. His bishop, Dr John Percy Phair, of Ossory, Ferns and Leighlin, told the press, 'Of course

I deplore mixed marriages. I do all in my power to discourage them. I think people should marry into their own faith and church. Then these things would not happen.' But the bishop knew that it was idealistic advice. The gene pool of the Protestant community had been greatly reduced, increasing the rate of mixed-religion marriages all around him. He might have instead have spoken up against the effects of the *Ne Temere* decree on his vanishing community. Phair at first offered conciliatory advice, urging the Protestants in Fethard to have a 'smiling face', as this was better than a 'sour and melancholy attitude'.[18] He stated that he would not condemn the Catholic bishop of Ferns, the Most Revd Dr Staunton, as he was 'a great friend of his'.[19]

This weak approach was criticised by Canon Lindsay in an article in *The Protestant,* which stated:

> The Right Reverend Prelate failed, and failed miserably, in an hour of crisis. When his voice should have been as the voice of a lion, he was a sheep bleating on the mountain. When will our leaders learn that the only opposition Rome understands is the resolute, convinced, uncompromising Protestantism?[20]

Phair wrote to Bishop Staunton to explain that Mrs Cloney's flight had nothing to do with the Church of Ireland people and that they could not get her back. He told Bishop Staunton that the boycott was 'doing very serious harm to the cause of Christianity in the country'.[21] He wanted the publicity to end, but Owen Sheehy-Skeffington took the opposite view: publicity was the language that the Catholic Church would understand.

Adrian Fisher was strong from the start. He wanted to approach the Papal Nuncio and the Taoiseach. He called on 'His Lordship, the Catholic Bishop of Ferns, to use his influence to stop this boycott at once'[22] and accused Father Stafford and his parish priest, Father Allen, of 'taking the law into their own hands'.[23] De Valera, meanwhile, urged Sheila to 'respect her troth and to return'.

The Roman Catholic Church needed to be challenged as, in the words of Fisher, it 'was so powerful then. Ireland was quite primitive in those times.' To explain 'primative', he told me an extraordinary story, later substantiated by Eileen Cloney, about Father Stafford:

One day he killed an elderly man. Ran into him and the body landed on the bonnet of his car. I walked to the village after this happened and I saw two elderly country women, simple souls, and I mean this in no disparaging way. I said it was a tragedy that poor old man who lived down the road. The immediate reaction of these two women was to put their hands in the air and say, 'Glory be to God, killed by a priest.' Extraordinary. I walked on. The Gardai did nothing about it. In England there would be an enquiry straight away.

A committee was established to administer a relief fund to aid victims. It was announced in *The Irish Times* and the *Belfast Telegraph*. Money came in mainly from Northern Ireland; not much from the south. After the *New Statesman* wrote about the boycott on 28 September 1957, donations came from England. The writer, Hubert Butler, visited Fethard and gave a donation. He also sent a small contribution from the wife of Terrence MacSwiney, who had died on hunger strike in 1920. Short Bros and Harland from Belfast sent a generous donation. A member of the Dublin and Wicklow Orange Lodge, Patrick Bentley, wrote to advise Revd Fisher to ask for funds in various papers, noting: 'You have been let down badly by your bishops. The only two who spoke were Messrs Phair and Tindall and their utterances were painful to read.' By 12 September, almost £1,100 had been subscribed.

The campaign never ended officially. However, on 24 September the *Belfast Telegraph* reported that the parish priest, Father Lawrence Allen, had paid an overdue bill to Leslie Gardiner's hardware shop, signalling his wish for the end of the boycott. It was at around this time that the vigilance committee formed to administer the boycott ceased to meet. However, the boycott did continue, with many Roman Catholics continuing not to buy from Protestants. But it was not a failure as far as the Catholic Church was concerned. It made clear to Protestants where they stood.

Many Roman Catholics were outraged, and one brave Catholic in particular needs mention. Donal Barrington, later a famous and highly respected judge, spoke up and told the Catholic Social Study Conference that the boycott was 'the most terrible thing that had happened in this part of the country since the Civil War'. But there was no general uproar. Most Roman Catholics did not protest, and the Roman Catholic hierarchy was unmoved. Protestants continued to be fearful and continued to exercise self-censorship as they lived from day

to day in their outsider community. The *Ne Temere* decree continued
to be enforced harshly and Protestant numbers continued to decline.

Sheila, meanwhile, did not settle down. The Roman Catholic clergy
continued to put pressure on Sean, and through him on Sheila, so
much so that Sheila feared they would win through in the end and
the children would have to go to the Roman Catholic national school.
So she left again with Eileen and Mary, this time to Goodwick, near
Fishguard in Wales. Sean came to see them at weekends, working on
the farm during the week. He wanted her to return, and after about
a year she gave in, but left Eileen behind with friends. Eileen was
miserable and was soon sent home. But Sheila was still very unsettled,
and suspecting she was about to take off again, Sean took the children
away to stay with his friends for a few months. She must have felt
pressure existed to have the children sent to the Catholic school.

It had dreadful effects on the children and their grandfather, Tom
Kelly. He was widely respected in the area where he sold and bought
cattle. He managed to sustain himself during the boycott, selling cattle
outside the parish. Eileen claimed that he was 'psychologically broken,
he was shattered. He was a decent man, looked out for people in hard
times, lent animals to widows, brought them a cow so they would
have milk. He was liked and fitted in.' A broken man, he died shortly
after the boycott ended.

An interesting light is thrown on Fethard by a letter written by
an old IRA man, John Ryan, a supporter of Fianna Fáil, to the then
Taoiseach, de Valera. He stated that the boycott 'was started by people
who are not of our party'. What party started it? Fine Gael supporters?
Labour? Fine Gael was silent on the boycott while Labour, in the
person of Brendan Corish, supported it. Ryan believed that 'the only
thing that is happening is to split the Catholics'. One Catholic in the
village ignored the boycott. He continued to sell petrol to Protestants
on the pragmatic basis that they paid their bills on time.

Approximately 40 years later, Gerry Gregg made *A Love Divided*, as
mentioned earlier. In an interview on 16 January 2004, he told me
that in 1990 he heard about the story of the boycott in Fethard-on-Sea
and decided to explore it. Gregg believes that from 1937 to the time
when Charlie Haughey was removed from power, Protestants lived in
an 'ice age', in a narrow Roman Catholic State that proved to be 'an
unappeasable host', in the words of W.B. Yeats. He instanced the disappearance of the Dublin artisan Protestant class, largely caused by the *Ne*

Temere 'without too much protest from the Church of Ireland which was prepared to see its working class go'. The people of Sean O'Casey's background went, people who were cabinet makers and wardrobe makers, plumbers and piano tuners. There are many Protestant churches in the inner city that are now FAS training centres, restaurants and shops.

Gregg feels strongly about what happened:

> All the aspects of the erosion of certain civil liberties are shown in a microcosm in Fethard-on-Sea. It also showed the weakness of the temporal authorities which did not intervene and show leadership … the Fethard story encapsulates the awful stifling power of the Catholic church and a very narrow interpretation of its teachings. Sean Cloney met Sheila Kelly in London and they got married in a registry office and in the Anglican church which allowed freedom of choice to bring up any offspring in whatever religion the parents chose, or in no religion. Very different in the Catholic church in London where they also got married: the "true" marriage was when Sheila would have had to attend instruction from a priest and then sign the *Ne Temere* decree.
>
> Sheila's refusal to obey the *Ne Temere* summons up all the Protestant virtues of free thinking, free will, conscience and a direct line to God telling her what is right and wrong. When she is confronted by this ultramontane reality that must have been triggered in a woman who is a descendent of Palatine refugees a question of where does this end was asked? She had a conscience and she believed that it was up to her and her husband to make the decision. One day, someone was going to say no; this is unfair, this happens in no other country in Europe, nor even in the Catholic heartland of Latin America. It is an Irish solution to an Irish problem. Sheila must have been brought up not to say anything in case it upset the priests and the Catholic neighbours. Normally it is the role of poets, writers and intellectuals to dissent from that cultural fog. But this was a woman in a little village who decided 'no; I'm not taking this'. Her actions speak louder than any words. My contention is that she also revolted against the whole system that was destroying the Protestant community in the Republic at that time and undermining its sense of itself, its sense of equality, its sense of history. If Yeats said they were 'no petty people', by the 1950s they were. They were a poor, pathetic people.

Gregg added:

Orkney was then light years removed from the Irish Republic in terms
of morality. For instance, if you fancied a woman and she fancied you,
you were encouraged to live together for six to twelve months and
that was in the fifties. So she would have been exposed to a form of
Christianity that was liberal, pluralist, non judgmental, believed in live
and let live.

Conor Cruise O'Brien 'isolated three people who deserved the credit
for creating intellectual space that a lot of people began to inhabit
in the '60s. The three individuals who stood up for the imagination
and arguably the principles of the Reformation were Seán Ó Faoláin,
Owen Sheehy-Skeffington and Hubert Butler.'

Seán Ó Faoláin was President of the Irish Association of Civil
Liberties and wrote to Fisher on 26 June 1957, enclosing a letter to
the 'national newspapers' in which he asked the local clergy, TDs and
councillors to end the boycott. These stand in stark contrast to the
silence from the Protestant churches.

What about political Ireland? Brendan Corish, the local Labour
TD, said he spoke first as a Catholic, and when de Valera made his
condemnatory speech in the Dáil on 5 July, Corish asked him 'to
ensure people will not conspire in this part of the country to kidnap
Catholic children'. De Valera ignored the remark. A Methodist Fianna
Fáil TD, Lionel Booth, addressed a Methodist conference in Dublin
on 11 June; shamefully he declined to criticise the Catholic Church
or call on the government to act. Instead, he used mealy-mouthed
words about giving leadership. Jimmy Kennedy was the local Fianna
Fáil TD in New Ross and he supported the boycott. John Joe Ryan,
meanwhile, had been a colleague of de Valera since 1916, and he was
quietly opposed, writing to de Valera to explain why the boycott was
senseless. Sir Antony Esmonde, the Fine Gael leader, said nothing
which Gerry Gregg could find. However, Archbishop McQuaid
became concerned, and the Vatican was contacted through the Papal
Nuncio and by the Irish Ambassador in the Vatican. Gregg pointed
out that: 'de Valera was in a situation where a Jewish Lord Mayor, Bob
Briscoe of Dublin, had been in America saying that Jews were very
well treated in Ireland so Fethard was giving the opposite picture as far
as the Protestant minority was concerned.'

There was also the fact that 'international journalists were descending
on the village in south-east Ireland and sending reports on an outbreak

of Counter-Reformation-style intolerance in a modern western democracy. De Valera was embarrassed by a furore that cast a poor light on the Republic's claim to be a more tolerant society than bigoted Ulster. In July he described the events in Wexford as 'this deplorable affair'. It was a cautious phrase, 'but it took some of the wind out of Catholic claims to be fighting for justice', in the words of Marcus Tanner.[24] De Valera did not ally himself with the boycott, so the State refused to get into bed with the church, and thus avoided 'playing with this ju-ju and letting it out of the bag', in Gregg's words. Gregg thought that: 'The forces of democracy were just about strong enough to hold in and restrain the forces that would have unleashed a Milosević-style ethnic cleansing. Imagine if Charles Haughey had been in power at that time as he had no respect for the State that was created.'

The local IRA commander was a composite figure in the film:

Local members of the IRA had been excommunicated in the 20s for taking an anti-treaty position and could never reconcile themselves, and that character was the compendium figure in our film. IRA members had never reconciled themselves to the church and may have believed that the church had contaminated their view of what a republic should be. There was a local IRA man called Andy Bailey who was involved in the IRA in the 1920s and he had no time for that sort of sectarianism.

Bishop Brendan Comiskey of Ferns did apologise full-heartedly in 1998, 41 years later; he asked for forgiveness and expressed 'deep sorrow'. He condemned the 'church leadership' at the time.[25] But Gregg commented on this as follows:

When you look at the crimes that were done in the name of Ireland in the 1970s, 80s and 90s, this little boycott pales. In terms of the island it took the culture nearly forty years to deal with the challenge of Sheila Cloney. She walked away from the confessional state and all the require-ments the Protestants were required to meet. So now I hope things will change as there are new Protestants here from Nigeria, 50,000 Chinese and 30,000 Muslims.

Gregg eloquently ended the interview by estimating that at least half a million people saw this film and:

it gave them the opportunity of what it meant to be Irish and the scary thing is that still forty years after it is a challenge to call yourself Irish and not be of the Catholic faith, not be of the Gaelic tradition, and not be of the political persuasion that looks to nationalism as the panacea for the island's solutions. We could ask the question for a contemporary Ireland, what does it mean to be Irish? Irish identity is now about race and ethnicity of a complex nature, and other things, so the challenge posed in 1957 by Sheila when she dissented must be met by a new generation of Irish people and I hope they meet it better that they did in 1957.

And what about the effects of the film? Eileen Kehoe is strong on this.

> When the film came out, no one mentioned it. People avoided us. I went on Gay Byrne's radio programme and on Pat Kenny and no one locally would mention it. This was forty years later. Some would even say, 'That never happened'. People who visited Fethard as summer visitors were told nothing had happened. No guilt admitted.

As to the effect on Eileen and her sisters? She believes that they were considered to be 'weird' and 'unacceptable', 'something to do with religion … very serious and no one talked about it'. They were in denial.

After all of Sheila's efforts to have her children raised in the Church of Ireland, Eileen has turned her back on organised religion, or what she calls 'man-made religion'. She is taken locally for a member of the Church of Ireland, but is not. She has cut the grass in the graveyard where her sister Mary and her grandfather, Tom Kelly, are buried but does not go to Mass in the church where all the trouble began. Her husband is a Roman Catholic, and to avoid more rows, they brought the children up as Catholics. But none of her children show any interest in the Catholic Church. Her daughter never goes and her partner has 'no time for his (Catholic) church'. Yet they had their daughter christened in the Catholic church in Kilmeaden, Co. Waterford. They 'need to place her somewhere', according to Eileen.

But for Eileen, the real lesson of Fethard was clear. Her beliefs are between herself and her Maker. She passed a turning point some time ago and she now feels immensely relieved. I could detect this in her voice. She told me she 'feels blessed at this stage'; it is 'brilliant' and it 'comes with age'.

Revd Adrian Fisher and his wife left Ireland for good. They applied to other Irish parishes but according to the Fishers, fear of the boycott spreading was a major factor in their not getting another parish. Fisher joined the Royal Army Chaplain Department and retired to Henley-on-Thames, Oxfordshire. He died there on 15 April 2014, aged 90.

Sheila Cloney died aged 83 on 27 June 2009 in Wexford General Hospital. She was a brave, strong woman.

Some Protestant Voices

A great deal has changed in Ireland since my parents returned in 1947. The country has moved away from the conservative, illiberal moral pieties of de Valera's dreamland to a more secular Ireland, which is part of the multiregional North Atlantic group of islands. Nationalist ideology taught in Catholic schools proclaims that revolution was needed to overthrow British colonialism, to set the country 'free' from 700 years of oppression, mainly based on myths and imagined wrongs, wounds nursed and paraded to innocent peoples around the world. Yet essential freedoms were denied after independence by the very victors who fought and died for 'freedom'. I have dealt with this in some detail in the first few chapters. Liberal changes became almost inevitable once British television arrived, and later on free secondary and tertiary education. Those changes came about gradually, however, and not through pressure from the tiny Protestant community, but rather because Roman Catholics – mainly women – had had enough of the imposition of narrow Roman Catholic doctrines. Censorship, divorce and contraception were tackled and reformed. The special position of the Roman Catholic Church was removed from de Valera's constitution in 1972, a constitution which recognised all other Churches as not having such benefits.

Ireland became an increasingly multicultural society, today characterised by a workforce of many immigrants from Poland, Lithuania, Ukraine and China. It is a country that claims to be pluralist by virtue of the fact that it has in its midst so many foreign workers speaking different languages. Far more Chinese and Polish is spoken today in Ireland than Irish.

Yet how pluralist is modern Ireland? How do modern Protestants view it? Are they becoming more outspoken? Or does the trauma of the 1920–23 period still cast its shadow over present-day Protestants? Have they metamorphosed into green Irishmen? Are they part of the seamless Irish society that Senator Martin Mansergh has proclaimed?

I decided to try to find out by interviewing some Protestants in various parts of the country to get some individual testimonies as to how they felt about Ireland. Are they outsiders, or an established class? I went to interview a few Protestants in the 1990s in the border areas, where Protestants ended up on the wrong side of the border following partition, and to others in Wexford and Limerick.

Let me start with a young married man named Charlie, a cultural development worker for the Ulster Scots community near Cavan, and also a member of the Orange Order. He has a strong Protestant voice, not typical of most Protestants generally in the Republic. On the strong feelings that arose during and after some of the Orange Order parades in the North, he believes the series of Drumcree parades in particular brought a huge propaganda victory to Sinn Féin in the south:

> It was a total disaster from the point of view of the way people view the Orange Order this side of the border. It endorses the view that Orangemen are violent thugs. We are finding it increasingly difficult now to bring in new members because anybody that is a wee bit middle-of-the-road will steer away. I know families that were all for joining the band, maybe two, three or four youngsters in a family, and when this thing blew up around Drumcree they wanted nothing to do with us. It is going to kill some of the Orange groups. Younger people going to work in a factory are going to feel very uncomfortable if they ask for a day off on 12th July to go and play with the band. It is harder for us to get a good turnout of the band on 12th July than on any other day of the year. If a Protestant is taking that day off, even if they wanted that day off for something else, they would be slow to ask.

Charlie explained the social nature of the Orange Order, emphasising that the Order has given opportunities for Protestants to mix while playing in a band or playing games.

Referring to parades in the counties of Cavan and Monaghan, Charlie mentioned that the closest you would get is in some small village like Drum, where there would be a church parade before or after the service. These parades were not welcomed in some areas, particularly the larger towns. Many feared that they would be 'targeted'.

There is a reason for this. Up until 1931, Twelfth of July parades had passed off peacefully in counties Cavan and Monaghan. But in 1932, all July demonstrations were cancelled in Donegal, Cavan and Monaghan due to the destruction of the railway line in Cootehill in 1931, as well as the election of a new Fianna Fáil government, which did not give official assurances of the right to parade. Thereafter, 'Orange activities in counties Cavan and Monaghan were restricted to church services and private meetings, and Lodges attended the Twelfth of July parades in Northern Ireland.'[1] In Co. Donegal, Orange parades were held in Rossnowlagh, a coastal village where some of the Cavan and Monaghan Lodges went.

We drove to a monument dedicated to the IRA outside the courthouse in Cavan. The inscription on the memorial reads: 'Volunteer, Kiaron Doherty, TD, Cavan-Monaghan, died in Long Kesh, 2nd August 1981, after 73 days on hunger strike.' On the front of the memorial was written: 'In commemoration of those men of the Irish Republican Army who gave their lives in the defense of the Republic.' Names are given of those who died between 1920 and 1924, presumably during the guerrilla war waged by Michael Collins, as well as on the side of the Irregulars during the civil war. On the back of the memorial is written:

Volunteer Patrick Dermody, Hilltown, Castlepollard, killed in action, 30th September, 1942, aged 33. Patrick McManus, OC South Fermanagh, IRA, died 15th July, 1958 in defence of the Irish republic, aged 28 years. James Carson, Banboy, Sinn Féin organiser murdered by British forces, 25th August 1956, aged 26. Jack McCabe, QMC, 30th September, 1971, faithful and fearless to the end.

'Very inclusive, isn't it?' said Charlie, as we drove away. There was no mention of the Irishmen who fought in the two world wars. He went on to talk about the Orange Halls, many of which were:

… cold with nowhere to park the cars except on the side of the road, you have roofs that need to be replaced, toilets normally none at all. One of the halls was burnt two years ago and they actually know where the petrol was bought and they suspect the man who did it. But no arrest was made. Sad thing is the best way to get a hall modernised is to have it burnt. They [the local council] won't fund a religious organisation. The Orange is not a singular religious organisation but consists of all branches of the Protestant religion, of like-minded people. They have the Protestant ethos of work, trying to avoid Sunday sport, in line with their religion. When you go into the mainstream Catholic community centres when concerts are going on, or whatever, that's not comfortable for Protestant people. The halls were the original community centres for the Protestant community.

According to Charlie, when applications for funds are made for a Roman Catholic community centre, the application form will state that Protestants will make use of it, when they 'have no intention of using that centre'. In one interview he gave concerning a request for a grant for a Catholic centre, the woman interviewing him was changing his answers as he responded:

'Well, that would mean you would be going to play badminton in that hall.'
    'No, I would play somewhere else.'
    'Ah, but you might.'
    And she would put down that I will. So I told her straight, 'You are not putting down what I tell you. Protestants would not use a cross-community hall.'

Much of the money for community centres comes from the Lotto, but an additional problem he raised was that some Protestants will not accept Lotto money, as they consider money raised from the Lotto to be gambling money. 'Presbyterians have serious problems with that. If they do draw down the money, it will divide the members and they would lose some, so to avoid that you do without it. That is why some applications don't go in. If we can't meet the criteria, it should be changed to be more welcoming to all opinions.'

However, since the interview with Charlie, the Department of Foreign Affairs in Dublin has provided funding to the Orange Order, particularly in Co. Donegal, and Minister Eamon O'Cuiv of Fianna Fáil opened an Ulster-Scots centre in east Donegal. He has been most supportive of the Donegal Orange Order Lodges.

Asked if his fellow Orangemen were associating with more militant Orangemen in the North, Charlie said, 'This side of the border I know no one who is an Orange militant and I know a lot of them. They are a community group that supports the bands and community activities.'

I moved on to ask about the Irish language. Charlie was 'not comfortable' learning Irish as 'it was not part of me'. He resented it being forced on him. He also played GAA games, and as he did not know the rules, he was made fun of. Again, it was not part of his culture. Charlie believes that the GAA games all revolve around alcohol, sponsorship coming from drink companies. There are bars in many of the clubs. He was also concerned that so many Irish activities revolve around the consumption of alcohol, from engagement parties to marriages to funerals. In contrast, Charlie believed that the Protestant community does not make the consumption of alcohol the centre of its social activities, and generally socialise over cups of tea.

On the recognition of bishops by the media, he pointed out that 'the Church of Ireland bishops are always referred to on the radio as the Church of Ireland bishop, but whenever they refer to the Roman Catholic bishop, they refer to him as, for example, the Bishop of Dromore. This means the Church of Ireland bishop is not the real bishop.'

He also noted that Protestant numbers had fallen drastically, as noted earlier in this book. In 1920, the town nearest to him was full of Protestant shops, but today there is only one left. 'This is the story of rural Ireland. In the north, by way of contrast, the Catholic people have gone from strength to strength, both in numbers and in prosperity.'

I next went to Co. Wexford for a meeting with a small Protestant farmer, whom I will call John. He told me that he, like his fellow Protestants, had learnt to keep his head down. It had been bred into him. He was of the opinion that the Protestants were persecuted not for their religious beliefs but for their political opinions. If they criticised 'the sectarian nature of the Irish State, or the rebels of 1916, they would be in hot water. It wasn't always that way. In 1798 when the rebellion took place in and around Enniscorthy, there were 4,000 loyalists living there. Today there are none.' His farmer friend, who lives nearby and to whom John introduced me, said that if it were not for the British, there would be no Protestants left in Wexford, and in the South generally, as they intervened to stop the massacre of Protestants during 1798. 'Part of the reason Protestants were murdered was because they administered British rule in Ireland, even the clergy could be magistrates.' But, he added:

> ... the British soon forget who their friends are, and even find them an embarrassment, and as a result they are not supporting the unionists in the

north and should not have allowed all the IRA murderers out of prison
without getting the IRA to put away their weapons and say 'the war is over'.

I asked John how he thought he fitted into the local community and
he told me that he was invited to the President's reception in Áras an
Uachtaráin on 12 July 1998. The then President, Mary McAleese, had
made a real gesture to the southern Protestant community by hosting
a reception on 11 July. She invited people from the Orange Order in
the South, as well as Protestant judges and professionals and journalists like Bruce Arnold. John was pleased to go. But he is convinced
that people in the area got to know of this, because he was given the
cold shoulder by some of his neighbours for about a year. It was not
clear why they should react in this manner. Perhaps it was because
neighbours were aware that some people from the Orange Order in
Northern Ireland had been invited and John was considered a sympathiser? Did John over-react?

John believed that Protestants like him had no political voice. He
had approached Ivan Yates, a local retired Fine Gael Protestant government minister, about the possibility of a united Ireland, something all
southern political parties sought. If we were really serious about this,
John suggested, concessions would have to be given to the unionists.
For instance, the South should go back into the Commonwealth of
Nations, should have a new flag and anthem, an all-Ireland parliament
located between Dublin and Belfast, a Human Rights charter. However,
Yates considered these suggestions to be unsellable in the South. He
did not want to even debate them in Fine Gael circles, where he was
respected and had considerable influence. Yet, as John pointed out,
Fine Gael has no plan nor discussion document to prepare for what
would happen if one day 51 per cent of the electorate in the North
votes to remove the border. Then again, no party has. It is a long way
off, if it ever happens.

John was convinced that Ireland had suffered considerably by
leaving the UK. As far as he was concerned, had the country remained
a part of the UK, it would have enjoyed an infrastructure comparable
to Scotland's, which he thinks is first rate. If it were not for the EU,
there would be no good new roads, no motorways. He also considered that if the UK had not been on Ireland's doorstep, the country
would have been as poor as parts of South America, with large families
living below the poverty line. The Irish health service is inferior to

the National Health Service provided in the North. However, the Irish road network has improved hugely since I interviewed John, with motorways connecting all the major cities to Dublin along with funding provided by a generous EU.

He is convinced, despite the party's pluralist rhetoric, that Sinn Féin wants the unionists out of the North. Unionists need only look to what happened to the Protestant loyalists in the South if they want to understand what would happen to them in a united Ireland.

> Look what happened after the Second World War in Europe. The Russians had tried to suppress Christianity in countries they conquered after 1945 but when they withdrew, Christianity made a comeback and is stronger than ever. Here this will never happen as far as the Protestant community is concerned as there are far too few left and their churches are closing down all the time all over the country. It has been a complete triumph for the Roman Catholic Church.

When some unionists in Northern Ireland whom he knows talk about the South, they say 'you Protestants must be very happy as we never hear you complaining'. Yet when he tells them that Protestants keep quiet because they fear consequences, unionists find this hard to accept.

> My example of going to the President's reception in the Park shows what my neighbours think about my tradition expressing itself. Then there was the murder by the IRA of Senator Fox in Monaghan when he spoke up, something which horrified John Bruton. But then Bruton is about the only truly pluralist man in the Dáil and look what they did to him.

However we should remember that Senator Fox was murdered in the 1970s, and that times had changed when John went to the Áras. Nevertheless, John's perception is that his Protestant tradition is not at ease in expressing itself.

I next travelled to Limerick to meet a scion of one of the Beamish families, who have been in Ireland for over 400 years. Ian Beamish is from Mellane near Dunmanway and went to school in Bandon Grammar, an old Protestant foundation secondary school with a proud tradition. He emphasised that his mother came from a poor Protestant family: 'It is a myth that all Protestants are wealthy. Most were not.'

Ian is in his 30s and works for Analogue, the large US computer parts manufacturer, in Limerick. His wife, from Limerick, is a devout member of the Church of Ireland. He is a member of the Orange Order.

His family memories go back to the War of Independence, when local people cruelly cut the hooves off the Beamish cattle and left them to bleed to death. But he added that the Beamishes were 'strong people' and that 'through their family history they hanged one or two people for attacking them'. There was a cake shop owned by the Wilsons in Dunmanway, a Protestant family. According to Ian's father:

> … when the lady who owns it was a little girl, the IRA came into the house, they had them all huddled, the head IRA man went over to take the bread, and the little girl said, 'Don't let him take that, Mammy,' and the IRA man put a gun in her mouth and told her to go back and sit down in the corner.

A boy with whom Ian went to school told him that his family also 'had all been huddled into a corner, his grandfather was pinned to the door with a gun at the back of his head, and was told, "Don't you dare say anything about what goes on in this house tonight."'

> The IRA had used that house as a stakeout to ambush an army patrol that was passing. The house was chosen to try to make the patrol believe the shots were coming from Protestants … Even to this day there is a man outside Dunmanway, one of my father's best friends, who heard gunfire (he lives in a mountainous area), and thought it was a guy shooting rabbits, but this was rapid fire, and he went up to investigate, and it was actually the IRA who were practising. They put a gun to his head and told him if he ever spoke about this, they would kill him. That's a threat he has lived with and that's only ten years ago.

Returning to the Troubles, Ian informed me that 'Michael Collins came from 12 miles outside Dunmanway. Sam Maguire was born in Dunmanway town and is buried in the local church. Maguire was in the British civil service and recruited Collins. Maguire got very sensitive information on Ireland and used to come over on the boat to Dublin to give it to Collins personally as it was too risky to post it. Based on some of this information, Collins organised the 'Bloody

Sunday' murders of the British Army intelligence men who were murdered in cold blood. Ian believed that Collins had let down Sam Maguire, as he did not give him the position he wanted as chief of the Irish civil service. Be that as it may, Maguire was rejected by his own local Protestant people and died of tuberculosis, an unhappy man.

Ian's grandfather had his own pub and farm and had built himself up over the years. He had also worked for Atkins, selling flowers and farm machinery in the local area, so a lot of farmers knew who he was.

> He was well respected and that's why when certain pressures were coming on Protestants in the town he used to get tipped off, you know. People would say to him out of the blue, 'I recommend not to be around and it could be in the afternoon and you'd better get out of town tonight,' and he said that he used to grab my father and wrap him up in blankets and go about four miles outside to cousins of ours. One night the IRA shot five Protestants in the town and one of them was eighty something, he was almost blind and he just answered the door and they shot him dead ... When my own father died, we had found bank accounts in England, Barclays. My mother said that through the years if the pressure ever got too much, he had to get out and he had a bank account waiting for him in England and he could leave overnight. He lived all his life with that in the back of his mind. He was self-employed and he had to keep his mouth shut. To stay in business and to survive you just had to keep your mouth shut.

Ian continued:

> I remember when the hunger strikes were on in the H block and I did not really understand what they were but I soon found out. I went to school in Bandon Grammar and going to school we were called 'Proddie woddie green guts'. I remember the day Bobby Sands died that the headmaster called an assembly and he just said if you need to ring your parents to collect you, go ahead and I would advise you to take your school ties off going home. I remember going down the town and getting kicked in the backside, and funnily Roman Catholics were also getting it, as it was an interdenominational school where there were Catholics as well.

I asked him why he joined the Orange Order.

Where I grew up a lot of the Church of Ireland people felt British. I felt proud that the community I grew up in had done everything to keep their traditions and religion and I felt very pro-British. I felt Britain was the cradle and fountain of everything I enjoyed in life. I can't be the only one who feels like this. I could never identify with the GAA, céili music, I could appreciate it but I could not identify with it. I wanted to be involved with far wider thinking and world. No one had taught me to be like this so it must be myself.

He saw an Orange parade on 12 July and thought that 'they must be proud to parade and are not afraid to walk out as Protestant and British. I felt that that was what I could identify with. My Dad said, 'Don't bring that on yourself.'

Dad was not in the Orange because he was in business and we would really be driven out. I answered back a few people in the shop, and my Dad told me we were going to have our windows driven in because of me. One day one guy called Margaret Thatcher a 'bitch' and I said isn't, she's one strong woman, isn't her ancestry from Kerry? Her grandparents are from Kerry. I remember playing with a little toy gun and I said 'I am going to join the British Army,' and said it was the finest army in the world and I got an awful doing for that. I just thought standing behind the shop counter, I am not going to make money like this and take this abuse ... I admire the way the Orange Order honours the war dead. No one lines up here on 11 November. I got a copy of the sash from a relative and I used to put it on and was told to turn it down.

Ian then rang the Orange Order in Belfast and was put in touch with the Lodge in Dublin. He was told not to go ahead as 'the fear factor came in again' but he 'did not care as he did not want to live his life like that'. He then joined and has 'no regrets since. The amount of people I have met who opened my world.'

Someone came into the shop once and said, 'I think it is so funny to see these people dressed like this on 12 July trying to be Englishmen'. I said, 'They are not trying to be Englishmen. They are witnesses for their faith. It's a walk. It is to remember what we fought for in 1690, the rule of law, parliament, democracy. It is very Irish.' The man, who was a clergyman who came from England said, 'It is not Irish, the

Famine is Irish.' So I said, 'Sorry, now, if you go down to that church and look at the tablet inside the door, that's our history, the names of the people from that church who are now dead who fought in two world wars. The Famine is part of history but that is also our history. Orangemen defend their church.'

Returning to the subject of the Orange Order, he went on:

> There used to be eight Orange lodges in Bandon. A man who is on the board of Bandon school was visiting relatives in northern Ireland and the old lady was very sickly and said, 'there is something under the bed and take it away but don't open it until you get home'. It was the original Orange banner from Bandon. He did not know what to do with it. They had closed the Protestant church, which was the largest one in Ireland, and they had turned it into a heritage centre. It is now on display.

When Ian and a few others went to discuss the Twelfth of July celebrations with Mary McAleese in Áras an Uachtaráin, he mentioned the banner and the president asked if she could have it to display in the Áras on the day. So Ian approached someone on the committee in Bandon, whose father was in the IRA, and he agreed. The whole Bandon committee was invited and all of them went. 'The celebration in the Park went off very well but unfortunately all the good we had done was ruined by events at Drumcree.' The Drumcree resistance to parades had been at its height in the 1990s and there had been high tensions in 1998/99.

> We have some republican clergymen in Co. Cork and one told people if you want to buy your poppies, go down to the Roman Catholic church and buy them there. So they did and came back. But people were not at all happy and some wanted to get rid of him. Particularly with the history of what happened to the Protestants in the area. Unfortunately the Church of Ireland is full of appeasing, wet clergy like that who are more interested in appeasement than in principles. That is why the Church of Ireland has got so weak. Rome matters more than their own.

Many southern Protestants, however, would not agree with these strong sentiments.

Kevin Myers and John Bruton have commented that there are very few Union flags flown in the South. Ian agrees:

I was down in the Blackpool shopping centre in Cork city. I was in there one day looking around and there were 22 flags in the centre and 3 of the flags were flying upside down. Canada was upside down with the maple leaf turned around and some of the flags you would not know where they came from. There was nothing from England, Scotland, Wales. They even had the Vatican flag flying. There was no Union flag, our nearest neighbours, our biggest tourists, so I said I would hop the ball here where Michael Collins and Roy Keane are big heroes. I just said to the lady behind the information desk there were 3 flags there flying upside down and she asked which ones. So I said, 'With all these flags, there is nothing to mark our nearest neighbour.' So she said, 'Which neighbour?' And I said, 'England, Scotland and Wales,' and I got a look as if I was joking and she said, 'You're serious? I don't think that would be appropriate here.' So I said, 'Why not?' So she realised I was not taking the mick and she said she would make a note and tell the manager. She wanted my details but I left it at that, as my name would be handed around. There's still a chip on the shoulder.

I was at work on Saturday after the Rangers and Celtic match and one guy turns to me and says, 'Those dirty Orange bastards,' and he looked at me. I said, 'That's a nice greeting to give me coming into work. If I had come in and insulted you, you'd have had me up for bigotry.' So he said, 'I did not mean anything by it, sure I was born over there. I have a British passport. I have two of them. I have a British and an Irish passport.'

So Ian told him that he was more British than he was, as Ian only has an Irish passport, though he very much wants a British one and is upset that the British did not agree to let Irish people have them as part of the Belfast Agreement. After all, anyone who wants an Irish passport in the North can have one. Apparently the right for Irish citizens to hold British passports was in the original agreement but later removed.

One day, someone suggested that Ian must be very disappointed in England, as they had lost the World Cup. He pointed out that he had been born in Ireland and, furthermore, his family had been here for 400 years and had no family connections in England.

Some other guy who was a lapsed Catholic said that a priest had said
that every town in Ireland should have a statue of Winston Churchill so
they could spit on it when they came out of Mass. The same man said
that all the world's problems can be blamed on English Protestants and
American Jews.

On mixed marriages, Ian believes that there is no longer 'the same
severity' about the enforcement of the *Ne Temere* decree and that
'about half the children who go to the Church of Ireland playgroup
my daughter attends are from mixed religion marriages'. He thinks a
lot of influence can come from the clergyman and he describes:

> ... an excellent clergyman in town now [Revd Hewitt], and all the
> mixed marriages he goes and visits and in fairness to him there are
> some coming back to church now. A lot has to do with the clergyman
> and that is what is wrong with the Church of Ireland ... we don't
> know our culture, we are not taught our history, it's not coming from
> the Church of Ireland anyway. I grew up in Dunmanway and my
> parents worked very hard ... when a bill was due, it was paid. We were
> called black Protestants and we used to think, why don't they like us?
> I remember I had played soccer and one guy asked me if I would play
> Gaelic and some of the lads were dead sound and others called us 'jaffas'
> after the oranges!

We moved on to the Irish language and unsurprisingly, he thought it
was taught 'with no love and no feeling behind it'. He mentioned that
a government department even brought fishermen from Connemara
to the area to help to revive the language, but it was a failure. Ian
associates the language with backwardness, as everything he read as
a boy was in English. They removed science subjects to give time for
Irish and it 'played no part in anything we did outside school'. His
nephew's background is Scottish and he was being forced to learn
a language that had nothing to do with his culture. 'It should be left
there for those who want to learn it, or for romantics or dreamers.
It was taught along with glorifying violence because the leaders of
1916 were in all schools with their names in Irish, even in Bandon
Grammar School.'

Growing up in Dunmanway, he was 'within a community within a
community', so the people clung to their own. The community was

'self-sufficient to an extent but when it came to politics, you just never got involved really because you'd always get the insult'. Ian's father wanted a golf course in Dunmanway, 'but it went to Skibbereen. He could not get the support of the community, only his own people'.

As far as Protestants in the Republic are concerned, Ian says, 'we are leaderless'. He believes that there is an attitude of 'we must be friends, we all have the one God'. He feels that too many of our clergymen were 'bending too much to fit in with them'. The leaders were not teaching 'our culture' in the schools, unlike Judaism or Islam. A lot has to do with Ireland's 'rugged individualism', or entrepreneurial spirit: 'look at all the inventions that came from Britain, and all the sports'. There is a spirit of 'questioning things', and not accepting laid-down doctrines.

Despite these characteristics, Protestant numbers have fallen, so they have little strength. Ian mentioned that 'the Anglo-Irish landlords left, like the Percivals in Castletownbere. They had to leave by boat as the house is right on the sea and they were picked up by a vessel out at sea.' All their possessions – including tapestries – were burnt to the ground. 'You look at all the fabulous treasures that were destroyed in the country just by pure hatred.'

> [In Bandon] they [the IRA] had taken the old Lord Bandon who was in his 80s, and old Lady Bandon stood up and sang 'God Save the Queen' repeatedly as the house burnt. That is one thing I admire about the old Protestant tradition. They had stiff upper lips and had real fight in them.

The middle classes left and the country was left to people who were not forward thinking; Ireland therefore did very badly, as it was somewhat inward looking. The attitude was 'I'd rather be poor than do business with Britain and Britain had a stepping stone to the world. A lot of poor people suffered because of separation and the self-sufficient economic theories of Arthur Griffith proved a disaster.'

We discussed the huge part that the Irish played in building the Empire, another fact that is not commonly known.

> Some were government officials. They are not recognised for their role in supporting the Empire, especially by the British Governments today. In fact the Irish left the British Commonwealth in a fit of nationalist pique, thanks to Sean McBride whose mother, Maud Gonne, was partly British and was treated abominably by McBride. Maud Gonne went

around in weeds for ever after her husband was shot in 1916, despite the fact she hated him. Perhaps only in Ireland could such self-serving, narcissistic behaviour be admired, especially from a Protestant. They are good at that, from Wolfe Tone to Childers.

Ian believes that once a Protestant becomes a nationalist they go to extremes to prove themselves. Ian has seen how in mixed-religion marriages, offspring can be brought up to not just reject their Protestant culture, but become hardened nationalists. He knows of one child of such a marriage who became a nationalist. We then discussed closer relations with Britain, which Ian considers to be:

> ... a slow, reluctant process. They don't want to admit there are any of us left here or that there were any atrocities towards us a long time ago, 80 years ago, but there has been a Chinese torture towards us, drip, drip, drip through their education system. They want every-thing that is British but do not want to put a British stamp on it. Everybody's watching BBC, the soaps, they are living just like any other British person, even the shops. *Homebase* opened up two weeks ago and you couldn't get into the place when it opened. People want these shops.
>
> The main problem is with the monarchy, the Queen and the Union flag, a red rag to a bull even if you explain that St Patrick, St Andrew and St George make it up. Mary Harney said we are closer to Boston than to Berlin but we are much closer to London. Irish people go to Canada, Australia and New Zealand and to England. If they can't live with English ways of life and laws, why go to England?

So why did we leave Britain?

> This country was in a serious recession for 70 years after it left Britain and everything was going very well before and in farming everything was excellent in the country. There was a boom time in business here. And the Irish who went to America, why didn't they come back and set up businesses here then if they were such perfect patriots.

Ian went on to mention some people in west Cork, who have worked very hard and are 'bent and twisted with arthritis. They had really hard lives and basic lives as well when they could have had so much more in an expanding world. They had pulled away from industrialisation and left the real world.'

The following letter from Ian and his wife Elizabeth was published in the *Irish News* on 3 February 2003 in response to Martin Mansergh's assertions that southern Protestants got a very fair deal, and it sums up Ian's attitudes:

Time to put the heating on for Protestants

HAVING read Senator Martin Mansergh's piece 'The south is a warm house for Protestants', my wife and I felt compelled to reply.

It appears that Mr Mansergh is at variance with himself, his identity and the culture to which he comes from. My wife and I are not ex-Ascendancy. He could claim this title. He is in fact more English.

In no way does Mr Mansergh reflect any significant body of opinion among living generations of Protestants in the south. Coming from Protestant backgrounds, we had to submit and come to terms with living in an Irish state as our businesses, livelihood and survival depended on it. Yes, we have integrated into the community — we are not assimilated.

How can we embrace the national anthem and flag of the south, as the two entwined have been adorned by people whose sole purpose has been to remove me and my cultural existence from my homeland. Feeling vulnerable, Protestants don't speak up so as not to attract any unwanted attention upon themselves for fear of consequences. When they do speak up they are called 'whingers'.

As Home Rule was on the statute books, the 1916 rising was unwarranted. Think of all the lives that have been lost unnecessarily since.

Why was there a pogrom of the Protestants from 1920–26? Why the *Ne Temere* decree which more than decimated the Protestant population? In the 1980s Dr Noel Browne's comments — 'a state where no Protestants need apply' — wasn't encouraging. Why the recent state funerals for dead IRA men when there has been no reciprocation for the victims those people had murdered?

Did Mr Mansergh's party consult minority religions when the wording for the last referendum bill was put together? No. Why wasn't a member of the Reform Group asked to attend the recent forum? Is it because we are not supposed to exist? Why have so many Protestant churches had to close? It wasn't because of the heating bills to keep them warm.

In Donegal, Protestants make up 10 per cent of the community and yet only one per cent are civil servants. In a recent survey (Derry-Raphoe) 78 per cent of Protestants believe that equal opportunities do not exist.

I'm discriminated against because I'm British and I'm not entitled to a British passport in southern Ireland yet Northern Ireland nationalists are entitled to Irish passports. [2]

I want to live in a genuinely plural, liberal democratic state capable of accommodating social, cultural and religious diversity whether you aspire to be Irish, British-Irish or British. The people of Scotland have the option of the normal range of politics – right, left and centre, all three being unionist parties with a small 'u' in addition to a nationalist party.

Is it too fanciful to ask Mr Mansergh to tolerate a similar evolution here where the Reform Movement can be tolerated alongside the main political parties in southern Ireland?

This state has been a cold house for Protestants for far too long. It's time to put the heating on, Dr Mansergh.

IAN AND ELIZABETH BEAMISH

Limerick

Protestant numbers have ceased to drop in the South. From 10.4 per cent in 1911, the population continued to decrease; it was 7.4 per cent in 1926, 5 per cent in 1960 and 3 per cent in 1991. However, there was a slight rise in 2011, when numbers increased to 3.5 per cent. This is largely due to an increase in the number of Protestant immigrants. Native Irish Protestant numbers, though, are not increasing significantly. In the 1950s, the Sparsely Populated Areas Commission closed 144 churches, and closures have continued since. It was reported that 6 churches closed in Cork city recently and 5 in Limerick city. Many Church of Ireland members do not attend services. It could be said that the Church of Ireland is fading away.

As for recognition of Protestant identity and its association with Britain, there is little doubt that people view Irish identity in a broader way. President McAleese said at the opening of Brakey Orange Hall in 2008 in Baillieborough, Co. Cavan that 'It is possible to be both Irish and British, possible to be both Orange and Irish. We face into a landscape new possibilities and understandings'.[3] Nevertheless, terms such as 'West Brit' and 'Anglo-Irish' are in common parlance, denying the Irish identity of southern Protestants, as is made clear in interviews in Heather Crawford's book *Outside the Glow*, where both Protestants and Catholics thought that Protestants are all too often seen as outsiders. Given the nature of the emotional and intellectual inspiration of the founding fathers of the Free State, this is not surprising. The inclusive dreams of Wolfe Tone and Thomas Davis were cast aside. Protestants were on the one hand required to be part of the nation and to be outside the nation on the other.

There have been major steps in recent years in recognising the Irish contribution to the British forces in the two world wars, with visits by Queen Elizabeth II to the Irish National War Memorial at Islandbridge in 2011. Bishop Paul Colton of Cork, Cloyne and Ross believed that the complexity of Irish history was being recognised, and this gave 'the lie to the heresy … that there was only one way in which you could meaningfully be said to be an Irish person – mythical Celtic, oppressed and Roman Catholic.'[4] The British Prime Minister, David Cameron, and the Irish Taoiseach, Enda Kenny, laid wreaths in May 2014 at war graves of Irish and British soldiers who fell in Belgium and Flanders in the First World War. This has led to an acknowledgement of those who followed the call of John Redmond to join the British forces in 1914.

John Redmond has been all but airbrushed out of Irish history following the unmandated insurrection of 1916, when a minority secret organisation, the IRB, which was part of a minority armed organisation the Irish Volunteers, took up arms in a hopeless military initiative to separate from the United Kingdom. The rebellion was countermanded by Eoin MacNeill, the Chief of Staff of the Irish Volunteers, but this order was ignored by the IRB leaders, Patrick Pearse in particular. Furthermore, Roger Casement, who had organised a shipment of arms from Germany that was intercepted by the British Navy, called off the insurrection.

What MacNeill said at the time is worth quoting:

> I do not know at this moment whether the time and the circumstances will yet justify distinct revolutionary action, but of this I am certain, that the only possible basis for successful revolutionary action is deep and widespread popular discontent. We have only to look around in the streets to realize that no such condition exists in Ireland. A few of us, a small proportion, who think about the evils of English government in

Ireland, are always discontented. We should be downright fools if we were to measure many others by the standard of our own thoughts.[5]

There were few 'evils', if any, 'of English government in Ireland'. Ireland enjoyed all of what were considered the major freedoms in 1916, and Home Rule was enacted by Westminster. Had John Redmond's Irish Parliamentary Party survived, it is likely that the outcome would have been more inclusive for southern Irish Protestants and that the nature of Irish identity would not have been, in the words of Bishop Colton, 'only one way in which you could meaningfully be said to be an Irish person – mythical Celtic, oppressed and Roman Catholic.'[6]

7

Some Donegal Voices

I continued my research on today's Protestant attitudes with a visit to Co. Donegal. The Protestant community there is larger than in any other county in Ireland, and beleaguered as it has often felt since independence, it has maintained its beliefs and different culture since 1922. This is partly because it is a border county in constant touch with fellow Protestants in the North.

Let me start with the sad story of Joe Patterson and his family, forced to leave Letterkenny for Vancouver in Canada in 1974. At that time he and his wife, Margaret, were 39, his son David was 10, and his two daughters 9 and 5. He had owned a farm of 150 acres and a thriving, long-established meat business.

Letterkenny is very near Derry, which had become a focus of bitter sectarian strife by 1970. The Pattersons were one of the few Protestant businesses in the town, and they were concerned about anti-Protestant sentiment crossing the border. That year, some of the butchers working in the Patterson business had joined a trade union, the Irish Transport and General Workers' Union (ITGWU). Shortly afterwards, 4 tonnes of meat and some cash were stolen. Joe saw his meat-packaging material being used by another company in Letterkenny, but never discovered how it got there. He was the only user of this product in Donegal.

He tackled the shop steward, who admitted responsibility for the missing meat and cash, but said he had no idea 'what happened to it'. Joe dismissed him. The next day the ITGWU members went on strike, supported by George Hunter, County Secretary of the ITGWU in Londonderry. The Gardaí were informed and supplied with the names of witnesses; they questioned the suspect but found no evidence of theft. Some time later, the suspect married a girl from Carrick-on-Shannon, where he bought a small farm. The Gardaí could not explain where he obtained the money for this purchase.

The Pattersons joined the Federated Union of Employers of Ireland, the strike was settled a week later and an agreement was signed by the ITGWU to avoid further strikes. But trouble soon flared up again. During the strike, Joe lost considerable business and had to take the difficult decision of laying off one of his employees. He called for a meeting with the union members, which was repeatedly refused over a six-week period. To protect his business, he laid off an ITGWU man, giving two weeks' notice. The next day the union members went on strike, again breaking the agreement with the ITGWU.

In Derry, George Hunter refused to take the calls Joe made every 20 minutes for 3 days. Eventually George arrived in Letterkenny in a state of great excitement, barged into the office, slammed his briefcase on the desk and used foul language in front of a female employee. Joe suggested that George should leave, compose himself and start again, which he did. At that point, Hunter admitted that the strikers had broken the agreement, the strike was unofficial and that Joe was free to lay them off. Aware that trade unions have 3 weeks to decide whether to support a strike, and wary of Hunter's 'business ethics', Joe decided to wait. He asked for a court injunction to prevent further pickets, but this alarmed the police, who advised Joe's solicitor that should the injunction be broken, offenders would have to be arrested, with the likely outcome of riots backed by nationalists in the Bogside in Derry. There might even be loss of life. For the Pattersons, it was a no-win situation. They withdrew the injunction. Hunter then lent official support to the strike, as Joe had suspected he would.

Following a threat to bomb his house, Joe sought a meeting with the senior IRA officer in Letterkenny, whom he had known for many years. Surprisingly, the response was positive and they met in the IRA man's home at night. Joe produced the threatening letter and was assured that the IRA was not involved. Yes, the IRA had been approached by the strikers and he, the local IRA man, had refused to help. Undaunted, the strikers went to the IRA headed by Martin McGuinness in the Bogside of Derry. Shortly afterwards, McGuinness paid a visit to Letterkenny to find out what was happening. Joe knew Martin McGuinness from visits to the abbatoir in Derry, where

McGuinness worked. The IRA's response to the strikers was that if Joe's family was harmed, they would pass the names of the offenders to the police in the North and South. Furthermore, the IRA offered protection, which he turned down.

Joe was threatened and persecuted. If his car was seen in Letterkenny, his wife often got a phone call, telling her where his body could be found. The police were aware of this and offered him a handgun under instructions from head office. He turned this down.

The strike lasted 8 weeks, ruining the Pattersons' meat business. It was finally settled by a Rights Commissioner, Mr Con Murphy. However, the representative of the Federated Union of Employers, John Quinn, announced to Joe just before the meeting took place that he would not support him. Trade union officials admitted religious discrimination, acknowledged the theft and accepted that the aim of the strike was to finish the Patterson business. The strike achieved its aim. When they reopened, few customers supported them and they closed shop on 2 June 1973.

Prior to that, with tensions rising in the North, business improved at the weekends in Letterkenny, with customers crossing the border. But word spread and few came to buy meat in the Pattersons' shop. Joe heard a woman outside his shop saying, 'We can't go into that Protestant shop, they are the ones who sacked the Roman Catholics'.

Before he first went to Canada his father, who was unwell, said, 'Joe, go to Canada, have a look around and then come home and take Margaret and the three children with you. There is nothing left here for you in Donegal.' He was to start a new life in Canada, as the de Burghs in Co. Limerick had done in 1924, as well as other Protestant families who had been driven out of the South, as detailed earlier in the book. Not one politician in the Irish Republic has tried to get justice for the Pattersons.

Sectarian acts were not confined to the Patterson business. There is a small confectionery manufacturer in the town called Oatfield, exporting worldwide, and particularly to Commonwealth countries. Joe explained:

> After our closure, many townspeople were shocked that this could happen to such a long-established business. There was some trouble at the Oatfield Sweet Factory (McKinney's). IRA slogans were painted all over the wall facing the main road. All the do-gooders, politicians in

the town were given big publicity when it was washed off. At that time there were 9 or 10 Protestant-owned businesses in the town.

A year after closing, Joe's solicitor pursued the case for a possible breach of contract, sending Mr Liam Hamilton a brief. Hamilton, a Senior Counsel, specialised in labour law but refused to act as he was on an annual retainer from the ITGWU. Instead he referred Joe to Diarmid, a fellow Senior Counsel, whom Joe met along with his solicitor in Malahide Hotel.

Arising out of this legal consultation, Joe was advised to pursue a claim and wrote to the Director of Public Prosecutions' office in Dublin. But there was no investigation. Joe refused to be silenced.

More recently, a Dublin-based solicitor, Greg Ryan, made inquiries through the Freedom of Information Act to the police, the Director of Public Prosecutions and Department of Justice on Joe's behalf, but all were refused. Joe explained that, 'Greg cannot go any further with this.

I next paid a visit to Jim McCracken, a retired schoolteacher from Donegal, now Development Officer with Derry and Raphoe Action Group, a cross-border group which seeks to encourage greater community involvement by the country's Protestant population. He has responsibility for Donegal, and he explained much of the background and findings of their report entitled *Protestants in Community Life*. Jim seemed anxious to portray Donegal Protestants as almost their own worst enemies. He thought they failed to engage thoroughly enough and often had a false perception of being neglected.

He explained that the Derry and Raphoe Group was funded from the North, a Development Officer being appointed in 1997. The Protestant community is scattered across Donegal, with concentrated areas and other settlements of very low numbers. The objective of the research was to find out what the Protestants want and how they really think.

The EU's special support programme, the Peace and Reconciliation Fund, funded the research for a 6-month period. A research director, Ruth Moore, was appointed in May 2000, with Pamela Smyth as her research assistant. Because most of Co. Donegal is rural, and people work in the summer months, it was not until September that the research started, meaning that there were less than 3 months for the project to reach completion.

During the group interviews, only one answer was permitted to each question, so the entire group had to agree. Consensus was essential, so nuanced replies were perhaps distorted by the necessity for concise answers. Ruth Moore submitted an 80-page report, which was greatly condensed in the University of Ulster by In Core, a professional body, and the resulting published report was just 12 pages. They attempted to distribute a copy to every Protestant household in Donegal.

Unlike some group members with whom I spoke, Jim believes that the findings were not watered down and faithfully reflected the views of Donegal Protestants. They took the report to five centres after publication: Dunfanaghy, Remelton, Saint Johnson, Glenealy and Rosnowlagh. At all meetings they asked for views from the different churches and no evidence of State sectarianism was apparent.

I referred to the report by Stephen Mennell, Professor of Sociology in UCD, and by Mitch Elliott, psychoanalyst, on Protestants in the South, which concluded that Protestants were an 'established outsider group'. I also mentioned that many Protestants resented the fact that to be considered truly Irish you had to be Roman Catholic and nationalist. Jim's reaction was that this is a 'perception' which when repeated 'over and over again', becomes a 'belief'.

We talked about why there were so few Protestants in the civil service, and Jim mentioned that he had been told that there were only seven Protestants in the Gardaí, which is completely wrong. It was a 'manufactured fact' to support a certain view. He considered that Protestants had exaggerated their plight and to illustrate his point he quoted Shakespeare's *Julius Caesar*: 'The fault, dear Brutus, lies not in our stars, but in ourselves.'

Jim illustrated the lack of local government discrimination by pointing out that when grants were going through in a rush, and Donegal County Council awarded sixty-four grants in a recent round, sixteen went to Protestant groups, which is 'far in excess of our overall representation' and a 'positive discrimination'.

I mentioned my discussions with the man from the Ulster-Scots Association in Monaghan, explaining that he had difficulties when applying for grants on the basis that they had to be for cross-community activities. Jim's reaction was that funding organisations 'cannot be seen to be promoting any particular religious organisation and that they have an all-funders charter', whatever one's religion. In the Protestant religion, by and large, each parish has a church hall:

> [This is] essential to the survival of the Protestant community … to maintain a witness and identity to the Protestant community. The Catholics do not have community halls in the same way so when they apply they do not mind if it is cross-community. Protestants do not want this and they certainly do not want bingo, gambling nor alcohol in the buildings. But Catholics might find this positive, rather than negative, as the environment would be properly controlled for their children.

I asked if céili music would be acceptable in Protestant halls and he could see nothing wrong with this. I mentioned that some Protestants rejected the GAA and céili bands as not being part of their culture. He responded that 'lots of Protestants' were into GAA and 'there was a Protestant President of the GAA for a number of years, Jack Boothman, Church of Ireland'.

Contrary to Jim's claim, practically no Protestant national schools play GAA in Donegal and very few – if any – Protestants have represented the Donegal team. But Jim did concede that it was difficult for church groups to get funding 'purely for the church hall'. As far as he is concerned, there is no question of the management of church halls being cross-community as the halls were owned by the vestries, but if the Catholics wanted to use it for, say a quiet social meeting following a funeral, it should be made available within the ethos of the Protestant religion; for example no alcohol would be permitted.

I told Jim that there were Protestants who would not accept money from the Lotto on the basis that they disapproved of gambling. 'All monies go into the Department of Finance income tax including speeding fines, lottery money, etc.', he responded. 'It is then distributed among the different departments. Lottery funding covers many things other than sports and recreation, like medicines, money for free transport.'

I asked him about the Donegal Protestants' attitude towards what some thought was a Roman Catholic, green, anti-Protestant State. He thought Protestants were 'holding back' and not applying for enough grants; in his opinion, they needed to be more forceful.

In the Donegal findings, 96 per cent of Protestants indicated that they socialise with their Catholic neighbours, 'maybe selling bullocks down the mart or in a farmers' group'. But Jim did emphasise that Roman Catholics do not realise that there are important and fundamental doctrinal differences between the various Protestant religions. They tend 'to lump them all together on the official forms under the catch-all word "Protestants"'.

We spoke about the Orange Order, particularly the peaceful parade at Rosnowlagh every year. Of the 12,700 Protestants in Donegal, Jim estimated that approximately 500 were Orangemen. He thought 'the voice was in excess of the number … I do have a big problem with the Orange Order saying, "We demand Protestant rights" when they are demanding Orange rights'. He has problems with how the Orange Order 'see their Catholic friends'. I mentioned that David Trimble was a proud Orangeman, but he considers that a big problem for the unionist party. 'The Donegal Protestant will vote for any party, including Sinn Féin', he noted, but he emphasised that there is a strong Fine Gael affiliation and 'Paddy Harte was Fine Gael and represented very well all sections of the community in Donegal'. Jim White, a Fine Gael Protestant in south Donegal, also represented the Protestants successfully.

I mentioned the *Ne Temere* decree and he thought that it was not as rigidly enforced in Donegal as in the rest of the country. He claimed: 'Overall it has not made any major differences to Protestant numbers, but this is controversial and will be challenged by people in Donegal … in east Donegal anyway'. I was told later by a Donegal Protestant that 'No Protestant in Donegal would agree with this analysis. We used to be 20 per cent of the population and the *Ne Temere* left us halved in numbers.'

I finished my research on Protestant experiences in Donegal by interviewing someone who lived there for most of his life and now works in Dublin. He is in his 30s, married to a Roman Catholic, and comes from a Protestant background. I will call him John. He started by emphasising that in society south of the border, there remained 'certain things that are divisive'. In terms of politics, the Protestant community did not have any allegiance to any party and if people talked about the civil war they would look on blankly, as they did not care one way or the other about the outcome. Not that this meant there was any less interaction with the majority community. It made no difference in people's day-to-day life.

He was surprised at some of the findings of the Derry/Raphoe report and felt that its most compelling finding was that a high percentage of people – 20 per cent – believed that their religion prevented them from getting on in their careers, despite the fact that they got on well with their neighbours. According to John:

> … you do not give any view which is divergent from the nationalist one. Because your view is divergent and because people view it as disloyal, I think you become self-censoring but we express them when we are gathered together. People who are neighbours and in business do not want the hassle of expressing their views.

This struck a chord with me – we are back to Hubert Butler's summation of southern Protestant social behaviour being manifested through 'amiable inertia'.

He described a scene in a bar where a news report comes on about some topical incident:

> … you might be in mixed company and you can just see people eyeing each other up and down but not in a confrontational way; the Catholics are thinking 'I know that these Protestant people who sit here with me have a completely different view on this, but they'll never express it.' If you asked Roman Catholics in Donegal how they view the Protestant community, do they think they are absolutely and totally behind the Irish Republic, I think even the reasonable ones would say, 'Well, they are not disloyal but they are not as keen about it as we are.' Do they view them as being less Irish? I think they believe Protestants have a way to go to persuade them that they are fully behind the country. Among the Protestant community there are those who see that and work very hard to blend in. They're not all quite 'Uncle Tom Prods' but there's an element of that present. There are those who say I am Irish, and they think of Wolfe Tone and Charles Stewart Parnell who were Protestants, and these people were nationalists. Finally there are those who say, 'I have a different heritage, I didn't come from a nationalist background, there are elements of it I find distasteful.' But they hold that view in private because to do otherwise would be social suicide, they are not going to fall out with anyone.'

I mentioned that Ian McCracken had said that Protestants had themselves to blame for not integrating more successfully. John's response

was that when the State was formed, the minority's views were totally
at odds. There were the Irish Volunteers and the Ulster Volunteers:

> … many people who live near me, their grandfathers were in the Ulster
> Volunteer Force and overnight they were betrayed, cut away from that
> and their whole political currency was rendered completely disloyal,
> virtually overnight. In that context there is a responsibility on the
> majority community, as it is the powerful entity, to assimilate, to reach
> out and allow those people to play a full role as citizens. I think there
> was a failure of the Irish state in this respect. It was a Catholic state for a
> Catholic people and there was a small minority of people who did not
> fit into that, and the Irish state did not give a damn about it.

He went on:

> [If there was to be] any settlement in Ireland, it was going to have
> to … embrace aspects of Irish history that is associated with Britain.
> The British connection can't always be negative, we were British for
> hundreds of years. There are people in Ireland, north and south, who
> believe that an element of British interaction doesn't necessarily always
> have to be something that is viewed in a negative way.

He thought things had changed significantly.

> The bottom line is that nationalists in the South are beginning to
> realise that their nationalism is going to have to be redefined to be
> more soft and open to people who view themselves currently as
> British. People realise that's the only way to achieve a united Ireland.
> That means that the small minority in the South, who still feel they
> have elements of British heritage and sympathies, will be regarded
> more sympathetically.

We discussed the way Irish history is taught and John recounted the
story of a holiday with a well-educated friend. They had a few late-night
drinks and his pal said that many Irish people are taught that 'the Famine
was genocide by the British'. John's reaction was forthright, describing
such views as an example of knee-jerk nationalism and historically inac-
curate. The British did react to the Great Famine in various positive
ways, from shipping in maize from America to setting up public works

and workhouses in the worst-affected areas. He pointed out that there
had been a real genocide in Armenia, and 6 million Jews died in the
Holocaust; two governments had calculatedly set out to eliminate two
races. It was simply untrue that British politicians, however misguided
and prejudiced towards the Irish, did this in Ireland during the famine.
John believed that the first thing the new Irish State did was 'to seek a
justification for itself. It expressed itself as the Ireland of the Gael and if
you weren't a Gael, you weren't really Irish'.

I brought up Hubert Butler's 'amiable inertia' description of
Protestant behaviour. John's reaction was that this is hardly surprising
if you look at the reaction of the majority community to those few
who stand up.

> Noel Browne called the Protestant community "acquiescent Uncle
> Toms". It was a wish and a fear of not being accepted that it led to
> the minority population in the south suppressing their views and not
> talking openly and taking stuff lying down. Let's face it, there were
> incidents like Fethard-on-Sea and such realities weren't widely appre-
> ciated until the 1990s when someone made a film about it. I have
> Catholic friends who could not believe that happened, but I knew
> about it and so did my Dad. Unfortunately, the Protestant community
> did not really rise up and say this is outrageous.

He had read about the attitude of the Roman Catholic Church to
evangelists in Limerick, such as the Mormons.

> Catholic priests were assaulting them on the streets and evicting
> them. Protestant people in the south of Ireland have felt afraid to
> react to anything, afraid to express a view, kept their heads down,
> the consequence of that is they have no sense of self worth. That
> is reflected in the fact that their numbers have ebbed so drastically
> so in a mixed marriage they would not assert themselves and their
> children were brought up as Catholics and that is the reason there are
> so few of them left.

We went on to discuss the border counties, particularly Donegal. He
described these counties as 'unusual', because they have the highest
number of Protestants in the 26 counties.

Because Donegal is close to Northern Ireland, it held on to its particular heritage. In Donegal, Monaghan and Cavan, they have a more distinct view of themselves as a minority community. The Orange Order is the most radical anti-nationalist expression you can get. The fact that it exists in the border counties more than 85 years after partition is proof positive that there are people of a different hue there.

John had no wish to hold a British passport: 'As long as the State recognises my Protestant heritage and the fact that I don't have to be a raving Brit-hating nationalist to be Irish, an Irishman is how I feel.'

We moved on to discuss sports and he mentioned that there are cricket, hockey and badminton clubs, as well as many Orange Order meeting halls in Donegal.

> Then there is the GAA. As the Protestant population is 14 per cent, then 14 per cent of the people who play GAA games should be Protestant. To the best of my knowledge, in 100 years a Protestant has not played Gaelic football for Donegal. If they have, then it's no more than maybe 1 or 2 and certainly not in the last 30 years. They say Protestants are welcome but the GAA is organised along parish boundaries in the Catholic Church. Protestant schools don't play GAA games, and the GAA never went into Protestant schools in an attempt to persuade them of the merit of playing Gaelic games. There has been no [Protestant] clergymen involved in the management of the GAA.

However, there are now some Protestant schools that play GAA games today. The main problem with the GAA is that it never embraced the Protestant community in Donegal 'because they view the Protestant community as distinctive and not of them … the GAA makes no effort to integrate the Protestants and nor do Protestants try to integrate themselves with the GAA.' I spoke to John after the GAA opened Croke Park to rugby and football matches. He sensed that the sea change in nationalism generally was beginning to permeate down to its most conservative elements. He welcomed this and warmly applauded those within the GAA who were redefining their cultural position.

On Anglophobia, he believes that anti-Englishness is 'shorthand for being anti-British'. Just because you are born in the North does not stop you from being British, just as the Scots and the Welsh are British. In Donegal, young people of his age 'have never had access to British passports'.

> [They] never experienced Donegal being part of Britain, so you cannot expect them to say I am British as that is not true. The question is do you feel sympathetic to the views of people in Northern Ireland who think of themselves as British? I would say if you asked that of Donegal Protestants, 80 per cent would say I feel sympathy and understanding with people in Northern Ireland who want to maintain their Britishness. By extension, then, I would ask them, is there some element of your identity which does not fit with Irish nationalism, that you are quite happy to have a British ancestry and identity, then most Donegal Protestants are quite at ease with the fact that their ancestors were unionists and that they are not Catholics. They don't associate being Irish with being Catholic.

Donegal Protestants still associate themselves very much with the Ulster unionists in culture and background and accent. They are all planters, with a huge Ulster-Scots community in Donegal. So John 'has a British heritage in my identity that I am happy with but I would not want other people to deny this and say I am less Irish because of this'. He believes it was not realistic to expect people in Donegal to think of themselves as British. At the same time, 'If you asked them if there should be a British aspect to an Irish identity, they would agree. The very fact that they have not generally got involved with the GAA says a lot.'

He believed that there was very little interest in the Irish language. During the first 30 or 40 years of the State, the Donegal Protestant community lobbied to remove compulsory Irish:

> ... de Valera made it an offence for your children not to be taught Irish if they lived in the county as many children crossed the border so they did not have to learn Irish. Basically the Donegal nationalist community thought the Protestants should have been welcoming Irish but Irish was associated with Catholicism, poor farmers.

We ended by discussing the possibility of Ireland being united. He thought that if the day came when unionists would be happy to be in a united Ireland, that would be fine, but the danger was forcing people into a united Ireland.

> My father said to me when the troubles were very bad, 'John, if things go bad in the North, and people are slaughtered, don't you expect that a mob will come up the road and burn us out as at the end of the day they see us as being British?' Like Serbia, when things boil up, we are not one of them. If the north went into a doomsday scenario, Protestants in the border area would be targeted. We still occasionally have Protestant churches vandalised in border areas, still have rare attacks on Orange halls. Why is that happening if these people are viewed as being fully Irish? That is because if someone is seen as not having a true Irish heritage stretching back to pure nationalism, he is less of a citizen. I often wonder how Protestant immigrants who are now coming in to Ireland from Africa and are filling up the Protestant churches will be seen. I think their arrival will refocus minds, challenge perceptions and will be a good thing.

He concluded that, thankfully, 'the days have gone when the IRA/ Sinn Féin approach of "Brits out" held any water. Cross-border and cross-community work would be in the best interests of the majority community. Half the new property built in Donegal was now being built by people from the North.' The Protestant community has never been *fully* accommodated. He believes that there is a clear reason for this. In Donegal, those of a unionist disposition (virtually every one of the 20,000 Protestant community in Donegal in 1920) were viewed as enemies of the fight for independence. It is impossible for any society to assimilate these people as fellow citizens right away. Crucially, though, the host society never had any interest in embracing these people.

An interesting illustration of this comes from a MA thesis by Donegal man Jim Tunney, entitled 'From Ascendancy to Alienation: A Study of Donegal's Protestant Community 1811–1932' and undertaken at NUI Galway. Tunney's research suggests that – incredibly to modern eyes – no political party wanted to be seen to get the Protestant vote immediately after partition. He adds that there was also significant resistance amongst the minority Protestant community to the teaching of Irish. Tunney also probes the motives that led 16,000 east Donegal farmers to petition the Northern government to take them and their land into Northern Ireland at the height of de Valera's economic war.

Interestingly, Tunney moves outside his timescale to suggest that a distinct Protestant core vote still remains in East Donegal almost a century after partition. He mentions a Bible-thumping Unionist pastor from Northern Ireland who put his name forward in the 1987 election in the East Donegal constituency and, with no canvassing or profile, pulled in 700 votes purely on the basis of his religion (more than the Labour Party candidate!).

So to conclude, Donegal Protestants, 86 years after independence, are a distinct community, left on the wrong side of the border. They have suffered a perhaps low-intensity pain as a result of their British background and culture arguably not being accepted in the nationalist community in which they live, the fate of any ethnic minority in post-independence Ireland. But as time goes on, attitudes are changing, particularly in the context of the Belfast Agreement, and there appears to be little discrimination today – though if the situation in the North deteriorates again, the community may be forced back to square one. At the time of writing, this seems unlikely.

8

The Triumph of Intolerance

In 1996 the Revd Brian Kennaway, Chairman of the Education Committee of the Grand Orange Lodge of Ireland, thought it appropriate to commemorate the first meeting of the Grand Orange Lodge of Ireland held on 9 April 1798 in Dawson Street, Dublin. He was supported by members of the Dublin and Wicklow Loyal Orange Lodge 1313. It was suggested that a parade should take place in Dawson Street, after which a plaque would be unveiled by the Lord Mayor of Dublin. Senator Mary Henry was supportive, as was the Lord Mayor of Dublin, Councillor Mary Freehill. The date proposed was Sunday, 28 May 2000.

This suggestion brought powerful religious, political and social attitudes to bear, both North and South, which eventually brought about the withdrawal of the plan, though the unveiling of the plaque took place in highly controversial circumstances. Not one Orangeman was present at the unveiling.

For Irish politicians, and the Irish people as a whole, it was arguably the first real litmus test for the Belfast Agreement in the Irish republic. Orange parades had taken place in areas near the border, notably at Rossnowlagh in Co. Donegal, which passed off with no controversy. The difficulty in Dublin, however, was the timing. Orange parades in Northern Ireland had become controversial, especially in Drumcree. It was not only the political classes in the Republic, but also the leadership of the Church of Ireland that linked a parade in the capital city with recent bitter events in Northern Ireland, which had taken place in a very different context.

The republic had become a rich country in a very short period of time, with an open economy to which came many of the world's best multinational manufacturers of high-tech products such as computer parts and pharmaceuticals. De Valera's economically protectionist Ireland had gone. But had his essentially monolithic culture also disappeared? This was the major question raised by the parade. In the words of Andrew Finlay and Natalie McDonnell (*Irish Studies Review*, Vol 11, No. 1, 2003), 'the proposed parade tested the rhetoric of multiculturalism'. Were the Belfast Agreement's clauses laying out conditions for a pluralist and tolerant society to be upheld in an increasingly multicultural Republic? It seemed doubtful, with both Dublin County Council and the Oireachtas being either opposed to the parade or silent. They were aware of the sectarianism engendered by some Orange parades in the North, and were nervous of a repetition in Dawson Street, with more extreme elements from the North travelling to Dublin to cause trouble, even riots. Mary Henry, and the Lord Mayor, Mary Freehill, were exceptions to this; two women who supported the parade.

A commercial consideration then came into play: Canon Empey wrote a letter to the Dublin and Wicklow Lodge on 18 April 2000, expressing concern that financial support might be withdrawn from Dawson Street traders if the service went ahead:

> Since we have a very small congregation consisting for the most part of people on old age pensioners [*sic*], I need the support and enthusiasm of our business neighbours to help us to maintain the fabric of the church. In this I am glad to say, I have had a large measure of success.

The Dublin and Wicklow Lodge accepted this decision gracefully.

The Church of Ireland leadership in Dublin was generally reluctant to get involved, with one spokesman reminding people that some Orangemen had burnt Roman Catholic children – the Quinn children – to death in Northern Ireland at around this time. Deplorable as this was, it had little bearing on the Dublin and Wicklow Lodge and on Protestantism in the South. In any case, as Mark Davenport from BBC Ulster, reported at the time:

> The Orange Order had had nothing to do with the violence which had been taking place across Northern Ireland that week. But it had less than nothing – if that's possible – to do with this particular attack. In fact the death of the children could well have happened in any other week in the year, in any other town, in any other country.

The residents who lived on the Garvaghy Road near Drumcree were influenced by Sinn Féin on the ground. The situation became politicised when Sinn Féin took control of events on the Garvaghy Road, a road on which most houses did not overlook the street the Orangemen wanted to walk down.

It was a complex, highly emotive situation, and it seems the Church of Ireland leadership in the Republic, above all anxious to distance itself from the Orange Order in the North, did not seem to want to support a parade in Dawson Street that had no connection with the events in Drumcree, although Archdeacon Gordon Linney was a notable exception. He explained to me that the Church of Ireland saw the parade in Dawson Street as a national issue rather than a local one. In the public mind, both in Ireland and abroad, the Drumcree parade was one which started after a Church of Ireland service in Northern Ireland and was associated with violence and sectarianism.

A Church of Ireland subcommittee was appointed to 'promote, at all levels of Church life, tolerance, dialogue, co-operation and mutual respect between the churches and in society and to identify and recommend specific actions towards that end.'

The subcommittee met eighteen times and received thirty-four written submissions and some face-to-face meetings were held with contributors.

The report was submitted to the General Synod in 1999. It arose out of the anxiety caused by events at Drumcree, which had the effect that 'the whole Church of Ireland has been seriously damaged in international esteem, internal cohesion and public reputation throughout Ireland'.[1]

The concern was simple: the Church of Ireland's relationship with the Orange Order was giving the impression that it was a sectarian body. Leaders of the Church of Ireland believed that it had moved away from some of the beliefs it had shared with the Orange Order. The emphasis now was on 'rapprochement and mutual respect between the denominations'.[2] The Church of Ireland was working for 'the visible unity of the Church'[3] and it was noted that 'the Church of Ireland has committed itself to working for Christian Unity'.[4] Yet the report, in its anxiety to emphasise ecumenism, seems to overlook the deep doctrinal differences between Roman Catholicism and the Reformed churches. The report states, 'Whereas the Orange Order adopts an anti-Roman Catholic stand, the Church of Ireland is fully engaged in inter-church relations with the Roman Catholic church in Ireland'.[5] Furthermore, it was emphasised that the Church of Ireland 'owes the Orange Order an apology for having moved on and changed without telling them'.[6] It could be argued that the Church of Ireland was naïve in their belief that the Roman Catholic Church was going to go down a road which would in any way compromise its doctrines and beliefs.

So what did this mean as far as Drumcree was concerned? A recommendation was made that the Church of Ireland had to 'give careful thought to the way in which it responds to situations in which one of its parish churches is seen repeatedly to be at the heart of serious and damaging controversy'.[7] These 'situations' had led to 'displays of hostility, hatred and lawlessness',[8] and the murder of the Quinn children was given as an example.

Resolution 3 of the report recognised the powerlessness of a bishop to intervene in the decision of the incumbent clergyman and his vestry at Drumcree.

> ... the Rector and Select Vestry of Drumcree [are] to endorse the pledges
> called for by the Archbishop of Armagh in respect of the conduct of
> those attending the annual parade ... the pledges are as follows:
>
> The avoidance of any action before or after the service which dimin-
> ishes the sanctity of that worship.
> Obedience to the law of the land before and after the service.
> Respect for the integrity of the Church of Ireland by word and action
> and the avoidance of all church property or its environs in any civil
> protest following the service.

If the pledges of the Archbishop of Armagh are not adhered to, the rector and select vestry should withdraw their invitation 'to the Lodges to attend Morning Service'.

The Church of Ireland wished to almost disown the Orange Order, as it had not 'moved on'. It was an embarrassment. But what was the Rector of Drumcree, Revd John Pickering, to do? Might he have done what the Revd Bingham did? Again, Mark Davenport of BBC Ulster commented on the situation:

> The Reverend William Bingham took a different tack to some other
> Orangemen. He did not tell his faithful, gathered in the Presbyterian
> church in Pomeroy that Sunday, that the dispute over Drumcree had

had nothing to do with creating an atmosphere in Northern Ireland in which some loyalists, armed with a whiskey bottle full of petrol, thought they could get away with setting fire to a house in which children slept. Instead he urged his flock and Orangemen everywhere to walk away from Drumcree, telling them that 'no road is worth a life'. The next day he was accused of betrayal by Joel Patton of the hardline Spirit of Drumcree group and there followed an undignified but suitably symbolic joust of black umbrellas between different sections of the Order. At Drumcree a few diehards lingered but most people voted with their feet.

In Dublin, the situation was being deeply influenced by the events at Drumcree, though in a quite different context. Eric Waugh was sympathetic to the plight of the Orangemen in Dublin. He wrote an article in the *Belfast Telegraph* on 19 May 2004, 4 years after the Dawson Street controversy. Waugh shows a Northern unionist's attitude towards the republic's intolerance towards its old unionist minority, one that many from the ex-unionist southern community prefer not to discuss, or may even oppose:

> To be Protestant and/or unionist down south is still to tread on thin ice. Two Orangemen tested its weight-bearing propensity four years ago when the then Lord Mayor of Dublin, Mary Freehill, gave support to their proposal that the Dublin and Wicklow Lodge should march down Dawson Street, the spot in the city centre where the Grand Lodge was founded in 1798.
>
> But, then, strangely, since the lodge had openly opposed the goings-on at Drumcree, all sorts of obstacles were put in their way. St Ann's Parish Church in Dawson Street was not available for an Orange service. The Round Room in the Mansion House would cost £4,500. It would cost another £1,500 for the police to close Dawson Street.
>
> Then the Lord Mayor said she would not actually be attending the parade herself. Businesses on Dawson Street complained about closing of the road – on a Sunday afternoon.
>
> The thirty-seven members of the lodge began to get threatening letters. One Dublin journalist set the mood. 'Apparently it is not enough for us to allow our neighbour to keep a dog,' wrote he. 'It must also be allowed to defecate in our rose bushes.' Another suggested the citizens of Dublin should lie down in Dawson Street in front of the parade. But a third warned that the people of the Republic had sent a clear message: there

would be no public demonstrations of Protestant tradition in that country, that the only good southern Prod was an assimilated one, willing to forget his heritage.

But Waugh's views were not quite accurate. Many letters to the papers supported the parade. Mary Freehill stood firmly behind it to start with, as mentioned previously. However, if the few members of the Dublin and Wicklow Orange Lodge were not supported by one of their own churches, it is understandable that Freehill's resolve would weaken. More importantly, she increasingly came under pressure from fellow Dublin Roman Catholic councillors, particularly those in Sinn Féin and Fianna Fáil, though Fine Gael councillors were also opposed.

Raised in the Cavan/Fermanagh border area in Ballyconnell, Mary Freehill understood Orangemen and understood that up North, knocks are routine. But at least Northerners of both tribes are aware of the deep political and religious differences between them. That is a difference between North and South.

So why did the plans for the parade go so wrong? I interviewed the two Orangemen that Eric Waugh refers to above, Brother Simpson and Brother Cox of the Dublin and Wicklow Lodge 1313 to try to find out. But first, a little history of the Orange Order in the Republic might be helpful.

Before 1916, the Orange Order had its headquarters for the island of Ireland at Nos 9 and 10 Parnell Square in the heart of Dublin. But in 1922, during the Civil War, the Dublin headquarters was attacked and badly damaged.

A large number of Protestants were living in Dublin at that time. In Rathgar and Rathmines, they made up about one third of the population, and more than a quarter of the population of Dún Laoghaire. Some were members of the Orange Order. Every year there was an Orange parade from Rutland Square to King William's statue in College Green, Dublin. This statue was removed in 1928, having stood there since 1701. Parades did go ahead up to the 1930s, but unfortunately some individuals took it into their hands to stop Orange parades. They moved to Cootehill, Co. Cavan, where the roads were blocked, the railways were stopped, telephone lines were cut and buses and lorries were commandeered by the invaders, armed with hurley sticks. In de Valera's Ireland, the last Orange march took place in Dublin in

1937. The parade was planned to end in Amiens Street, on its way to Belfast, but it was attacked and stopped. After that incident, the Orange Lodges went into terminal decline. Parades in the South are now few and are concentrated near the border.

Derek Simpson explained the background to the request for a church parade in Dublin, emphasising that this particular form of parade is quite different from the traditional Twelfth of July processions. It involves a Reformed Church service taken by a clergyman, or a minister, from one of the various Protestant churches. It would be a memorable occasion, celebrating the pluralism of a confident, newly wealthy Irish State. It was anticipated that the political establishment would support it.

Mary Freehill agreed the wording for the plaque with Brian Kennaway, and Dublin Corporation agreed to pay for it, having responsibility for the placing of plaques in Dublin. A church service was planned in St Ann's church in Dawson Street as Canon Adrian Empey, the rector, had previously been supportive of the Dublin and Wicklow Lodge when welcoming an Orange service in St Stephen's church in Dublin in 1995.

However, as we have seen, Canon Empey and his select vestry turned down the request. Canon Empey clarified his position in a letter to *The Irish Times* on 13 April 2000, explaining why a church service was being refused. He feared that it 'would reinforce the popular misconception that the Orange Order was connected to the Church of Ireland ... Through Drumcree, people have the impression we are linked which, emphatically, we are not ... To have permitted the service would only have reinforced the perception, and that was also the unanimous view of the vestry.'

Canon Empey wrote a letter on 6 March 2000 to Brother Ian Cox of the Dublin and Wicklow Lodge, saying that 'the people of Dublin did not have their city shamed in the eyes of the world in the way that the Church of Ireland was disgraced by the episode at Drumcree'.

In an email to me, Adrian Empey wrote on 4 October 2004:

I appreciate that an effort was being made to demonstrate that we in the Republic were prepared to be 'inclusive' of all the traditions on the islands – including, of course, the Orange tradition – but the high-jacking of Drumcree by sinister elements also raised difficult issues for the Church of Ireland which had nothing to do with keeping our heads down. The church was also struggling to come to terms with its part

over the centuries in creating or accommodating sectarian attitudes. As
you know, that report has since appeared, and we are all obliged to act
on its recommendations.

I accept – and always have – that the order played an unacknowl-
edged role in restraining sectarian strife in many localities, and that we
shall never know how bad things might have been without quiet and
dignified restraint of that kind. However, the Drumcree thing was really
run by very different elements.

The nature of these 'elements' is not clarified by Canon Empey. Mark
Davenport has suggested that they were not connected to the Orange
Order.

The reluctance of the Church of Ireland to support a service opened
the way for Dublin County Council's negative attitude. Almost all
of the councillors sought to prevent the parade. Some letters to the
papers used the refusal of Canon Empey and the vestry of St Ann's to
justify their opposition to the parade. If the Church of Ireland refused
to accommodate the Orange Order service, why should the Dublin
councillors, the Irish State and the Irish people?

As for the report, Empey refers to in his email, it was published at
the direction of the General Synod in 1999. In the words of Canon
Empey in an email to me on 31 March 2005:

> … as far as I remember it was presented at the General Synod in the
> same year. This is a lengthy report, running to 179 pages. The short title
> is *The Hard Gospel*. According to the General Synod Report of 1997,
> following a major debate on the issue of sectarianism the following
> motion was adopted:
>
> That this synod affirms that the Church of Ireland is opposed to
> sectarianism and requests the Standing Committee to initiate an
> examination of church life at all levels, to identify ways in which the
> church may be deemed to be accommodating to sectarianism, and as
> a means of combating sectarianism, to promote, at all levels of church
> life tolerance, dialogue, co-operation and mutual respect between the
> churches and in society, to identify and recommend specific actions
> towards that end and then to report progress in the matter to the
> meeting of General Synod in 1998.

The context of that debate was, of course, the events at Drumcree.

Canon Empey was a co-signatory to the letter sent by 'Catalyst' to the rector of Drumcree parish church in 1998, asking him 'not to accept requests from the Orange Order to participate in the church service' (*Irish Studies Review*, Vol.1, 2003). The Catalyst request put the Revd Pickering in a difficult position. What Pickering did instead, as I have indicated, was to tell the Orange brethren to comply with the law of the land and behave with dignity and restraint.

The Protestant churches in the Irish Republic have had to come to terms with living on the margins of an adamantine form of Roman Catholicism. It has not been an easy task, and it has generally been faced with forbearance and diplomacy, but to argue – as Canon Empey did – that 'the church was also struggling to come to terms with its part over the centuries in creating or accommodating sectarian attitudes' is surely to beg the question of tolerance for the Orange Order in Irish society. In reality, the foundations, even the inspiration for the Irish State, are sectarian. The Roman Catholic Church was 'an institutional pillar' and formed 'the inner life of the State'.[9] It claimed it was the one true church, and in few countries in the world did this belief proclaim itself in more powerful terms than in Ireland, whose 1937 Constitution gave the Church a privileged position and enshrined some of the social and moral doctrines of Rome. Well before the Free State had come into being, Protestants in the 26 counties had lost political power. That had ended with Catholic emancipation in the nineteenth century, and the various land acts in the late nineteenth and early twentieth century removed the large landholdings of the Protestant Irish ascendency, some 13 million acres. To hark back 'over the centuries' is to enhance, even enliven, the often thinly disguised Protestant guilt. Perhaps a more appropriate stance for the Church of Ireland in today's Ireland, where many Roman Catholics are disillusioned and looking for alternatives, would be to assert the theological values of the Reformation: individualism and rejection of the invasiveness of the Roman Catholic church, now in disgrace.

Mary Freehill progressed the plans for the day with Ian Cox of the Dublin and Wicklow Lodge. From the start, she had made it clear that there was to be both a parade and an unveiling of a plaque on the same day and she would be present for both events, laying the plaque herself. In a letter to Ian on 19 January 2000, she wrote:

Thank you for your letter of the planned Parade in Dublin on May 28th next. Please keep me informed as your plans progress.

I have written to Mr Peter Morley in the Roads and Streets Department asking that arrangements for the plaque to mark the site of the original Grand Lodge be progressed in time for May 28th.

She was well aware of strong opposition from her fellow councillors, particularly from Sinn Féin, and told me in an interview on 16 May 2005 that 'I have no doubt whatsoever that Sinn Féin wound it up … I knew it because they circulated literature at some sports events asking people not to support the parade'.

Freehill's opinion on the refusal of St Ann's to allow a service was that it 'gave fuel to the opposition'. But she insisted on continuing her talks with Ian Cox and Derek Simpson adding, somewhat to my surprise, 'I suppose in a way I was not expecting the two gentlemen to be as Machievellian as Sinn Féin'. She meant by this that both Ian and Derek were 'saying in the end that I was not really supporting them'. In fact, Ian and Derek believed that she was being pressurised by the Labour Party and was retreating. Councillor Freehill denied this, but it became apparent that she was being put under pressure by other parties. When asked after a council meeting if she would be marching herself, she replied she would not be 'next or near the Orange Order' and 'that was an unfortunate way I said it and it might appear I was changing my position and I will admit it might have appeared that way but it was in the context of a difficult meeting'. She seems to have been distancing herself. On 19 May 2000, *Phoenix* magazine wrote that 'she delivered the sharpest political U-turn in memory' but Freehill insisted that she had never intended to walk in the parade in the first place. Now it seemed that she did not want to participate in the ceremony in the Mansion House after the plaque was unveiled. Both Derek and Ian had failed to understand this and were taken aback.

The plan was for the Orange Order to rent the Round Room in the Mansion House, where they would meet for a service and reception. But the cost was high and Mary Freehill believed that it discouraged the Orange Order from proceeding. It was an important factor, but it was not the crucial one, as Derek made clear to me. When St Ann's was refused, she offered the Oak Room in the Mansion House for a service, but it was not big enough for the 400 people expected. 'I didn't have the giving of the Round Room as that was in the hands of a separate company, Sports and Leisure, and it would have to be rented.' I challenged her about Ian Cox's assertion that the Round Room could not be rented, as the private company that owned it had not signed a contract with Dublin County Council to allow it to be let. This may have been because it was being refurbished at that time but 'certainly the officials were not against it and John FitzGerald was very supportive, the City Manager. But there is no doubt about it a lot of the council were against me supporting the march, even against me unveiling the plaque.'

The council meetings were then being held in the Mansion House and she 'remembers when all of the leaders were there and they were nearly all of them putting pressure on me. Pat Carey from Fianna Fáil, Christy Burke from Sinn Féin, Joe Doyle from Fine Gael and all saying "Would you ever give this up, Mary, would you ever forget about it".' But she made it clear she was going ahead with the unveiling of the plaque.

Freehill also made it clear that she would support the parade, but would not participate in it: 'I don't even agree with the Orange Order. My position in all of this was people having the right to march. It is part of our culture, whether we agree with it or whether we don't … let's be tolerant.'

Those who were to participate in the parade would have come mainly from Northern Ireland, England, Canada and Australia, as well as the Republic of Ireland. The banners were to be confined to the crosses of St Patrick, St George and St Andrew. Only Canadian and Australian flags were permitted. The parade would take 20 minutes and men, women and children were invited to participate. It was planned to use the excellent Temple Band from the North, which had won an all-Ireland band competition. The service after the parade was one to which all were invited, and a collection was to be taken for the Romanian appeal fund.

At this stage, Brothers Simpson and Cox held a meeting with the Department of Foreign Affairs (DFA) to request financial assistance, as well as moral support (though why the DFA was involved in a domestic matter puzzled A. Simpson and Cox). At this meeting, Derek and Ian were astounded to hear that someone had advised the DFA that the Lodge had breached a contract with the Church of Ireland over the service that they held in 1995. Adrian Empey had taken this service. Derek and Ian told me that it was untrue, but also, more worryingly, it meant that the Church of Ireland seemed to be running a secret campaign to stop help being offered to the Orange Order by the State. Why advise the DFA of a private dispute between Canon Empey and the Dublin and Wicklow Lodge? Derek asked Adrian Empey for an explanation.

Derek told me that there had not been any complaints after the service in 1995. The Orange Order had agreed at the time that the service was not to be publicised, except in the *Orange Standard*, and this condition was fully met. But somehow RTÉ's John O'Mahony radio programme got wind of the service and mentioned on Sunday on air that the service was going to be held.

The leak did not come from a member of the Dublin and Wicklow Lodge and Derek has been unable to find out from RTÉ where they got their information. At any rate, a member of the Lodge, John Quincy, heard the comment on air before the service took place and told Adrian Empey that the programme had incorrectly mentioned that Adrian Empey's brother, Walton Empey, the Archbishop of Dublin, was to take the service. At the time, Adrian did not make a fuss about the leak, but he revisited it 5 years later when Derek asked Canon Empey for an explanation in writing, to no avail. He copied his letter to Empey to the Primate, Robin Eames. There was no response.

The upshot was, in Ian's words, that he and Derek were 'very courteously shown the door and treated like parlour guests' by the DFA.

Mary Freehill went on to say that difficulties arose:

[Derek Simpson and Ian Cox] used me and started to blame me by saying that I had started to pull back. I did not expect such Machievellian behaviour from them. But I suppose they did not understand my background. I was born and raised in the Cavan/Fermanagh border area. I grew up in a town, Ballyconnell, a very middle class town and I'd say a third of the population would have been Protestant. There was a Presbyterian church, Church of Ireland church, a Methodist one, a Masonic Hall. In a small town it encapsulated the Plantation of Ulster. We got on very well, there was great regard for one another. My father would always be teasing people saying there is a bit of a stalwart in you. Very good humoured. I grew up in a tolerant society.

I asked whether the whole idea was premature, being in the shadow of the Garvaghy Road; that it was simply the wrong time to have a parade. She replied: 'Isn't that always the way? When is the right time?

As long as you have somebody trying to turn it to their advantage there always will be a problem.'

As for the Garvaghy Road:

> There was the difference between night and day between the Orangemen walking down the Garvaghy Road and walking down Dawson Street, and the President, Mary McAleese, said that to me also. She was very supportive and very helpful. She made it her business to say, 'I think what you are doing is great.' But you see, she was into all of that and had been working to improve the understanding between the different communities.

Mary Freehill and President McAleese led the way here, questioning both the Church of Ireland and the councillors who linked the Garvaghy Road to the proposed Dawson Street parade. It was perhaps naïve to believe that these events could be separated, certainly as far as the Church of Ireland was concerned.

The following Sinn Féin motion was carried by the council:

> The Dublin City Council defends the right to freedom of speech and assembly which includes the rights of bodies such as the Orange Order to parade peacefully in the streets of the city. In the spirit of mutual respect for diverse traditions and the right of communities and mindful of the planned Orange parade and plaque unveiling in Dublin, the City Council calls on the Orange Order to enter into direct dialogue with the chosen representatives of the people of the Garvaghy Road in Portadown to lift the siege of that beleaguered area to finally resolve the issue through negotiations.

Fianna Fáil councillors supported this motion, which was designed to stop the plaque going up, not to stop the parade. Mary Freehill had got permission 3 years earlier to put up the plaque so the decision could not be rescinded. Mary Freehill explained:

> The parade did not need anyone's permission: that was the whole point. You do not have to obtain permission to have a parade. However, it is necessary to get permission from Northern Ireland to have a parade as well as notifying the Gardaí. The senior Gardaí were extremely helpful and believed they could handle it.

I asked if the Lodge was therefore wrong to pull out if the Gardaí were convinced they could handle it, and Mary wondered if Derek and Ian faced a problem of 'diminished support'. The Grand Lodge seemed to be split and their Education Officer, Brian Kennaway, decided not to come to the unveiling. He threw a different light on what was happening in an email to me on 24 March 2005. He believed that a very senior ex-officer of the Grand Lodge had deliberately linked Dawson Street to the Garvaghy Road, which was unhelpful. If a parade could be held in Dawson Street, he asked, why not on the Garvaghy Road? But if the Grand Lodge put its foot in it by making this unwise, provocative comparison, it was still supportive of the parade, just clumsy in its approach to a delicate situation in another jurisdiction. As Brian Kennaway wrote:

> But there are extremes on both sides. On the nationalist side you have Sinn Féin and their raison d'être is to prove that they cannot get on with these people and in some ways you have the same thing being said by the DUP who may not want people down there being too nice to the Orange Order.

With no encouragement from the Church of Ireland, no support from Dublin city councillors and the political classes as a whole, and in the face of coolness from the DFA, Derek and Ian decided to postpone the parade to avoid possible violence.

Ian had heard that leaflets asking people to oppose the parade were being distributed at football matches, something that Mary Freehill confirmed, and he feared that should the parade go ahead, there would be a demonstration where bottles or missiles would be thrown, perhaps injuring bystanders, including children.

On the day that the plaque was unveiled by Freehill, the so-called Sovereignty Movement, a seemingly Sinn Féin organisation, appeared with a huge, elaborately designed banner declaring that the Orange Order was Ireland's Ku Klux Klan. Designer and nationalist Robert Ballagh appeared, as did Sinn Féin's Mary Lou McDonald, who was vocal. Both Julitta Clancy of the Meath Peace Group and Tomás MacGiolla challenged them vigorously on the street.

The plaque was unveiled on 28 May by Mary Freehill and a reception followed in the Mansion House. Freehill told me that she was disappointed that the brethren of the Dublin and Wicklow Lodge failed to turn up to the unveiling of the plaque and to the reception. I tend to agree, as the signal they were giving – which no doubt was not intended – was that they disapproved of her and the work of her team in the Mansion House. No TDs lent their support by coming to the ceremony – no one from Freehill's own Labour Party other than Prionsias de Rossa , nor from Fine Gael, nor from the PDs. I asked her to comment on this, but she had no explanation. She did emphasise, though, that Ruairi Quinn was fully supportive. Why didn't Bertie Ahern attend? Or his Minister for Foreign Affairs? The President, Mary McAleese? Was this not an act of 'building bridges'?

Mary Henry went, to her great credit, but no other senator, who numbered among them the Protestant senators Martin Mansergh, David Norris and Shane Ross. I went, with the writer and columnist Bruce Arnold. Bernie Lowe, a Fianna Fáil councillor in Dun Laoghaire/Rathdown, whom I knew, spotted me on television and berated me later on. I was taken aback, and pointed out that it was a peaceful parade to commemorate the first meeting of the Grand Lodge in Ireland, and that if Fianna Fáil was serious about pluralism, which it proved itself not to be by opposing the parade in Dublin City Council, it would not only have welcomed this event, but sent the Taoiseach. She was unimpressed, and brought up the flight of unionists from Northern Ireland around 12 July every year.

Mary Freehill is convinced that Sinn Féin brings a highly confrontational brand of politics to the Republic, one that comes as second nature to them in Northern Ireland. She believes it is 'Machiavellian' in its behaviour; above all it seeks to get votes and more members. They see these kinds of issues as an opportunity to create discontent and get members into their party. She elaborated:

> It is not principled. It is totally pragmatic and Machiavellian. That is the kind of politics that they have evolved in Northern Ireland. It is all about conflict. They haven't passed over the point of saying, well, look down here now, we have got to figure out how we can get on and make peace rather than live by conflict. It is about the threat outside and how we can get people together.

As if a few dozen brethren in the Orange Order constituted a threat to the Irish state! I suggested that it was deeply sectarian and directed at further weakening a compliant Protestant population.

Some time later, Mary Freehill spoke at a meeting in Monaghan town, where Sinn Féin representatives wanted her to meet afterwards with some women from the Garvaghy Road.

> So I agreed to meet them and there was a man who introduced himself as a journalist and wanted to interview me before I went into the meeting. He wanted to interview me about the Orange Order so I said I was there to talk about directly elected mayors. So I went into the meeting and they wanted me to go to the Garvaghy Road, which needless to say I wasn't going to agree to but anyway I invited them down to Dublin. The people they had from the Garvaghy Road were actually Sinn Féin members but introduced to me as community workers. The reporter wrote on the front of the Star paper that I had got very annoyed and used language that I simply had not used. I sued the paper afterwards and won. What actually happened was that this guy was only out of Long Kesh about six weeks, and how and where he got a journalist card is another question, but he was part of the entourage to try and trap me. I just mention that because that is the day-to-day politics of Sinn Féin and probably, I don't know, the DUP. That is the guttersnipe level that it operates at. Here we just get on with it. The same thing happened down in Cork. I was on the radio with the Sinn Féin representative in Cork, Doolan, and with the Fine Gael representative, Covenney. It was very interesting listening to Doolan, it was all very much Northern Ireland politics and the distance they were from each other.

As I have mentioned, the comparison with the Ku Klux Klan was the main thrust of Sinn Féin's argument against the parade. Nicky Kehoe, a Sinn Féin councillor, wrote in a letter to *The Irish Times* on 14 April 2000:

> The Orange men state that they are an expression of 'Protestant' culture in the same way that their views and actions are an expression of 'white' culture. Orange men and racists have a constitutional right to march, but the rest of us have a constitutional right to say what we think of the organisation organising the march.

There was another angle to the Sinn Féin approach, however. Councillor Larry O'Toole claimed in an interview on 19 August 2000:[10]

It was going to be used ... you know that Orange parades are accept-able in Dawson Street, Dublin, then they're acceptable in the Lower Ormeau and that's why I don't believe we could take any march in isolation from what was going on in the Garvaghy Road. Don't forget that a month after the march in Dublin ... the Drumcree thing was going to start all over again.

O'Toole thus considered that the parade in Dublin was not a natural event, like the one in Rossnowlagh, but was to be used as a kind of PR stunt. It was being promoted by people like Brian Kennaway in Belfast as a means of getting the Orange parade down the Garvaghy Road. As the Sinn Féin banner had stated, the Orange Order was the Ku Klux Klan. There was never a word said about the Roman Catholic fundamentalism that had taken hold in Ireland since 1922, nor the virtual suppression of the Orange Order all over the Republic and the disappearance of large numbers of Protestants to friendlier shores.

Garret FitzGerald had recognised that pluralism had not taken root in the republic when he wrote that it is 'at variance with a traditional inherited value system [that] for historical reasons has not had occasion in the past to distinguish clearly between religious and secular loyalties'.[11]

For Sinn Féin to cast the Orange Order as an alien tribe has little relevance. In the words of the article written by Andrew Finlay and Natalie McDonnell, such an attitude 'would have offended against the pluralist rhetoric at the heart of the GFA, which was invoked by supporters of the parade'.[12]

Senator Mary Henry wrote to *The Irish Times* on 29 March 2000 to encourage pluralism: 'This march will say more about us here than about the Orangemen ... no matter what our views on the Orange marches, the process of reconciliation and the development of a tolerant Irish society has to take place here as well as in Northern Ireland.'

Mary Freehill wrote:

It's nothing to do with whether I agree or disagree with the Orange Order. I voted for the Good Friday Agreement and in that agreement I voted for parity of esteem and [of the] people [who] exist on this island. I mean what are you going to do? Push them off? I mean they're there.[13]

William Binchy, Regius Professor of Law at Trinity College, Dublin, challenged the sectarian approach of Sinn Féin when he wrote to

The Irish Times on 25 March 2000: 'If a member of the Orange Order feels ... secure walking down Dawson Street, that will be no defeat for Republican ideals but rather a small step towards their practical fulfilment.'

Sinn Féin is preoccupied, even obsessed, with achieving a united Ireland. Here is what one writer to *The Irish Times* said about the parade in the context of this aspiration for unity in a letter dated 3 March 2000:

> Those of your correspondents who have expressed fury at the prospect of Orange men parading in Dublin wish (presumably) to see the creation of a United Ireland. They should ask themselves whether that prospect is enhanced by making it clear to Northern Protestants that they hate their culture.

So what is the future of Orangeism in the Republic? Brother Simpson is quite confident of a revival of the Dublin-Wicklow Lodge. Numbers are growing and more young men are joining; there are members from Cork, Limerick, Carlow and Kildare. He believes that Orangeism has a healthy future in the Republic, and there are some 30,000 members on the island. It is a diverse organisation with rural and urban people, including some professional people like David Trimble, though the professional people are drifting away. It is changing and becoming less political.

It is a sectarian organisation by definition, as is the Ancient Order of Hibernians. It bans its members from marrying Roman Catholics and attending Mass. The former rule was not always on the books, but in the interests of the greater good, both should go. The Order needs to reflect changes in modern Ireland and encourage inclusiveness. In the words of Roy Garland in the *Irish News* on 14 March 2005:

> Orange people must reverse the old profile by dropping the negative emphasis on opposing Rome and instead promote the welfare of their fellow men in keeping with a more charitable emphasis. In line with this, the Orange Order has recently promoted a more festive approach to celebrations and has tried to reach out to the wider community. Recent reports say Orangemen have welcomed members of the Hindu community and provided them with refreshments in a Belfast Orange Hall.

The organisation was started to defend the Protestant faith and to oppose mixed-religion marriages. It encourages the Protestant churches to uphold the 39 Articles and the Westminster Confession. It also maintains important cultural aspects such as the Orange bands and social gatherings.

Brother Simpson put it this way:

> The Orange Order believes that there are erroneous doctrines in the Roman Catholic Church and these can be identified and pointed out, based on teachings in the Bible. The Order consists of members of the Baptists, the Methodists, the Presbyterians and the Church of Ireland. The Church of Ireland seems obsessed with getting on with the Roman Catholic Church and many believe the 39 Articles are out of date and no longer of relevance. The Church of Ireland is fading away and were it not for the fact that Roman Catholics are sick of the paedophilia scandals and the way the bishops have responded and are turning to the Church of Ireland, it would disappear. The Protestant churches should concentrate on other issues like the right to have a nondenominational or Protestant education. In the border areas some school buses are being taken off the roads because the numbers of Protestant children are tiny so the children are ending up in Roman Catholic schools.

Perhaps the last word needs to go to the writers of the *Irish Review* article previously referred to:

> The parade organisers' claim that they belong to a minority that has been ill-treated mirrors the crucial distinction that Larry O'Toole made when attempting to reconcile Sinn Féin's opposition to the parade with the party's general valorisation of tradition and specific support for multicultural principles. He asserted his commitment to defend the cultural rights of minorities that have been ill-treated, but refused to extend this to the Orange Order or to Southern Protestants: the Orange Order is a threat to the Catholic minority in Northern Ireland, and the Republic's Protestant minority has not been ill-treated. We have no wish to adjudicate on these conflicting claims to victimhood; indeed, to attempt to do so would be to pander to the dangerous "me too-ism" that identity politics seems to encourage. It is far more important that we register an objection to the notion – shared by the organisers of the parade, its principle opponents and too many

others – that admission to the emerging multicultural order in Ireland is dependent on one's ability to claim social or cultural victimisation.

As Ireland gets wealthier and continues to face a substantial influx of refugees and immigrants of different races from all over the world, it needs to progress from the homogeneous society it has been, to at last learn tolerance for all the different identities in its midst. This means learning to leave other traditions and cultures to practise their beliefs and customs. Part of that respect for other traditions is strongly demonstrated by allowing, even encouraging, a peaceful parade of uppity Protestants in Dawson Street. I suggest that decision should not be based on any claims of victimisation, and it should be respected by all Protestant religious denominations, particularly by the Church of Ireland, which has assumed a mode of 'rapprochement'. Let us remember that the parade was not cancelled, it was postponed. It is now 15 years later and much has changed. Perhaps a very different response would be forthcoming if the Dublin and Wicklow Loyal Orange Lodge 1313 decided to parade in Dublin, perhaps this time in the city's main thoroughfare, O'Connell Street. By linking a parade in Dublin with one in Drumcree, our politicians ensured that our unionist neighbours were confirmed in their belief that the republic was far from fostering the spirit of the Belfast Agreement. It seemed to show itself to be as Gaelic, Catholic, green and intolerant as ever. Mary Freehill and President Mary McAleese, as well as Mary Henry, were noble exceptions who did not seek to avoid the central message of the Irish flag: to cherish the orange and green traditions on this island, North and South.

Epilogue

Over recent decades the Republic of Ireland has undergone fundamental changes, particularly in the economic and religious spheres, but also in social and cultural areas. Economic nationalism was abandoned in the 1960s. Facing economic meltdown in the 1950s, the State turned its back on the failed policy of economic self-sufficiency behind protectionist tariff barriers. The dreams of the founding fathers that a free Ireland would be a prosperous once it was free to encourage native industries and develop its rich, unexplored mineral resources were just that, dreams.[1] Agriculture was southern Ireland's only significant natural resource.

Economic nationalism floundered and by 1956 'the Republic's growth rate was clearly the slowest of the Western European countries … and semi-literate Portugal appeared to be doing rather better'.[2] D.K. Whitaker, the Secretary of the Department of finance, drew up a report which called Irish economic protectionist policies a failure and instead recommended attracting foreign direct investment by tax incentives and other supports. The Taoiseach, Sean Lemass, took up his proposals and made them policies in the 1960s. The result was that between 1987 and 2001, the Republic of Ireland went through a half-generation of quite unprecedented growth, with GNP growth rates routinely exceeding 7 per cent and occasionally touching 10 per cent.[3]

Today, thanks to its attractively low rate of corporation tax, Ireland is home to most of the largest pharmaceutical companies in the world and to leading manufacturers of computer parts as well as Apple, Intel, Google, Facebook and Dell. These transnational companies employ up to 165,000 people, of whom some 115,000 are well-educated Irish nationals. They export 90 per cent of total Irish exports, indigenous companies only 10 per cent. It is an impressive success story. However, these highly profitable companies contribute practically no corporation tax to the Irish exchequer and should the EU change the favourable corporation tax regime they enjoy some are likely to up and leave. Transnationals, by their very nature, locate where economic conditions make for maximisation of profits. They are not motivated by loyalty to nation States. But should some decide to move out of Ireland, the loss of employment of perhaps at most 115,000 jobs for Irish nationals, or 7 per cent of the total Irish workforce, would be hardly a death blow to the Irish economy.[4] It is the indigenous sector of the economy that pays the corporation tax and provides the vast majority of jobs. In an EU environment of pressure for increased tax harmonisation, perhaps the indigenous service and manufacturing sectors need more nourishment by government in the years ahead.

During the first 50 years or so of the Irish State, from 1921 to 1970, Irish nationalism and Catholicism were virtually indivisible. This excluded, even suppressed, the Protestant minorities, as well as other sects and free thinkers. De Valera's 1937 constitution embodied the then popular principles of Catholic teachings and sought to make the Free State incorporate Catholic moral teachings in its legislation. Article 44 recognised the special position of the Roman Catholic Church 'as the guardian of the faith professed by the great majority of [the State's] citizens and article 41 prohibited divorce'. The word 'secular' was notably absent from this constitution, unlike the Indian constitution written only a decade later. There was legislation for film censorship in 1923, censorship of publications in 1929, legislation against contraception in 1935. Archbishop John Charles McQuaid of Dublin 'prevailed upon the national broadcasting services [RTÉ] to carry the twice daily ringing of the angelus bell'[5] which it does today, refusing to acknowledge the Angelus prayer embodies religious dogmas that all other churches find unacceptable, if not heretical. This reflected the 'absolutist position of the Catholic Church, rather than the more flexible, but certainly not permissive, attitudes of other Churches and communions.'[6] In other words, they could like it or lump it, '… in the South majority religion was flaunted without any reference to the sensibilities of the small Protestant minority.'[7] Vincent Comerford believes a 'puritanical mindset' was at work:

> It was highly prescriptive and dogmatic, promoting the assumption that everything was either obligatory or forbidden, and so did not place

a high value on individual freedom of choice. Intolerance was epito-
mised in a readiness to demonise dissidents and opponents and to brand
people and institutions as untouchable, without concern for the human
dignity or rights of individuals, including the right of reply.[8]

The historian Ian D'Alton thinks exclusivist Catholic nationalism led
Protestants to retreat into what he calls their own Free State, arguing that:

> [if] the Irish Catholic Free State was uncongenial, then the only option left
> to those for whom Ireland had to be their patria was a liveable-in Protestant
> Free State. In terms of southern Protestants' developing sense of identity,
> this held considerable significance, since it was one which was referenced
> to themselves – at last, and at least, they had ownership of it. That was chal-
> lenging – but also invigorating. Furthermore, it was dynamic, representing,
> more often than not, an attainment of equilibrium with the contemporary
> – and it is their own contemporary; they're waving, not drowning. If it was
> the strange death of unionist Ireland, it presaged a resurrection. In that sense,
> their so-called identity crisis was never really a crisis at all.[9]

This is a seductive argument in which there is undoubtedly some truth,
though perhaps it does not paint the whole picture and needs challenging.
Protestants do not form a monolithic community. Along the border
areas there are Church of Ireland, Presbyterians and Methodists who
have different views and some relate to Northern Ireland and feel they
were left on the wrong side of the border in 1922. Protestants further
south also vary. In terms of 'victimhood', it should be remembered that
nonconformists like Presbyterians were also subjected to the strictures of
the penal laws. There is an urban/rural divide. In the major cities arguably
Protestants have integrated better than in isolated rural areas. Some in rural
areas have experienced past hostility and are not wholly at ease in their
environments. They opted out of an 'uncongenial' State, retreating into
their own world, their own 'Free State', opting for what could be called
a ghetto of the mind. They play cricket, badminton and bowls and keep
their ethos alive in their schools and churches. But to argue that this did
not cause 'an identity crisis' is surely avoiding the much-debated question
of what constitutes an Irish identity? We have seen from some Protestants
interviewed in chapter six, and from other research, in particular Heather
Crawford's interviews with Protestants, that the question of identity is a
real difficulty for many southern Protestants.[10] It signals that Protestant

identity and beliefs are 'other'. And they certainly are. No doubt there are
Protestants who are content to be 'other'. They would argue it is positive to
be outside the 'glow' which Heather Crawford writes about, the 'glow' of
Catholic nationalism, made up of unquestioned obedience to the Catholic
Church, its shameful treatment of women embodied in de Valera's constitution much influenced by the ethics of the Roman Catholic Church,
the acceptance of the expensive force-feeding of a all but dead language
which Irish people have decided they do not want to speak, a nationalism
whose foundation stone and lifeblood is Anglophobia based on distor-
tions of Irish history. However, an exclusivist form of nationalism has, by
definition, involved an identity crisis for many Protestants, as Ruane and
Butler have made clear in their study of west Cork Protestants.[11] One
only has to read the still unaltered preamble to the 1937 constitution of de
Valera to get the message of Irish national exclusivism:

> We, the people of Eire, Humbly acknowledging all our obligations
> to our Divine Lord Jesus Christ, Who sustained our fathers through
> centuries of trial, gratefully remembering their heroic and unremitting
> struggle to regain rightful independence of our Nation ...[12]

Many Protestants continue to believe today that 'a culturally revivalist,
Catholic regime [was] hostile to their culture, religion and economic
interests'.[13] Very many Protestants chose to leave, their numbers going from
164,000 in 1926 to 104,000 in 1961. But above all there are 'doubts that
some Catholics still raise about whether Protestants are "really Irish" and
Protestant resentment of this.'[14] Edna Longley's thinks that Catholics are
born Irish, whereas Protestants have to 'work their passage to Irishness'.[15]
And arguably this journey is taken without a ticket. But significantly,
unlike advanced nationalist Catholics in Northern Ireland, we might also
note that, drawing on the European Values Study, 1999–2000, Bernadette
Hayes and Tony Fahey came to the conclusion that: 'Protestants are closer
to the ideal of the model citizen than are Catholics',[16] meaning they
are law-abiding and loyal to a State that has not gone out of its way to
embrace them. Southern Church of Ireland Protestants have followed the
advice of the Archbishop of Dublin, John Gregg, who had 'stressed the
pragmatic necessity of offering "to the Irish Free State ... our loyalty and
goodwill" ... he condemned those "who think of us as an alien minority
... his community had "an identity genuinely Irish", although he empha-
sized that it was "not necessary to be Gaelic in order to be Irish".'[17]

How has the Catholic Church changed and, more significantly, how have people's attitudes to the Catholic Church altered in recent times? Mary Kenny, a conservative Irish Catholic journalist living in England outlines the changes in direction made by Catholic Church 50 years ago as follows:

> The liberalisation of Ireland really began 50 years ago, with the launch of Vatican II, when Pope John XXIII opened the Vatican Council whose purpose was to renew the Catholic Church, and indeed, modernise it.
>
> The trendy word was '*aggiornamento*' (bringing things up to date) and it was, believe it or not, widely used in the inns and taverns of Ireland wherever lively conversationalists gathered. Almost overnight, it seemed, the tone of Catholic values softened, just as, almost overnight, nuns threw off their wimples and their seventeenth-century habits to wear more simplified, modernised garb.[18]

Yet this view needs challenging. After Vatican II there can be little doubt that the Roman Catholic Church in Ireland failed to adequately reform. Its undemocratic governance continued and it tolerated sexual deviants amongst its clergy. It remained aloof until the recent devastating revelations of the media, resulting in the beginning of disillusionment and a process whereby Ireland started to become a modern, increasingly secular State in which the Catholic Church has lost much influence and credibility.

Recent revelations of the harsh treatment of innocent children in Catholic institutions have shocked Catholics. As has the behaviour of the Catholic hierarchy when it was aware of the many incidents of paedophilia by its priests. Instead of reporting such behaviour to the gardaí, the offenders were moved to new parishes and inevitably continued to abuse children under their care. The Magdalene Laundry abuses caused outrage and were the subject of the film *The Magdalene Sisters*. The treatment of pregnant unmarried women was portrayed in the film *Philomena*, which tells the story of a mother who searched for her son who had been adopted by American parents. She got little help from the nuns and had a painful and dangerous breech birth. By the time she located him he had died. Many mothers and children died while in the care of the Sisters of the Sacred Heart of Jesus and Mary in the Sean Ross Abbey Mother and Baby Home in Roscrea, Co. Tipperary where Philomena had her baby.

Recently a mass grave was found where up to 800 babies were buried in the Tuam Bon Secours Mother and Baby Home which was run by nuns. 'The infants were buried without coffins in the grounds of a former Bons Secours home for unmarried mothers between 1925 and 1961. The unmarked grave was discovered accidentally in 1975. Death records show many of the infants died from malnutrition and infectious diseases.'[19] These scandals were not confined to Catholic homes: the discovery of the unmarked graves of 219 children in Mount Jerome Cemetery from the Bethany Protestant Home for children of unmarried mothers in Rathgar, Dublin, shocked Protestants. Other Protestant homes also had scandals.

Following the revelations of these scandals, a more questioning Catholic laity has largely deserted the Catholic hierarchy and clergy, particularly in urban centres, with less than 50 per cent attending Mass on a regular basis today. Many rural parishes, however, continue to command strong support.

In this changed, more secular environment, Protestants are no longer looked at as heretics but arguably they are still considered as 'other'. Any public expressions of pro-Britishness would be considered unpatriotic. However, the reality is that many Protestants think 'the British connection had been positive for Ireland and remained essential to its prosperity'[20] and the history of an independent Ireland has made their point. Exports from indigenous companies very largely go to Britain. There is scarcely a family in Ireland who does not have relatives living in England, often for generations.

Ironically, today certain Protestant values are admired by many Irish Catholics. Their married priests are mostly envied and the consecration of the Revd Pat Storey as Bishop of Meath and Kildare at a ceremony in Dublin's Christ Church Cathedral on 1 December 2014, the first female Church of Ireland Bishop, was positively covered by the most of the media. The *Church of Ireland Gazette* editorialised in August 1998: 'the Church of Ireland has found itself at the centre of a new pluralism in recent years … A Church which was very uncertain about its future now has a confidence and optimism inconceivable 20 years ago.'[21]

Many Protestants prospered, and continue to prosper, in an independent Ireland. Only 26 years before this editorial was written, 100 Protestants from the elite Protestant lay establishment wrote a short letter to the papers showing an almost unquestioning attitude to the nature of the State in which they prospered, declaring:

We want it known in Northern Ireland – for it does not seem to be – that Southern Protestants have every opportunity here to play a full part in the affairs of the community. Protestants hold positions of trust at least in proportion of their fraction of the population. Opinions and points of outlook are exchanged easily and without acrimony whilst the respect of one man for another is habitually related to the man rather than to his religious views.[22]

Tellingly, beside this letter is an article written by a prominent Catholic journalist, John Horgan, who pointed out that the average income of the signatories was 'significantly higher' than that of their fellow Protestants so they were not representative of the Protestant community as a whole. Not only this, but Horgan correctly thought that these high-profile Protestants were opting out of expressing concerns about 'the erosion of human rights' and the 'contraception, divorce provision and adoption legislation',[23] all of which were highly conservative. Horgan believed that many southern Protestants he knew had a 'don't rock the boat mentality' but that 'Protestantism was all about rocking boats'.[24]

Horgan was right in that this group of 100 had prospered in an independent Ireland, whether as academics in Trinity College, Dublin, in business, medicine and the arts. They had much reason not to start 'rocking boats'. Protestants with lower incomes might not have signed such a letter.

There were, however, two men who did 'rock the boat', the writer Hubert Butler in Kilkenny and Dean Griffin in Dublin's national cathedral, St Patrick's. In his classic essay 'Portrait of a Minority' Butler wrote: 'So now our amiable inertia, our refusal to express grievances or cherish hopes about Ireland, are really delaying our ultimate unity and the reconciliation of our two diverging communities'.[25]

As Edna Longley wrote, 'Butler healthily broke interdenominational Taboos and "rocked the boat". There is sometimes a fine line between boat rocking and coat trailing, but it's better to be damned if you do than damned if you don't.'[26]

Dean Griffin, who was raised in the South in Co. Wicklow, spent 22 years in Londonderry from 1947 and then a further 22 years as Dean of St Patrick's Cathedral. He protested strongly about the *Ne Temere* decree and was critical of the role of the Roman Catholic Church in Irish politics. He supported the removal of the constitutional ban on divorce and worked with David Norris to get homosexuality decriminalised. Significantly he wrote in his book *Enough Religion to Make Us Hate*:

> In the overwhelming Roman Catholic ethos of the new independent Ireland Protestants, a beleaguered minority, felt vulnerable, not really accepted as the 'genuine article, associated in the public mind with the British ascendancy. Understandably they kept a low profile, their heads down, especially when it came to religion and politics.[27]

Southern Protestants have had a tradition of not 'rocking the boat' and there are reasons for this, as we have seen. But there are reasons in today's more tolerant and secular Ireland for 'rocking the boat'. As we have seen, some Catholics deny that Protestants are 'really Irish'. However, Irish Protestants have been in the Republic since the Reformation and before and many are descended from ancient Gaelic families such as the O'Haras in Sligo and the O'Briens in Co. Clare. They deny that Catholics have a monopoly on Irishness.

Catholics in Northern Ireland have seen legislation put in place to end discrimination as part of a larger programme. In 1976, fair employment legislation, designed to address discrimination in employment on grounds of religion, was introduced, as well as other human rights legislation. Their economic status has improved and numbers have grown. In contrast in the Republic, Protestant economic standing has weakened and their numbers have decreased sharply. They now live in pockets confined to Dublin and the Pale, the border counties, with a scattering of Protestants in west Cork, Galway (particularly in Tuam), Waterford city, Co. Wexford and Kilkenny city. Since Independence in 1921, the only new Church of Ireland churches were those re-built to replace ones destroyed from 1920–23 in Kilmallock, Co. Limerick and one in Cathal Brugha Street in Dublin. Much later in Sneem, Co. Kerry the church was radically renovated and St Mary's church in Crumlin, Dublin replaced an earlier church. In Killorglin, Co. Kerry, a fine modern church, St Michael's, opened in 1996 to replace St James's church, which was in poor condition. It has a community centre. However, the general overall picture is quite gloomy. When Marcus Tanner, the writer and journalist, visited some Church of Ireland churches recently, he wrote:

> ... to visit the churches in the west of Ireland was to see a Church near the end of its life. There were broken spires, smashed windows and overgrown

churchyards. At Askeaton, the centre of the Second Reformation in County Limerick, where Bishop John Jebb had confirmed hundreds of converts in the 1880s, trees grew through the church roof. At Tourmakeady, the grave of Bishop Plunket, leader of the Second Reformation in Connaught, has disappeared under a forest of weeds and the nearby church was an impenetrable, ivy-clad ruin. When Peig Sayers wrote her popular account of life on Great Blasket Island, off the coast of Kerry (generations of school children were required to read this book and thus discouraged from learning Irish), she recalled a time when the Protestants of Dingle had been numerous enough to constitute a threat to Catholics. When I attended a Sunday service in Dingle it might not have taken place had I not turned up.[28]

Native Protestant numbers fell from some 300,000 in 1911 to 142,280 in 2011, a fall of 49 per cent.[29] Church of Ireland native Irish numbers increased by 5 per cent between 1991 and 2011 and Irish Presbyterians increased by 8.7 per cent in the same period. These figures show a small growth in numbers of native Church of Ireland Protestants as opposed to recent Protestant immigrants from the UK and elsewhere. Native southern Protestants constitute only 3.5 per cent of the population, a similar figure to the 1991 census. In other words, a stagnant population number for 10 years. Comparative figures do not exist for Methodists between 1991 and 2011. No doubt the losses in mixed religion marriages have declined as more young Catholics ignore the demands of their Church but inevitably some children in such marriages are raised as Catholics. Regrettably there are no statistics available to give an accurate picture. However, in contrast, in 1911 in the six counties which became Northern Ireland, Catholics numbered 430,161, while the figure was estimated at 651,700 in 1991, 737,472 in 2001 and 817,385 in 2011.

There has been widespread joining up of parishes under one priest and dioceses under one bishop. In the parish of Cloyne in east Cork, where I was raised in the 1950s, famous for Bishop Berkeley, there were once four churches. Today two have closed and are boarded up. There is the ancient Norman cathedral, built in about 1250, now struggling for funding with a congregation of perhaps two or three dozen on Sundays. The graveyard is overgrown and neglected. Local Church of Ireland families have almost all entered mixed religion marriages and their children are mostly Catholics, or non-religious; my own family is not exempt from this. The influence of Bishop Lucey was a factor in the past. He was a conservative who strictly enforced the *Ne Temere* decree in the diocese of Co. Cork when he was bishop from 1951 to 1981. However, the replacement of the *Ne Temere* by the *Matrimonia Mixta*, discussed earlier, seems to have made little difference.

However, against this picture of decline and decay, there are many Church of Ireland churches throughout the country that have survived and are cared for lovingly by parishioners who are resilient and treasure their religious tradition.[30]

The Protestant-owned manufacturing companies have all but gone. They flourished behind tariff barriers but once these were removed and when Ireland joined the free trade European Economic Community, almost all of them succumbed to outside competition or takeovers. They had afforded employment to Protestants, especially W.R. Jacobs and Guinness Brewery, which gave rise to resistance from Catholics organisations, as mentioned in chapter four. Other Protestant companies that closed, or were bought, include Willwoods, Lambs Jams, Lairds, Lemons and Goodalls. Such Protestant employment citadels, some of which made products that became international brands like Guinness, Jacobs and Jameson, arguably were a tribute to Protestant entrepreneurship. One semi-State organisation, Coras Trachtala, the Irish Export Board, recognised Protestant business acumen and experience and recruited a number of Protestants, particularly in its early days.

Is one of the primary inspirations of Irish nationalism, the romantic nationalist belief in 800 years of English crime and oppression in Ireland, dying? According to Stephen Howe: 'Early directives on primary education in the new Free State urged the main aim in history teaching should be 'to inculcate national pride and self-respect … by showing that the Irish race has fulfilled a great mission in the advancement of civilisation'.[31] However, Howe points out that '… other influences outside the formal educational process reinforced the same version of the past.'[32] Howe suggests that 'In political terms, the educational orthodoxies of cultural nationalism and of the Free State may have succeeded in their aims – and they may have done so in part … because they corresponded to genuine popular feelings and desires.'[33] Also '… this vision of history served important State-building, cohesion-affirming and psychologically comforting functions in a weak and insecure new polity.'[34]

Moving forward, Howe believes essentially that despite recent work by 'revisionist' historians such as Roy Foster, Francis Shaw (on 1916), Conor Cruise O'Brien and F.S.L. Lyons in *Culture and Anarchy in Ireland 1890–1939*, the impact on the Catholic, nationalist narrative has been weak. Roy Foster has acknowledged that 'by 1972 new textbooks were being used in schools and universities and new questions were being asked. But what might seem most striking is how little this affected the popular (and paradoxically Anglocentric) version of Irish history held by the public mind'.[35]

Howe takes Irish historians to task though for their 'insularity':

> Neither conceptual boldness in integrating Irish themes into wider international currents, nor comparative work of any degree of sophistication … has been much in evidence. An implicit or explicit belief in Irish exceptionalism seems widespread even of scholars most critical of nationalism. Revisionism has been an attempt to broaden the definition of the nation, to qualify its appeal, or to liberalise it, not to supplant it or step outside it altogether. The other side of this coin perhaps follows naturally: that modern Irish historical writing has little international influence.[36]

Irish historians have, in essence, been disappointing in terms of international influence.

Some comparison of the original form of secular republicanism that was the ideal of the 1798 rebels with what eventually emerged in Ireland might be instructive. Compared, for example, with France, the Irish seem to have departed significantly from the secular ideal, possibly because Irish republicans became characterised by the things they were against rather than what they favoured. Was Republicanism embraced by the early twentieth-century Irish revolutionaries just because it was not the British system, rather than any real love of republican ideals.

As regards the relationship between Church and State, the difference may be that the French Catholic Church was identified with the old monarchy, whereas in Ireland the Catholic Church had the later advantage of having once being suppressed by the British monarchy, though by 1914, Catholics and the Roman Catholic Church enjoyed all the civil and religious freedoms of Protestants in Ireland.

How does this relate to the tiny Protestant minorities, forced to go down the Catholic, nationalist road since 1921 and before? We have seen the results. Exceptionalism meant exclusivism. Protestants after all have until recently been looked on as the remnant of Britain's garrison in Ireland, as the upholders of the British presence and policies. Yet by

the end of the nineteenth and early twentieth centuries they were a
spent force, as we have seen. When the Free State came into being, they
were a powerless minority, albeit with important privileged positions in
commerce, the legal profession, medicine and manufacturing, positions
which after almost a hundred years of independence have faded away.

One interesting cultural issue is the tendency of middle-class
Catholics, particularly urban, to adopt what might once have been seen
as 'Protestant culture' activities and the so called garrison sports – rugby-
and cricket-playing schools, tennis and hockey clubs. When Protestant
schools opened their doors to them, admiration for 'Protestant ethos'
meant no shortage of Catholic parents wanting to enrol their children.

How are Protestants seen in today's Ireland? It is hard and ill-advised
to make sweeping generalisations as Protestants are by definition far
from a monolithic people. Some value the British connection of the
past and see themselves as Irish and British. Mary McAleese, when
President of Ireland, 'urged a new sense of culture of acceptance and
inclusion be built, following the success of the Belfast Agreement.

In Church of Ireland churches throughout the State Remembrance
Day is marked by selling poppies and prayers for the dead. The British
Legion has carried the torch. Until recently the Catholic Irish who
served and fell in two world wars have been forgotten. But not so today.
Kevin Myers is a shining light in making this happen, revealing the
innumerable Irish men who fought in the First World War through his
ceaseless research. He has unearthed countless Irish families, Catholic
and Protestants, who, in a sea of nationalist fervour following 1916,
had too often sought anonymity post the First World War. His recently
published book, *Ireland's Great War*, is a study of Irishmen who played
a part in the defeat of the Central Powers. Myers also did much to
expose the disgraceful neglect of the Memorial Gardens designed by
Edwin Lutyens at Islandbridge, Dublin, where HM Queen Elizabeth
II laid a wreath on 18 May 2011, Kevin Myers being present, not
invited as an individual by the organisers, he went with the Royal
British Legion delegation.[37]

A peace park was built at Messines in Belgium by people of Ireland
and HM Queen Elizabeth II and President Mary McAleese opened
it in 1998. President McAleese acknowledged that: 'Respect for the
memory of one set of heroes was often at the expense of respect for
the memory of the other.'[38] In 2003 she said:

The old vanities of history are disappearing. Carefully hidden stories like those of the Irish who died in the First World War are coming out of shoe boxes in the attic and into the daylight. We are making new friends, we are influencing new people, we are learning new things about ourselves, and we are being changed.[39]

The 'one set of heroes' no doubt refers to the extreme, self-appointed fanatics who led a doomed rebellion in 1916 when up to 200,000 of their fellow Irishmen and women were fighting with Britain in Europe.

But surprisingly Mary McAleese seems to draw the line on where and how far to extend new friendships. She opposes Ireland re-entering a huge club of friends, an anti-colonial organisation (not that Ireland was a 'colony', as Stephen Howe has pointed out[40]), the Commonwealth of Nations, radically changed since Ireland left it in 1949. Leaving the Commonwealth in 1949 was perhaps childish and counter-productive. Foreign policy was created and guided after 1949 by the advanced nationalist, Sean McBride, Minister for External Affairs. The then Taoiseach, A.J. Costello, seems to have been persuaded by him, claiming that leaving the then British Commonwealth would 'take the gun out of Irish politics'. Thirty years of needless violence later followed in Northern Ireland.

Young Irish people have emigrated for over two centuries to Commonwealth countries including Canada, Australia and New Zealand. They willingly helped to build many of the fifty-three countries in today's Commonwealth, which consists of 2.2 billion people. Some 21 million people of Irish descent live in Commonwealth countries today.[41] It says more about Ireland than the Commonwealth that Ireland has not re-entered a club of countries that share a common past. We also might bear in mind that Irish economic and social mismanagement resulted in many Irish people relocating to the Commonwealth. The pretence among the political elite that Ireland's place is primarily in the Continental continues, when the languages, cultures and customs of countries in the EU are such that Irish people are not attracted to work in there. It seems, however, that re-entering is a bridge too far for Fine Gael, especially as it took Ireland out. It also appears not to be a consideration of reconciliation for any political party and the Department of Foreign Affairs takes a surprisingly strong negative attitude in the face of hugely improved Anglo-Irish relations. Some might argue that Ireland's long history of being ruled by Britain is different from the experience of all other countries in the

Commonwealth, but after almost a century of independence a more informed and mature view might indicate reconciliation.

Going back to the time when the Normans were invited to help an Irish chieftain, Dermot MacMurrough, it is clear that the Irish warring classes were in alliances with their English counterparts to gain control over rival Irish kingdoms. Moreover it suited as and where appropriate the Irish warlords to bring their vassals to heel when they got out of hand by using their English warlords if necessary.

But as time moved on Ireland became an integral part of the Empire that they played a huge role in building and most Irish people were proud of being part of the Empire until the extremists of 1916 decided to become 'freedom fighters'. Freedom from what? The country descended into a bloodbath, finally emerging as a theocracy masquerading as a democracy. Perhaps the question needs to be asked of all those who oppose Ireland's Commonwealth membership, like Mary McAleese, why would Commonwealth members welcome into their fold a country with a long history of hatred of England since 1916.

Mainly thanks to the work of ex-President Mary Robinson, and later of Mary McAleese, in May 2011 HM Queen Elizabeth II paid a State visit to Ireland, the first visit of a British monarch since 1921. Mary McAleese was President during this visit, which marked reconciliation and perhaps a beginning of the end of past grievances and misunderstandings. The Queen spoke about Britain's involvement in Ireland, saying: 'With the benefit of hindsight we can all see things we wish had been done differently or not at all.' The visit was hugely successful, marked by spontaneous warmth of the Irish people for a hugely popular monarch.

It could be argued that a new way forward is needed. Perhaps we now at last need to lay aside arguments about historical origins, narrowly defined identities and ancient quarrels and claims. Old arguments about real and perceived wrongs have embittered our political and social landscape for far too long and it is time to replace them with the recognition of the multiple relationships of the people on the two islands, bound by history for millennia. We share a common heritage with the Scots, the Welsh and the English.

Perhaps as part of this process southern Irish Catholics, and Irish historians,[42] need to get over their belief in Irish exceptionalism, in believing they were the MOPE (most oppressed people ever) and that the centuries of dominance by a once world power demanded a strong, unmandated violent reaction. This obsessive dwelling on historical wrongs is a barrier to diplomatic progress. The 'you started it' justification is used. As we know, the Irish invited the Normans to invade, unlike the Saxons in England who were conquered by a Norman invasion in 1066. They have somehow put that behind them. And many other countries in the British Empire broke away, from India to Kenya to South Africa, without leaving a lasting legacy of popular enmity, of Anglophobia, inflamed by admiring those violent unmandated few at the expense of peaceful constitutionalists. Instead today countries once in the British Empire embrace the benefits of a departed imperial master such as democracy, the rule of law, free press, strong infrastructures (the British brought rail networks, particularly in India) and the primary world language, English. They value friendships with a much-changed United Kingdom and the expression of this reality is marked through membership of the Commonwealth of Nations.

History is a tale of invasions and conquests that resulted in the confluence of cultures and the mingling of traditions. The popular culture of Ireland is largely Anglophone and American. Irish people are deeply interwoven with English people over many generations by blood and in economic/business life.

The 1916 commemorations were of concern to many, if not most, southern Protestants. This merits little surprise, bearing in mind the Roman Catholic nature of the Rising and its later consequences for the Protestant community in the twenty-six counties. Very few Protestants took part in the Rising and the one Protestant, an Ulster Quaker once prominent in the IRB, Bulmer Hobson, opposed armed rebellion which led to: '… barren conflicts over verbal differences of politics which only the contestants, and not many of them, could understand, that these conflicts developed a fanatical bitterness which found its outlet in a civil was …'[43]

Hobson believed martyrdom was 'indulgent and damaging'.[44] He was cast aside by those who took leadership roles after 1916 and 'a disillusionment set in that was rapid, intense and permanent'.[45]

Another Protestant, Warre Bradley Wells, editor of the *Church of Ireland Gazette* in 1916, was a witness to much of the fighting around Sackville Street where the Church of Ireland premise was located in Middle Abbey Street. He wrote that the Rising was 'a complete failure with no approval from the mass of the Irish people'.[46] In the special edition 25 April–5 May, he editorialised:

The pity of the citizens murdered, the young English soldiers shot
down on Irish soil, the callow lads led into treason: the shame of this
stab in the back of our brave soldiers in Flanders and Salonika; and the
horror of Dublin, fired by the hands of her own sons, and of Irish blood
shed by Irish hands.[47]

The same edition of the *Gazette* published a letter from the 'Archbishop
of Dublin, the Most Revd John Henry Bernard, dated 3 May and
published by *The Irish Times* in which he appealed for martial law to
continue: 'Many armed rebels are at large in Dublin still, and can only
be averted by the adoption of the sternest measures … no one who lives
in Ireland believes that the present Irish Government has the courage to
punish anybody'.[48]

Dr Susan Hood wrote in the archive section of the Church of Ireland
library, which published the special 25 April–5 May edition in April
2016, that during the rebellion were, perhaps surprisingly, no sectarian
incidents:

Such colourful insights to events as they unfolded sit side by side
with the Gazette's articulation of a middle-ground opinion seriously
concerned about the long-term consequences for Ireland as a whole.
At pains to point out 'the religious element did not enter in any way
into this unfortunate rebellion' with 'no whisper of old sectarian feuds',
it remarked moderate unionist and nationalist Ireland '… have learned
in an awful personal experience what war means … Easter week has
taught us the terror of the sniper'.[49]

The rosary was recited many times in the GPO by the insurgents,
something that would have been abhorrent to the nationalist icon,
Wolfe Tone. The Catholic hierarchy as a whole was reluctant to oppose
the rebellion. Eamon McCann wrote:

It is said that 'the bishops condemned the Rising'. This is at best an
exaggeration, repeated today in efforts to project the Rising as a secular
event. In fact, there were 31 Catholic bishops in Ireland in 1916, of
whom only seven explicitly condemned the rebels. Most of the rest
kept cannily quiet, before placing themselves soon at the head of the
national movement which was to arise from the Dublin rubble.[50]

George William Russell was another Protestant separatist from Ulster who had lived in Dublin from the age of 11. He was a writer, painter, and poet, editor of the *Irish Statesman* and friends with many of the leading Irish writers in the early nineteenth century. He was deeply involved in the Theosophical Society which led him to believe that a new messenger would come to bring in a new era for Ireland. Like Hobson and Wells, he opposed 1916, saying: 'I do not approve of the rising at all. I hate physical force employed in almost any cause ...They were all mad and most of them on both sides bad shots and half demented, the whole thing was dreadful.'[51]

Russell cast a socialist light on the motivation of the insurgents, believing not so much that they fought for a new separate nationalist state, as to redress profound economic grievances among working-class Dubliners:

> It was labour supplied the personal element in the revolt. It had a real grievance. The cultural element, poets, Gaels, etc. never stir more than one per cent of a country. It is only when an economic injustice stirs the workers that they unite their grievances with all other grievances.[52]

Dublin workers were 'badly housed, badly paid.'[53] Russell joined the disillusioned voices which came into being after the Treaty. He was particularly critical of Fianna Fail, which took power in 1932 under Eamon de Valera. He complained about 'squalid Catholic materialism' and 'smug Catholic self-satisfaction'. After Lady Gregory died in 1932 he praised her, writing to Yeats that 'the Anglo Irish were the best Irish, but I can see very little future for them as the present belongs to that half-crazy Gaeldom which is growing dominant around us' and was convinced 'the long cultural revolution wrought by his generation had in fact ended in defeat'.[54]

Russell turned his back on the Ireland that had evolved after 1921 and went to live in Bournemouth after his wife died in 1932. He died the following year and was buried in Dublin after a huge public funeral, attended by his enemy, Eamon de Valera.

What of the reaction of southern Protestants to the many commemorations? The Presbyterian Minister of Arts, Heritage and the Gaeltacht, Heather Humphreys, in charge of the commemorations, was anxious that an inclusive theme was adopted, rather than a Catholic, Gaelic emphasis, more in line with the outlook of the new, young, modern

Ireland. She expressed her wish that 'reconciliation' would be the theme
for the various traditions on the island.

This message was powerfully driven home by the erection of a Wall
of Remembrance in Glasvevin cemetery in Dublin, inspired by the
International Memorial of Notre Dame de Lorette in France. It was
officially opened by the Taoiseach on Sunday, 3 April 2016 with representatives of all religious denominations present. There was a reading by
a member of the Humanist Association of Ireland.

The names of all who died in Easter week 1916 were included on
the memorial by the dates of their deaths starting on Easter Monday, 24
April 1916. There are 488 names, 268 civilians, including 40 children
under 17.[55] All the British and Irish soldiers serving in the British Army
are included with the names of the insurgents. Not surprisingly, Sinn
Fein sourly described the wall as 'totally inappropriate'.

On 26 May 2016 the deaths of British soldiers during the Rising
was remembered with a wreath-laying ceremony followed by a minute's
silence and the raising of the Tricolour to full mast. The British ambassador, Dominick Chilcott, laid a wreath in remembrance of British
soldiers who died and members of the British and Irish armies were
present. The Minister for Foreign Affairs, Charles Flanagan, was anxious
to promote reconciliation between all political traditions on the island
and wanted mutual respect for 'the different traditions and the multiple
narratives across our islands' and wrote:

> The Ireland 2016 Centenary Programme includes events that reflect
> on how Easter 1916 was experienced by those who participated in, and
> were affected by, the Rising; not only the experiences of the men and
> women that mobilised during Easter week, but also those of civilians, of
> children, of the Irish diaspora and other groups involved in that seminal
> moment in our country's path to independence.[56]

However, there was an incident during the commemoration. A protester,
a member of the Irish Republican Prisoners Welfare Association, was
grabbed and pushed away by the Canadian ambassador, Kevin Vickers, a
national hero in Canada who had shot dead a terrorist, Michael Zehaf-
Bibeau, in October 2014 outside the Ottawa House of Commons. The
protester found it 'unpalatable to be commemorating British soldiers
killed in 1916 … He also wanted to highlight the case of the "Craigavon
Two", Brendan McConville and John Paul Wootton, jailed in 2012 for

the murder of PSNI officer Stephen Carroll who was shot dead in Craigavon, Co Armagh, in 2009.'[57]

According to Kevin Myers, the Canadian ambassador's action was 'gallant'. He attended the commemoration:

> It wasn't much, surely, to expect that such a ceremony could be allowed to pass off without incident, even if almost no one from Dail Eireann had the decency to attend. The only reason that the demonstrator was prevented from creating more havoc was the timely intervention of the Canadian ambassador.
>
> What if the protester had been armed? He had the drop on everyone yet not one single state firearm was drawn as he rose, shrieking slogans. Contrary to popular myth, some republicans have screamed abuse as they attacked. I was seated just behind him, and I thought a serious attack had begun, with the British ambassador and the half-dozen uniformed British Army officers as possible targets.
>
> What was the subsequent response of Official Ireland? Not criticism of An Garda Siochana and its commissioner for allowing such a protester to evade security. Oh no. Instead, Kevin Vickers, the hero of the hour, was turned into a comic turn on RTÉ. Soon, the letters page of *The Irish Times* pullulated with complaints about his prompt and gallant intervention.[58]

What was the reaction to the military nature of the commemorations by Protestant church leaders? After all there were no less than thirteen separate military ceremonies, emphasising the violence as politics nature of the insurgency, arguably excessive in the context of an Irish Republic as an enthusiastic member of the post-nationalist EU.

The head of the Methodist Church in Ireland, Revd Brian Anderson, called for an attitude of 'viewing the future inclusively'.[59] He hoped the two major commemorations in 1916, the Rising and the Battle of the Somme, would no longer divide 'our two communities'.[60] A similar note was struck by the Church of Ireland Primate, Archbishop Clarke, who said 1916 had to be commemorated 'well and properly and constructively' but people need to remember the Somme 'North and South because we tend to think of it as a Northern Irish thing'.[61] Both Archbishop Clarke and his counterpart, Archbishop Eamon Martin, visited Glasnevin cemetery and the Irish Peace Park in Messines and the Somme in the summer of 2016.

However, controversy arose over the announcement that the Dublin Church of Ireland Cathedral, Christ Church, might have to close its front gates to avoid the large crowds using the grounds as a picnic site, even a public toilet, on Easter Sunday, 27 March, and six other inner Dublin Church of Ireland churches also closed due to traffic restrictions being imposed during the commemorations. The parades were planned to last over two hours. All Roman Catholic churches in the city centre, in contrast, held Easter Sunday masses, partly because their priests lived close to their churches, unlike Church of Ireland rectors, and partly because their congregations lived near their churches, unlike Church of Ireland parishioners, only 5 per cent of whom live in the inner city.

There was no consultation with any churches likely to be effected by the parades when the plans were being drawn up. It was not until January 2015, that it became clear that the route of the various parades between the two canals would be cordoned off to prevent traffic entering the city centre. The Church of Ireland Archbishop, Michael Jackson, asked why the parades could not take place on Easter Monday, as the Rising started on Easter Monday, 24 April, not on 27 March, the day it was commemorated. There appears to have been no official response but suggestions have been made that the government feared Sinn Féin would make the running if the state did not mount major commemorations on Easter Sunday.

The former Taoiseach, John Bruton, wrote to Minister of Justice Frances Fitzgerald and the Garda Commissioner to complain about the proposed closure of seven Church of Ireland churches, stating 'Easter Sunday is the most important day of the Christian year' so 'access to Christian services should be prioritized over other events'.[62] John Bruton's hostile views on 1916 are well known but this was a helpful intervention which had effect.

Consultations with the government, the Garda, the Archbishop and Archdeacons of Dublin followed and arrangements were made to open Christ Church Cathedral on Easter Sunday for the celebration of the Eucharist at 10 a.m. and at midday the bilingual liturgy was said to commemorate the Rising. 'During the service the parade is passing the Cathedral, the congregation will pray for the country and its leaders and remember those who died in the Rising.'[63]

The government had stated that it was 'its earnest wish … that people would be able to attend their usual places of worship on Easter Sunday if at all possible'.[64] But this was not to be. Four Church of Ireland churches had no services on Easter Sunday and Archbishop Jackson and senior clergy 'remain of the view that, given the large numbers of people expected to watch the parade, it is not practical to have every Church of Ireland church in the city open on Easter Day'.[65] Archdeacon Pierpoint was quite clear that the traffic cordons would make it very difficult for Church of Ireland parishioners to 'battle' their way to church. He emphasised that the Gardaí did 'all in their power' to help the churches to keep open' and there was no ill will during and after Easter Sunday.[66]

The rector of one of the four churches that closed, Canon Mark Gardner, decided he could not go on foot from one of his churches, St Audoen's, and back again to his other church, St Catherine and St James 'in the time available'. On the commemoration of the Rising, he wrote:

> I feel no affinity with the commemoration of the rising and my own memories of 1966 and what I have learnt about those events a hundred or so years ago convince me that it was a series of ghastly mistakes compounded by one government after another. I feel the loss of the Public Record Office particularly keenly. In 1966, every school had to display a copy of the Proclamation and even as a child I felt it intrusive. The destruction of the pillar added to an already oppressive atmosphere.[67]

On the Proclamation, John Bruton argued in his address at Iveagh House, Dublin, on 28 March 2016 that it was not based on consent and ignored the wishes of Ulster Protestants who wanted to stay in the UK, being British, not Gaelic Irish by choice and not because they had been subject to 'careful fostering' by 'an alien government'.[68] Bruton thinks 1916 put gunmen in charge 'as dictators with powers of life over death over many areas … there was no law but the law of force' quoting P.S. Hegarty in *The Victory of Sinn Fein*. The deaths of 488 people would have been avoided if patience had been exercised. After all, Home Rule was on the Statute books and Westminster would have 'freely granted' Dominion status in 1931 under the Statute of Westminster when Canada and Australia obtained Dominion status. Professor Geoff Roberts supported John Bruton in his letter to *The Irish Times* of 31 March 2016, believing there would have been 'a peaceful and democratic transition to Irish independence' in the course of time.

The ex-attorney general, Paul Gallagher, came out strongly against the Rising following the 2016 commemorations. He believes the insurgents had 'no legitimacy whatsoever' and the leaders were 'a self-absorbed group of brave idealists who had never represented anybody'. More seriously, perhaps, 1916 held back Ireland as 'for over 70 years following 1916 we were a country that did not realise our potential. We were obsessed with the past, we were obsessed with who did what in 1916. It itself was used to discriminate between people. I regret greatly the lost years and I believe that Ireland between 1920 and 1980, perhaps even 1990, was a wasteland for so many people.'[69]

He also made it clear that 1916 had an influence on the Troubles in Northern Ireland, stating: 'all of these thugs and murderers claimed they were doing this in a cause that deserved to be revered, in a cause that they said justified anything, in a cause they said was going to improve the lives of all the people who undoubtedly were being discriminated against'.[70]

Professor Ronan Fanning disagrees, believing 1916 was a just war as there was no evidence of Home Rule being brought into effect before 1916, if indeed ever. John Bruton, as we have seen, takes a different view, as does the biographer of John Redmond, Dermot Meleady, who thinks that Fanning's belief was proved wrong in 1916 when Britain did try to introduce the Home Rule Act unsuccessfully. He also wrote about the consequences of the 1919–21 IRA violence for many Protestants, something that few historians have highlighted.

Precious economic resources that had made Ireland a richer country than most in Europe were lost in the exodus of up to 40,000 of the southern unionist population due to burning of houses and lesser forms of intimidation.

It is worth mentioning that Bulmer Hobson thought that it was the First World War and the Irish Volunteers that moved support to Sinn Fein away from the Irish Parliamentary Party, rather than the blood sacrifice and the executions of the 1916 leaders.[71]

There was much debate in the media and at various conferences around the country about the Rising commemorations. RTÉ covered the centenary on radio and television, arguably to excess, presenting near hagiographies of the seven men who signed the Proclamation. However, RTÉ did organise a balanced debate which took place in the GPO before Easter Day which gave an opportunity for an exchange of views between those supporting and opposing 1916.[72] In addition, the permanent interpretive centre exhibition in the GPO, which was the headquarters of the Rising, is balanced and well designed 'with the government reflecting the present mood of a mature society sick of violence' especially thirty years of Northern Irish violence.[73]

On Newstalk FM Sir Bob Geldoff attacked 1916 in an interview with Ivan Yates on 24 March. The academic Seamus Murphy S.J. wrote eloquently about the theological and liturgical nature of the Rising, stating: 'The lack of democratic legitimacy is no mere legal technicality; it is precisely the thing can never be fully part of us … the Rising represented nobody but its leaders.' He believes it was the liturgy of the Rising that captured the imagination and support of the people:

> The sacrament is a sign that effects what it signifies; the Rising's liturgy was indeed effective … in the preface to *Ghosts*, Pearse remarked 'There's only one way to appease a ghost. You must do the thing it asks you'. The command of Pearse's ghost has been obeyed in this centenary of the Rising, and his bloody sacrifice reenacted sacramentally. It will not be without effect.[74]

Journalists Patsy McGarry and David Quinn argued that the rebellion did not meet the criteria for a just war. McGarry believed the Rising was 'immoral, undemocratic … the only begetter of and justification for the Irish republican violence since then.'[75]

Kevin Myers, a longtime, well-informed opponent of 1916 wrote:

> It is surely blasphemy to associate the days of Easter … with an unprovoked violent rising in which hundreds of innocent people were killed. The belief that the April insurrection was in resistance to British oppression is still widespread. It is completely inaccurate.[76]

Myers has enlightened many people on the treasonous nature of 1916 with its attempt to imperil Britain's war efforts and strategy. He pointed out that the German strategy was to attack the British not only in Ireland by sending 20,000 rifles for the insurgents, but also to attack the British ports of Great Yarmouth and Lowerstoft. Both plans failed. The German ship carrying arms to southern Ireland, the *Aud*, was captured by the Royal Navy and scuttled while the German battleship SMS *Seidlitz* hit a mine on its way to attack East Anglia and had to return to its base at Wilhelmshaven. The remains of the taskforce then half-heartedly bombarded their targets of Lowestoft and Yarmouth, and though destroying some 200 houses, killed only three people.'[77]

There is agreement among some historians that 1916 led to the Treaty in December 1921 when the twenty-six counties became the Free State and substantially more independence was forthcoming than under the terms of the third Home Rule Act. Indeed, Declan Kiberd has argued that the Rising 'blew away the world of haut-bourgeois parliamentary nationalism' and there had been 'a frustrating postponement of Home Rule after years of teasing foreplay'.[78] 'Foreplay' it hardly was, more it was determined, long, peaceful work to secure devolved government democratically. However, it is hardly disputable that the Anglo-Irish guerrilla war from 1919 to 1921, rather than the 1916 Rising itself, brought about the negotiations which concluded with the Treaty in December 1921. Perhaps, then, it is at least arguable that it is incorrect to attribute the founding of an independent Irish state primarily to the rebellion in 1916. One legacy seems certain, however, dying for Ireland '… is out of fashion; the young want to live for it.'[79]

Various forms of nationalism gave rise to a history of conflict in Europe during the nineteenth and twentieth centuries, Ireland was unexceptional, north and south, where identity by blood, religion and land led to intense hatreds and unbending prejudices. Though much has changed, the island is still profoundly divided, as journalist Eoghan Harris pointed out in an article in the *Sunday Independent*:

> People in the Republic have as little interest in Northern Ireland politics as they have in Northern Ireland's football team. The reverse is also true. And thereby hangs a huge tale of hypocrisy. The Republic is profoundly partitionist in practice. All we really want in Northern Ireland is peace … in spite of the peace process, we are still politically bigoted about Northern Protestants.[80]

Also many are unwilling to admit that leaving the UK proved to be a disaster in many ways. Ireland was strong in 1921. It had a system of local services, old-age pensions, universities, free primary education, an excellent network of railways and farm prices were good. In this positive environment mythical and mystical interventions came to violently drive a move for independence. In the words of Conor Brady:

> Poets and the pamphleteers invented a mythical land, peaceful, once ruled by Gaelic kings and queens. Before the advent of the rapacious invader, it was peopled by hero warriors, gods and mystics. Its laws were just, its

rulers wise. Once we could get rid of the Brits, a 20th-century version of this idyll would be re-attained. Ireland would be 'a nation once again'.

He went on:

> In reality, what we got was not a golden age or a land flowing with milk and honey, but a Free State that was scarcely self-sufficient, that fell progressively behind European living standards and that failed to provide a livelihood for more than a million people, who were forced to emigrate.[81]

Though much progress has been made in improving Anglo-Irish relations, partitionist attitudes remain firm. In the context of the EU and its influence in an Irish context, particularly following the economic crash, it is indisputable that the Irish Republic lost much sovereignty, even seeing an end to its sovereignty.

Anglicanism shows toleration, doubt, the importance of individualism, and a willingness to allow debate. But perhaps in practice Irish Protestants have been 'one of the most inarticulate minorities in the world'[82] ('inarticulate' is questionable; 'quiescent' is perhaps nearer the mark).

As we have seen, those who stayed on, the great majority being unsympathetic to advanced Irish nationalism, understandably kept their heads below the parapets. Perhaps they should have been more critical, but we can ask, to what avail? The few that were outspoken went unheeded as we have seen. And they had their livelihoods and ways of life to protect, embodied in their schools, hospitals and sports. Many prospered. If they found Irish nationalism alienating they had a friendly country to go to across the Irish Sea, or further afield in Canada, Australia and New Zealand.

It is, however, a tribute to their inner strength and resilience that those who stayed on quietly survived against the odds, retaining both their sense of Irishness and patriotism. The signs are that their long winter of isolation, and even suppression, is now ending. The ice is melting. From 1977 until the early 1990s there was only one Protestant TD in the Dáil. Today two members of the Cabinet are Protestants, there is one other Protestant TD and the Chief Justice is a Protestant. There is a sea change in attitude towards those who fought in two world wars. There is still much room to go, as we have seen, but recent improvements serve to underline how narrow the situation was before.

The Protestant tradition seems to have been laid aside as of little consequence in this debate about what constitutes Irish nationality, Roman Catholicism taking centre stage. This Protestant tradition is northern European in nature. It rejects 'an authoritarian, centralist mindset: an unwillingness to make individuals accountable for performance; and an anarchic character with a mistrust of authority – frequently well founded'.[83]

One important indication of changed government attitudes is that in recent times we heard the first official expression of regret for the attacks on Protestant civilians in the period 1919–23. It came from the late Brian Lenihan, late Minister for Finance, in his speech at the annual Michael Collins commemoration at Beal na Blath in which he said, '... and many people with little or no connection to the struggle died or suffered by accident, or because of where they worked or where they worshipped.' The murders in the Bandon Valley in 1922, are implied by Minister Lenihan, the subject of much heated recent debate characterised by attacks on Peter Hart's findings, as discussed in chapter 2. Indeed, a few historians have been anxious to present this mini program as being non-sectarian. As previously stated, Michael Collins had no doubt the motive was sectarian, in retaliation for the massacres of Roman Catholics in Belfast.

Finally, once there is widespread acceptance that southern Protestants are as Irish as their Catholic neighbours, through a long tradition that embraces Swift, Grattan, Wellington, Parnell, Bulmer Hobson, Sean O'Casey and Oscar Wilde, the end of the road is in sight for an inclusive, pluralist, secular Ireland. Vincent Comerford has argued that the 'national category in respect of Ireland ... [has] no essential common character ... Such a perspective is of little use for the purposes of chauvinist nationalism or intransigent unionism. But it is, arguably, a better key to understanding the fascination, wealth, the ever-changing complexity, the infinite variety and the endless contradictions of a long-lasting nationality such as Ireland's.[84] In such a broad form of interwoven nationality lies the deeply enriching southern Protestant legacy.

Appendix

THE VICTIMS AND THE SURVIVORS

The myth that the killings in the Brandon Valley in April 1922 were a carefully targeted campaign against a dozen or so people is still bandied about. Those targeted were well known as spies and informers, so the story goes. Therefore the killings were of a military nature that had nothing to do with religion; they were a pre-emptive strike against the agents of an invader just evicted but fully expected to return.

This would have been a catastrophic massacre, involving up to 30 victims if the IRA had been efficient and got their entire intended quarry.

Those Killed Outright

In Ballygroman, beginning in the early hours of Wednesday morning:

Michael O'Neill of Kilbrittain, an IRA man, was killed while trying to force entry, along with 3 others, into Ballygroman House, the home of Thomas Hornibrook.

Thomas Hornibrook, a 78-year-old widower and owner of Ballygroman House.

Samuel Wood Hornibrook aged about 45, Thomas' unmarried son by his first marriage.

Herbert Woods, a nephew of Edward Woods, who was married to Matilda, daughter of Thomas Hornibrook by his second marriage.

In Dunmanway on the Wednesday night:

Francis Fitzmaurice, a 70-year-old solicitor and land agent, of Carbery House.
David Gray, aged 37, a chemist.
James Buttimer, aged 81, a retired draper.

In Ballineen/Enniskeane area on Thursday night:

Robert Howe, aged about 60, a farmer of Ballaghnure.
John Albert Chinnery, a 32-year-old farmer, of Castletown.
***Alexander McKinley**, aged 17, of Ballineen.
John Buttimer, a 59-year-old farmer, of Caher.
James Greenfield, aged 45, a farm servant employed by John Buttimer.

In Clonakilty on Thursday night:

***Robert Nagle**, aged 16, a night school student and post office assistant.

In Killowen area on Saturday night:

***John Bradfield**, a 69-year-old farmer.

The Escapees and Survivors

In Dunmanway on Wednesday night:

William Fitzmaurice, brother of Francis Fitzmaurice.
James McCarthy, the publican whose pub was attacked.
William Jagoe, draper.
William Morrison, teacher.
George Applebee Bryan, shopkeeper.
Daniel Sullivan, a retired RIC man.

In Glandore on Thursday evening:

Arthur Stewart Travers.

In Skibbereen on Thursday night:

Jasper Travers Wolfe, aged 50, solicitor.
William Good Wood, aged 60, auctioneer.

In Ballineen/Enniskeane area on Thursday night:

Willie Daunt, aged 27, farmer and cattle dealer of Derrigra House, Ballineen.

Robert and Joseph Bennett of Ballineen, were not around when the killers called.

*★**Ralph Harbord**, a 26-year-old curate of Murragh rectory, was seriously injured but survived.

William Buttimer, aged 22, farmer's son, of Caher, west of Ballineen.

In Clonakilty area on Thursday night:

Thomas Nagle, aged 66, a bootmaker of Barrack Street, Clonakilty. When the gang could not find him, they shot his 16-year-old son instead.

William Perrott, a farmer near Clonakilty. A visit was paid to his property on Thursday night, but he had made himself scarce.

Richard Helen was kidnapped from O'Donovan's Hotel, Clonakilty, on Thursday night, but escaped from his captors as they led him away.

In Killowen area on Saturday night:

William Bradfield, aged 53, was asked for but absent. The gang shot his crippled brother instead.

Henry Bradfield, aged 81, a cousin and neighbour, was also visited but was absent.

Thomas Bradfield, brother of the murdered John Bradfield, fled when his brother was killed. He returned a fortnight or so later, but received a death threat the same day and left for good that night.

Although there is no evidence of him being directly attacked, he could be considered potential victim number 30. With one brother killed and another targeted, there is a reasonable probability that Thomas too might have been on the list.

Notes

PREFACE

1 Patrick Buckland, *Irish Unionism*, Vol. 1, (Dublin, 1972), p.285.
2 Roy Foster, 'Something to Hate' in *Irish Review*, xxx (2003), p.5.
3 Marianne Elliott, *When God Took Sides* (Oxford, 2009), p.20.
4 Ibid., pp. 215–216.
5 R.B. McDowell, *Crisis and Decline* (Dublin, 1997), preface.
6 Richard Tillinghast, *Finding Ireland* (Indiana, 2008), p.23.
7 Charles Townshend, *The Republic: The Fight for Irish Independence, 1918–1923* (London, 2013), p.452.
8 McDowell, *Crisis and Decline*, p.136.
9 BBC Four, 16 December 2013.

CHAPTER 1

1 *Census of Ireland 1926*, Vol. III, table 1b, p.1.
2 Ibid., table 1a.
3 Patrick Buckland, *Irish Unionism 1: The Anglo-Irish and the New Ireland 1885–1922* (Dublin, 1972), pp. 285–6.
4 Ibid., p.284.
5 Ibid., p.285.
6 Ibid.
7 Peter Hart, *The IRA at War 1916–1923* (Oxford, 2003), p.223.
8 Ibid., p.240.
9 R.B. McDowell, *Crisis and Decline*, p.132.
10 Kent Fedorowich, 'Reconstruction and Resettlement: The

Politicization of Irish Migration to Australia and Canada, 1919–29'
in *English Historical Review*, November 1999.

11 Enda Delaney, *Demography, State and Society: Irish Migration to Britain, 1921–1971* (Liverpool, 2000), p.72.

12 Hart, *The IRA at War*, p.226.

13 Delany, *Demography, State and Society*, p.72.

14 *General Report of the 1926 Census*, Vol. 10, p.47.

15 Kurt Bowen, *Protestants in a Catholic State*, p.35.

16 *General Report of the 1926 Census*, p.47.

17 *Preliminary Report of the 1926 Census*, p.7. However, it is not explained how this figure of 37 dependents per 100 men is arrived at for Dublin city.

18 Hart, *The IRA at War*, p.227, footnote 14.

19 Kevin Myers, *Ireland's Great War* (Dublin, 2014), p.5.

20 J.J. Sexton and R. O'Leary, 'Factors Affecting Population Decline in Minority Religious Communities in the Republic of Ireland' in *Building Trust in Ireland: Studies commissioned by the Forum for Peace and Reconciliation* (Belfast, 1996), p.314.

21 Ibid.

22 For Ireland overall, the modern consensus lies between 27,000 and 40,000. K. Jeffery, *Ireland and the Great War* (Cambridge, 2000), pp.33, 35; J. Horne, 'Our war, our history', in J. Horne (ed.), *Our War: Ireland and the Great War – the 2008 Thomas Davis Lecture Series* (Dublin, 2008), pp.5, 6, estimates the number to lie between 27,000 and 35,000.

23 Ian d'Alton, paper given at the Parnell Summer School, 13 August 2014 entitled *Sentiment, Duty, Money, Identity? Motivations for the Southern Protestant Involvement in Two World Wars*.

24 *Census of Ireland*, Vol. X, Chapter 4, p.46. However, the figure of 12 per cent is high as it is arrived at by subtracting ALL people born outside Ireland to get a figure for native Protestants. There were Catholic British soldiers born outside Ireland, Scots in the 26 counties who were Catholics, and American-born Catholics.

25 *Census of Ireland*, Vol. III, table 1b, p.1.

26 Email from Ida Milne to the author on 21 January 2013.

27 Ida Milnes' PhD thesis and subsequent email correspondence give a figure of 14,256 victims of flu in the 26 counties, so perhaps 10 per cent (this being the proportion of Protestants in the 26 counties in the 1911 census) died of flu.

28 Fitzpatrick, 'Protestant depopulation and the Irish Revolution' in *Irish Historical Studies*, November 2013, p.659.

29 Ibid.

30 Thanks to Donald Wood for drawing my attention to this in his
   email of 22 November 2016 when he referred to the Registrar
   General's report, 1926.
31 *The Irish Times*, 7 February 2015.
32 Ibid.
33 R.B. McDowell wrote, 'It is fair to say … that the pressure exercised
   on unionists … partly accounts for the striking fall in the Protestant
   population of the 26 counties between 1919 and 1923.' *Crisis and
   Decline*, p.136. Fitzpatrick quotes McDowell instead as writing
   that the new government's 'direct discriminatory action against
   Protestants' led to 'voluntary' emigration rather than involuntary
   emigration; this would have been after 1923. McDowell cites cases
   from the Irish Grants files in The National Archives at Kew of
   Protestants forced out by intimidation.
34 I am indebted to the independent researcher Don Wood for his
   analysis and questioning of David Fitzpatrick's article, as well as the
   paragraphs above, which he emailed to me. He is currently writing
   about the Protestant decline in numbers.
35 Bowen, *Protestants in a Catholic State*, pp.30–31.
36 Miriam Moffitt, *The Church of Ireland Community*, p.54.
37 Ibid.
38 Ibid.
39 Andrew Bielenberg, 'Exodus: The Emigration of Southern
   Protestants During the Irish War of Independence', *Past and Present*,
   218, p.218.
40 Ibid., p.219.
41 Sexton and O'Leary, *Building Trust in Ireland*, p.301.
42 Enda Delaney, *Demography, State and Society*, p.72.
43 Ibid., p.73.
44 B.M. Walker, *Irish History Matters: Politics, Identities and Commemoration*
   (Stroud, 2019), pp. 191–222.
45 Bielenberg estimated the number of 'involuntary Protestant
   emigrants was 2,000 to 16,000', see 'Exodus: The Emigration of
   Southern Irish Protestants During the Irish War of Independence
   and the Civil War' in *Oxford Journals Past and Present*, 218:1
   (February 2013), pp. 199–233.
46 Email from Don Wood to author, 10 November 2015.
47 *Census of Ireland 1926*, Vol. III, pp.8–9.
48 *The Irish Times*, 6 July 1923. This letter is one of a number in
   the letters pages of *The Irish Times* concerning the departure
   of Protestants. The debate was continued in The Cedar House
   Lounge Revolution website at http://cedarlounge.wordpress.

com/2009/10/29/corks-bloody-secret-a-small-dispute/

49 W.E. Vaughan and A.J. Fitzpatrick (eds), *Irish historical statistics: Population 1821–1971* (Dublin, 1978), pp. 67–71.

50 Ibid.

51 Bielenberg, *Exodus*, p.207.

52 Ibid., p.227.

53 Ibid.

54 David Fitzpatrick, *Politics and Irish life 1913–1921* (Cork, 1998), p.40.

55 R.B. McDowell, *Crisis and Decline* (Dublin, 1997), p. 10.

56 *The Irish Times*, 15 February 1929.

57 Fergus Campbell, *The Irish Establishment 1879–1914* (Oxford, 2009), p.299.

58 Ibid.

59 Hart, *The IRA at War*, p.3.

60 Lloyd George to Law, 12 Jan 1918, B.L., 82/8/4. House of Lords Record Office (Parliamentary Archives).

61 Peter Hart, *The IRA and its Enemies* (Oxford, 1998), pp.273–292.

62 Ibid., p.290.

63 Sexton and O'Leary, 'Factors Affecting Population Decline in Minority Religious Communities in the Republic of Ireland', p.263.

64 Diarmaid Ferriter, *The Transformation of Ireland* (New York, 2005), p.229.

65 *Church of Ireland Gazette*, 7 September 1921.

66 J.B. Leslie (ed.), *The Irish Church Directory and Year-Book for 1920* (Dublin, 1920); J.B. Leslie (ed.), *The Irish Church Directory and Year-Book for 1930* (Dublin, 1930)

67 McDowell, *Crisis and Decline*, p.135.

68 Marcus Tanner, *Ireland's Holy Wars* (London, 2003), p.312.

69 Richard English, *Irish Freedom* (London, 2006), p.296.

70 Dooley, *The Decline of the Big House in Ireland* (Dublin 2001), p.106.

71 Ibid., p.111.

72 Ibid., p.106.

73 Elliott, *When God Took Sides*, p.217.

74 *The Irish Times*, 10 May 1922.

75 McDowell, *Crisis and Decline*, p.132.

76 *Morning Post,* 26 January 1924.

77 R.B. McDowell, *Crisis and Decline*, p.139.

78 Dooley, *The Decline of the Big House in Ireland*, p.201.

79 Ibid., p.142.

80 Ibid., p.202.

81 Ibid., p.202.

82 R. Dudley to Lord Dunalley, 27 May 1923 (NLI, Dunalley papers, 29,810 (19).

83 McDowell, *Crisis and Decline*, p.148.

84 Dooley, *The Decline of the Big House*, p.205.

85 McDowell, *Crisis and Decline*, p.140.

86 Ibid., p.140.

87 *Freeman's Journal*, 17 July 1924.

88 Letter from Wood-Renton to Cosgrave, 27 February 1926. F 19/2/26, NA Dublin.

89 F 19/2/26, NA Dublin.

90 Ibid.

91 Ibid.

92 *Morning Post*, 18 June 1925.

93 Ibid., pp.91–92.

94 Mr David Griffin of the Irish Architectural Archives (IAA) in Dublin advised me that he has been in touch with TNA in London, which believes that it may have copies of the Shaw-Renton Commission reports. The *Shaw Scrapbook* in the IAA contains some details of awards published in various editions of *Iris Oifigiul*. Fuller details are available in the National Library of Ireland.

95 David Fitzpatrick, *Terror in Ireland 1916–1923* (Dublin, 2012). See No.6 – David Fitzpatrick, *The Price of Balbriggan*.

96 N. Brennan, 'Southern Loyalists and the Irish Grants Committee, 1921–31' in *Irish Historical Studies*, xxx, No. 119 (May 1997), p.407.

97 Ibid., p.150.

98 Ibid., p.151.

99 Brennan, *A Political Minefield*, p.414.

100 McDowell, *Crisis and Decline*, p.160.

101 Brennan, *A Political Minefield*, p.415.

102 McDowell, *Crisis and Decline*, p.160.

103 Brennan, *A Political Minefield*, p.417.

CHAPTER 2

1 Augustjein, Joost (ed.), *The Irish Revolution 1913–23* (Palgrave, 2002), Historiography p.11.

2 Peter Hart, *The IRA and its Enemies*, p.308.

3 Tom Wall, 'Getting Them Out, Southern Loyalists in the War of Independence' (drb, Issue 9, Spring 2009) www.drb.ie/essays/getting-them-out – See more at: www.drb.ie/essays/a-house-built-on-sand#sthash.G53VpqEj.dpuf

4 Buckland, *Irish Unionism*, p.204.

5 TNA CO 762, 37, de Burgh.

6 Letter sent to me by Susan de Burgh in Vancouver.

7   CO 762, 37, de Burgh.

8   Email from Susan de Burgh, 9 October, 2007.

9   CO 762, 37, de Burgh.

10 Email from Susan de Burgh, 9 October, 2007.

11 Buckland, *Irish Unionism*, p.202. Buckland gives many other examples of outrages committed against Protestants in pp.202–203.

12 Ibid., p.202.

13 Ibid., p.203.

14 Ibid., p.204.

15 PRONI 989A/8/23

16 Buckland, *Irish Unionism*, p.206.

17 Delaney, *Demography, State and Society*, p.73.

18 Hart, *The IRA and its Enemies*, p.304.

19 Ibid., pp. 313–314. Hart lists 15 cases in the reports of the IGC TNA CO 762. I found further cases of Protestants who had nervous breakdowns in IGC reports from Co. Tipperary claimants. The majority were women.

20 James S. Donnelly Jr, *Big House Burnings in County Cork during the Irish Revolution, 1920–21*. In Éire–Ireland 47: 3&4 Fall/Win 12.

21 *Cork Examiner*, 2 June 2001.

22 Donnelly, *Big House Burnings*, p.178.

23 Tom Barry, *Guerrilla Days*, p.14.

24 Ibid., p.214.

25 David Leeson, *The Black and Tans: British Police and Auxiliaries in the Irish War of Independence, 1920–1921* (Oxford University Press, 2011).

26 Buckland, *Irish Unionism*, p.214.

27 James Donnelly, *Big House Burnings* in Éire-Ireland 47: 3&4 Fall/Win 12 p.182.

28 James S. Donnelly Jr, *The House Burnings in County Cork during the Irish Revolution, 1920–21* Éire-Ireland 47:3 & 4 Fall/Win 12 p. 182.

29 TNA CO 904/196

30 Hart, *Unionism in Modern Ireland*, p.92.

31 Lionel Fleming, *Head or Harp* (London, 1965).

32 Ibid., pp.67–68.

33 TNA CO 762 32, Good.

34 Ibid.

35 Hart, *The IRA and its Enemies*, pp.273–292.

36 Éire-Ireland, Volume 49, Issues 3 & 4, Fall/Winter 2014, pp.7–59 (Article)

37 Hart, *The IRA and its Enemies*, p.292.

38 Charles Townshend, *The Republic* (London, 2013), p.371.

39 Ibid., p.375.

40 Cork Constitution of 13 May 1922.

41 Townshend, *The Republic*, p.371.

42 *Éire-Ireland* 49: 3 & 4 Fall/Win 14. P. 53.

43 *The Times*, 13 May 1922.

44 John M. Regan, *History Ireland*, January/February 2012, p.13.

45 Éire-Ireland 49: 3 & 4 Fall/Win 14. p.42.

46 http://year-of-disappearances.blogspot.ie/search?updated-max=2014-11-26T10:01:00-08:00&max-results=7&reverse-paginate=true

47 Ibid.

48 Eric Hobsbawm, *On History* (London, 2013), p.187.

49 Niall Meehan, *Troubled History: A 10th Anniversary Critique of Peter Hart's 'The IRA and its Enemies'* (Aubane Historical Society 2008), p.12.

50 See appendix for names of targeted men.

51 See appendix for list of names and details.

52 Letter from Doris Matthews to the author, 19 July 2009.

53 Éire-Ireland 49: 3 & 4 Fall/Win 14. p.39.

54 Ibid., p.40.

55 Hart, *The IRA and its Enemies*, p.283.

56 *The Irish Times*, 10 November 1994.

57 Letter to *The Irish Times*, 10 November 1994

58 Collins, *Jasper Wolfe of Skibbereen*.

59 Marcus Tanner, *Ireland's Holy War*, p.292.

60 *The Irish Times*, 17 February 1923.

61 *Poblacht na h-Éireann*, 4 May 1922.

62 Augustjein, Joost (ed.), *The Irish Revolution 1913–23* (Palgrave, 2002), Historiography, p.160.

63 *Church of Ireland Gazette*, 17 June 1921.

64 *The Irish Times*, 9 October 1922.

65 Ibid.

66 Ibid., 6 November 1922.

67 Ibid., 10 May 1922.

68 George Seaver, *John Allen FitzGerald Gregg: Archbishop* (London, 1963), p.121.

69 Michael Hopkinson, *Green against Green: The Irish Civil War* (Dublin, 2004), p.60.

70 *The Irish Times*, 6 November 1922.

71 A search was carried out online of the archives of the Nenagh Guardian and *The Irish Times*, to no avail.

72 TNA CO 762/37/8, Revd Henry, Newport.

73 Ibid.

74 Ibid.

75 Ibid.
76 Ibid.
77 Ibid.
78 Ibid.
79 Ibid.
80 Crockfords Clerical Directory 1937.
81 TNA CO 762/19/1, Sanders, Glen of Aherlow.
82 Michael Lynch, *Below Aherlow* (Waterford, 2002), p.97.
83 *Cork Examiner*, 29 July 1924.
84 TNA CO 762/19/1, Sanders, Ballinacourtie.
85 Ibid.
86 Ibid.
87 TNA CO 762/18/8. Neville-Clarke, Thurles.
88 Ibid.
89 Ibid.
90 Ibid.
91 Ibid.
92 *Tipperary Star*, 3 March 1923.
93 *IT,* 6 July 1923.
94 TNA CO 762/162/1, Sweetnam, Clonmel.
95 Ibid.
96 *Nenagh Guardian*, 23 April 1921.
97 *Tipperary Star,* 23 April 1921.
98 *Cork Weekly News*, 25 June 1921.
99 *Nenagh Guardian*, 25 June 1921.
100 TNA CO 762/111/8, Conlough, Clogheen.
101 *Census of Ireland 1926,* Vol. III, p.28.
102 *General Report on the Census of Ireland 1911*, p.125.
103 ibid., p.106.
104 See my MPhil dissertation, Trinity College, Dublin, September 2012 for a detailed examination of the intimidation of Protestants in Co. Tipperary 1920–23. Available from the author.
105 *Census of Ireland 1926,* Vol. III, p.11.
106 *Nenagh News and Tipperary Vindicator*, 15 April 1922.
107 Peter Hart, *The IRA at War*, p.237.
108 Telephone conversation with Declan Mullen on 3 August 2012.
109 *Nenagh Guardian*, 10 May 1924.
110 Dunalley papers, Doupe to Lord Dunalley, 14 August 1922. (NLI, Dunalley papers, MS 29, 810 (17)). The reference to 'the refugee system' is the Irish Distress Committee in London.
111 Ibid.
112 TNA, CO 762/39/10, Otway-Ruthven, Nenagh.

113 *Nenagh Guardian*, 19 July 1924.

114 TNA, CO 762/39/10, Otway-Ruthven, Nenagh.

115 Miriam Lambe, *A Tipperary Landed Estate: Castle Otway 1750–1853* (Dublin, 1998), p.55.

116 Gemma Clark, *Fire, Boycott, Threat and Harm*, unpublished doctorate, Queen's College, Oxford 2010, p.139. It has recently been published as *Everyday Violence in the Irish Civil War* (Cambridge University Press, 2014).

117 TNA CO 762/57/4, Burkett, Nenagh.

118 Ibid.

119 Ibid.

120 TNA CO 762/57/4, Burkett, Nenagh.

121 Ibid.

122 Ibid.

123 *General Report on the Census of Ireland 1911*, table xxix, p.148.

124 *General Report on the Census of Ireland 1926*, table 7, p.8.

125 Interview with Adrian Hewson in Roscrea on 18 July 2012. Hewson is a Church of Ireland teacher and history graduate of Trinity College, Dublin.

126 TNA CO 762/99/3, Vaughan, Roscrea.

127 TNA CO 762/137/6, McKenna, Roscrea.

128 Ibid.

129 Ibid.

130 Ibid.

131 *General Report on the Census of Ireland 1911*, p.148, and *General Report on the Census of Ireland 1926*, p.9, table 7.

132 Dudley Levistone Cooney, *So Civil a People* (Tullamore, undated), p.16.

133 Reports of the Diocesan Boards of Education of Diocesan Council of Cashel and Emly 1915–16 and 1924–5 in RCB library, Dublin.

134 Ibid., 1924–5 report.

135 *Census of Ireland 1911*, Vol. 3, p.28 and *Census of Ireland 1926*, table 8A, p.10, and xxix, p.149.

136 *Census of Ireland 1911*, table xx, p.106.

137 *Census of Ireland 1911*, Vol. 3, p.94, dependents in Military barracks, Co. Tipperary.

138 Tom Garvin, 'Peter Hart: The IRA and Its Enemies', in *The Irish Review*, xxii (1998), p.176.

139 Ibid.

140 McDowell, *Crisis and Decline*, p.99.

141 TNA CO 762, 71 Bury

142 Denis Kennedy, *The Widening Gulf*, p.118.

143 *Church of Ireland Gazette*, 16 June 1922.

144 *The Witness*, 16 June 1920.

145 CO 762,71.

146 CO 762,37.

147 CO 762, 71.

148 CO 762, 37, Stone.

149 CO 762, 37.

150 Ibid.

151 CO 762, 37.

152 CO 762, 193.

153 CO 762 58.

154 CO 762, 94.

155 Tanner, *Ireland's Holy Wars*, p.293 and *Church of Ireland Gazette*, 13 October 1922, p.630.

156 *The Irish Times*, 8 May 1923.

157 Tanner, *Ireland's Holy Wars*, p.313.

158 Ibid.

159 F.S.L. Lyons, *Culture and Anarchy in Ireland 1890–1939* (Clarendon Press, 1979), p.163.

160 Ibid., p.315.

161 Fitzpatrick, *Politics and Irish Life 1913–1921*.

162 Delaney, *Demography, State and Society*, p.73.

163 Miriam Moffitt, *The Church of Ireland Community of Killaloe and Achonry 1870–1940* (Dublin, 1999), pp.9–10.

164 'A Short History of the United Empire Loyalists', https://www.uelac.org/PDF/loyalist.pdf.

165 Michael de Nie, Sean Farrell (eds), 'The Protestant and Catholic Communities of Tipperary since 1660' in Kennedy, Liam, *Power and Popular Culture in Modern Ireland* (Dublin, 2010), p.89.

166 Bowen, *Protestants in a Catholic State*, p.58.

167 Patrick Buckland, *Irish Unionism*, p.285.

CHAPTER 3

1 Dooley, *The Decline of the Big House*.

2 Richard English, *Irish Freedom* (London, 2006), p.51.

3 Ibid., p.51.

4 Ibid., p.53.

5 Ibid., p.54.

6 James Lydon, *The Making of Ireland* (London,1998).

7 *Irish Independent*, 16 August 2003.

8 Dooley, p.191.

9   Mark Bence-Jones, *A Guide to Irish County Houses* (London, 1988), p.268.
10 Dooley, p.191.
11 Iris Oifiguil, 1923, pp.1 and 101, National Library of Ireland.
12 Dooley, p.256.
13 CO 762/193, TNA.
14 CO 762, 71, TNA.
15 Ibid.
16 Email from Gregory McReynolds, 4 June 2009.
17 CO 762, 3
18 Dooley, p.189.
19 Fleming, Head and Hart, p. 92.
20 Albert Thomas, *Wait and See* (London, 1944).
21 Ibid.
22 Albert Thomas, Wait and See, p. 89.
23 Ibid., p. 90.
24 Elizabeth Burke-Plunkett, *Seventy Years Young, Memories of Elizabeth, Countess of Fingall* (Dublin, 1991).
25 Tarquin Blake, *Abandoned Mansions of Ireland* (Cork, 2010).

CHAPTER 4

1   Richard Tillinghast, *Finding Ireland* (Notre Dame, 2008), pp.42–43.
2   Mark Finnane in *Irish Historical Studies* (November 2001), p.519.
3   Kurt Bowen, *Protestants in a Catholic State* (Kingston and Montreal), pp.156–157.
4   Brian Walker, *A Political History of the Two Irelands: From Partition to Peace* (New York, 2012), p.76.
5   Ibid.
6   Ibid.
7   Reg Hindley, *The Death of the Irish Language* (London and New York, 1990), p.15.
8   Hindley, p.12.
9   Ibid., p.13.
10 Tom Garvin, *Nationalist Revolutionaries in Ireland* (Dublin, 1987), p.79.
11 Roy Foster, *Modern Ireland* (London, 1988), p.518.
12 Jack White, *Minority Report: The Protestant Community in the Irish Republic* (Dublin, 1975), p.188.
13 Hindley, p.211.
14 Ibid., p.218.
15 Ibid., p.211.

16 Tom Garvin, *Nationalist Revolutionaries in Ireland* (Dublin, 1987), p.86.

17 Ibid., p.99.

18 Ernest Blythe, 'The Significance of the Irish Language for the Future of the Nation', p.24.

19 Ibid.

20 Hindley, p.208.

21 Bowen, *Protestants in a Catholic State*, p.169.

22 E.Cullingford, *Yeats, Ireland and Fascism* (London, 1981). Speech by de Valera in New York.

23 Clair Wills, *That Neutral Island* (London, 2007), p.26.

24 Ibid., p.28.

25 Ibid., p.24.

26 Lord Midleton, *Ireland – Dupe or Heroine* (London, 1932), p.114.

27 Wills, p.312.

28 Stephen Howe, *Ireland and Empire* (Oxford, 2000), p.34.

29 Hubert Butler, *Grandmother and Wolfe Tone* (Dublin, 1990), p.138.

30 Walker, p.60.

31 George Moore, *Hail and Farewell* (1976), p.587.

32 R.B. McDowell, *Crisis and Decline* (Dublin, 1997), preface.

33 National Archives of Ireland, jus/2008/117.

34 Ibid.

35 Ibid., 2008/117/557.

36 Ibid., Report 5 March 1935.

37 Ibid.

38 Ibid

39 Ibid.

40 Ibid., Report of Superintendent Muldoon.

41 Ibid.

42 Ibid.

43 Dennis Kennedy, *The Widening Gulf* (Belfast, 1988), p.172.

44 Ibid., p.173.

45 Brian Walker, p.66.

46 Henry Patterson, *Ireland Since 1939* (Dublin, 2006), p.104.

47 Elliott, *When God Took Sides*, p.227.

48 Ibid., p.229.

49 Walker, p.75.

50 Ibid., pp.75–76.

51 W.B. Stanford in *Faith and Faction in Ireland Now* (Dublin APCK), p.7.

52 Ibid., p.21.

53 F.S.L. Lyons, *Ireland Since the Famine* (London, 1985), p.742.

54 *Sunday Independent*, 23 November 2014.

55 Ibid.

56 Ibid.

57 Ibid.

58 *Sunday Independent*, John-Paul McCarthy, 23 November 2014.

59 Richard Davis, *Arthur Griffith* (Dundalgan Press, 1976), p.xxxi

60 Lord Hailsham, *A Sparrow's Flight* (London, 1990), p.229

CHAPTER 5

 1 Walker, p.134.

 2 Don Akenson, *An Irish History of Civilisation* (London, 2006) Vol. 2., p.395.

 3 Letter from Dr Jameson in *The Irish Times*, 13 January 2014.

 4 Ibid., p.15.

 5 Ibid., p.16.

 6 Ibid., p.16.

 7 'Trends in the Religious Composition of the Population in the Republic of Ireland 1946–71', Economic and Social Research Institute, Dublin and Population Studies, 49, (1995), 259–279.

 8 Richard O'Leary in *The Economic and Social Review*, Vol. 30, April 1999, p.126.

 9 Kenneth Milne, *The Laity and the Church of Ireland, 1000–2000* (Dublin, 2002) p.227.

10 V. Griffin, *Mark of Protest* (Dublin,1993), p.30.

11 A. Clifford, *The Constitutional History of Eire/Ireland* (Belfast,1987), p.310.

12 Arthur Aughey, *Building Trust in Ireland*, p.22.

13 *Church of Ireland Gazette*, 2 April 2010.

14 *The Irish Times*, 30 June 1957.

15 Hubert Butler, *Escape from the Anthill* (Dublin, 1986).

16 Interview, 18 July 2007, Henley-on-Thames, England.

17 Letter to *The Irish Times*, 11 June 1957.

18 Letter to *The Irish Times*, 12 June 1957.

19 Letter to *The Irish Times* from Canon Lindsay of St Bartholemew's, Belfast, 11 June.

20 *The Protestant*, July/September 1957.

21 *Belfast Telegraph*, 26 June 1957.

22 *Irish Press*, 12 June.

23 Adrian Fisher's notebook, Archive P 164/32, UCD Archive library.

24 Marcus Tanner, *Ireland's Holy Wars* (Connecticut, 2003), p.340.

25 *Belfast Telegraph*, 1 June 1998.

CHAPTER 6

1 Walker, p.103.
2 The Reform Group attempted to persuade the Foreign and Commonwealth Office (FCO) to allow those adults in the South who wanted British passports – not being entitled to them – to be given them. A legal opinion was sought, but failed to be considered positively.
3 *The Irish Times*, 27 November 2008.
4 Walker, p.198.
5 F.S.L. Lyons, *Ireland Since the Famine*, p.359.
6 Walker, p.198.

CHAPTER 8

1 Church of Ireland Sub Committee Report, April 1999, p.4.
2 Ibid., p.5.
3 Ibid., p.22.
4 Ibid., p.27.
5 Ibid., p.17.
6 Ibid., p.5.
7 Ibid., p.7.
8 Ibid., p.20.
9 Aughey, pp. 21 and 24.
10 *Irish Studies Review*, Vol. II, No.1, 2003.
11 Garret FitzGerald, 'Ireland's Identity Problems,' *Etudes Irelandaises*, Vol. 1 (December, 1976) pp. 141 and 142.
12 'Pluralism, Partition and the Controversy Generated by a Proposed Orange Parade in Dublin', *Irish Studies Review*, Vol. II, No. 1, 2003.
13 *Irish Studies Review*, Interview 23 August 2000.

EPILOGUE

1 Arthur Griffith, the leader of Sinn Féin, believed that there were undiscovered coal resources that, once mined, would lead to prosperity for an independent Ireland. Such resources have not been found over 90 years after independence.
2 Tom Garvin, *Preventing the Future* (Dublin, 2004) p. 133 and 136.
3 Ibid., p. 153.
4 C.S.O. Statistics 2014 Quarter 4. www.cso.ie/en/statistics/labourmarket/
5 R.V. Comerford, *Inventing the Nation: Ireland* (London, 2003), p.117.
6 Ibid., p.114.

7 Ibid., p.117.

8 Ibid., p.114.

9 Ian d'Alton paper to the Irish Historical Society.

10 H.K. Crawford, *Outside the Glow: Protestants and Irishness in Independent Ireland in the Twentieth Century* (Dublin, 2010).

11 Ruane, Joseph and David Butler, 'Southern Irish Protestants: An Example of De-Ethnicisation?', *Nations and Nationalism*, 13 (4) (2007), pp 619–35.

12 Bunreacht na hÉireann, Constitution of Ireland, Preamble, p.2.

13 Ibid.

14 Ibid., p.131.

15 Enda Longley, 'The separation of political Irishness and culture in Ireland', *Irish Times*, 9 August 1989.

16 B. Hayes & T. Fahey, 'Protestants and Politics in the Republic of Ireland: Is Integration Complete? In M. Busteed, F. Neal & J. Tonge, *Irish Protestant Identities* (Manchester, 2008), p.82.

17 Kurt Bowen, *Protestants in a Catholic State* (Kingston, Canada, 1983), p.116.

18 *Irish Independent*, 11 October 2012.

19 http://motherandbabyhome.com/

20 Joseph Ruane, *Ethnopolitics*, Vol.9, No.1 (March 2010), p. 130.

21 Markus Tanner, *Ireland's Holy Wars*, p.418.

22 *Church of Ireland Gazette*, 2 June 1972.

23 Ibid.

24 Ibid.

25 Edna Longley, *Untold Stories* (Dublin, 2002), p.111.

26 Ibid.

27 Victor Griffin, *Enough Religion to Make us Hate* (Dublin 2002), p.2.

28 Tanner, *Ireland's Holy Wars*, p.421.

29 Vaughan and Fitzpatrick (eds), *Irish Historical Statistics: Population 1821–1971* (Dublin, 1978), pp.49, 66–68; COI 2011 website: www.cso.ie/multiquicktables/quickTables.aspx?id=cd702 Note these figures represent Church of Ireland, Presbyterians and Methodists in 1911 and 2011.

30 When the author spoke to the lady Church of Ireland priest in the parish of Fethard-on-Sea some years ago, she offered the opinion that when you take into consideration the boycott of Protestants there (see Chapter 5) 'it is surprising we survived'.

31 Stephen Howe, *Ireland and Empire* (Oxford, 2000), p.82.

32 Ibid.

33 Ibid., p.83.

34 Ibid.

35 Ibid.,p.85.
36 Ibid., p.84.
37 Email to the author of 24 May 2016.
38 *The Irish Times*, 12 November 1998.
39 Walker, *A Political History of the Two Irelands*, p.194.
40 Howe, *Ireland and Empire* (Oxford, 2000).
41 While President, Mary McAleese held an annual reception for Orangemen, north and south, at Áras an Uachtaráin in her efforts to 'build bridges'. It was at one such reception that the President informed the author that she opposed Commonwealth membership.
42 Stephen Howe in *Ireland and Empire* argues that 'An implicit or explicit belief in Irish exceptionalism seems widespread even among the scholars most critical of nationalism', p.84.
43 Francis Flanagan, *Remembering the Revolution* (Oxford University Press, 2015), p.1.
44 Ibid., p. 2.
45 Ibid.,
46 Ware Bradley Wells, *An Irish Apologia: Some Thoughts on Anglo-Irish Relations and the War* (Dublin,1917) cited in *Remembering the Revolution*, p.70.
47 Church of Ireland library archive http://library.ireland.anglican.org/index.php?id=128
48 Ibid
49 Ibid
50 *The Irish Times*, 9 April 2015.
51 Flanagan, *Remembering the Revolution*, p.128.
52 Ibid. p.122.
53 Ibid.
54 Ibid. p.155.
55 See Joe Duffy's book *The Children of 1916*, which was a bestseller at Christmas 2015.
56 *The Irish Times*, 26 May 2016
57 Ibid., 27 May 2016.
58 *The Sunday Times*, 5 June 2016.
59 *The Irish Times*, 9 February 2016.
60 Ibid.
61 *The Irish Catholic*, 21 January 2016.
62 *The Irish Times*, 2 March 2016
63 *Church of Ireland Gazette*, 11 March 2016.
64 *The Irish Times*, 16 February 2016.
65 Ibid.
66 Telephone interview with the author on Wednesday, 13 April 2016.

67 Email to author 1 April 2016. The Pillar was Nelson's Pillar in the middle of O'Connell Street, Dublin. It was blown up by a splinter group of the IRA on 8 March 1966 (the IRA disowned the act stating they were interested in ending imperialism, not its symbols). The then Taoiseach, Sean Lemass, did not condemn the act.

68 See the Proclamation.

69 *The Irish Times*, 20 May 2016.

70 Ibid.

71 Francis Flanagan, *Remembering the Revolution* (Oxford University Press, 2015), p.2.

72 Those supporting the Rising were Eamon O'Cuiv, the grandson of Eamon de Valera, Professor Ronan Fanning of UCD and Michael McDowell, grandson of Eoin MacNeill, the Chief of Staff of the Irish Volunteers and those opposing were Ruth Dudley-Edwards whose book The Seven had just been published, journalists Kevin Myers and Patsy McGarry.

73 Ruth Dudley Edwards, *Prospect*, May 2016.

74 Seamus Murphy SJ, *Studies*, Spring, 2016.

75 *The Irish Times*, 26 March 2016.

76 *The Dorchester Review*.

77 Ibid.

78 *The Times Literary Supplement*, p.15, 22 April 2016.

79 Ruth Dudley Edwards, *Prospect*, May 2016.

80 *Sunday Independent*, 8 May 2016.

81 *Sunday Times*, 29 May 2016.

82 Hubert Butler as quoted in *The Irish Times*, Arts and Books Review, 14 March 2015, p.11.

83 Conor Brady, *The Sunday Times*, 2 August 2015.

84 R.V. Comerford, *Inventing the Nation: Ireland* (London, 2003), p.117.

Bibliography

1. ARCHIVAL SOURCES

National Archives of Ireland, Dublin (NAI)

Records of the Department of Justice.
Records of the Department of the Taoiseach.
Records of the Ministry of Finance.
Returns of the Census of Ireland (1911), http://www.census.nation-alarchives.ie/ (online database).

National Library of Ireland (NLI)

Dunalley Papers of the Prittie family, Lords Dunalley, 1665–1937.
Correspondence re strike by labourers on the estate of Robert Sanders of Ballinacourty, Co. Tipperary [1920].
Haicead, Patrick, In bloody protest (Nenagh, 1996).
Iris Oifigiúil (The Dublin Gazette) Criminal Injuries decrees under Criminal and Malicious Injuries (Ireland) Acts, 1922–1923.

Public Record Office of Northern Ireland (PRONI)

Papers of the Southern Irish Loyalist Relief Association.

The National Archives, Kew (TNA)

Records of the Colonial Office, Records of the Irish Office.
CO 762: Irish Grants Committee: Files and Minutes.
PRO 30/67: First Earl Midleton papers.

Parliamentary Archives

Houses of Parliament, London SW1A OPW. Command no. 8279. The Royal Commission on the Rebellion in Ireland. Report of Commission.

The Central Statistics Office, Dublin

Returns of the Census of Ireland (1926).

The Architectural Archive, Dublin

Scrapbook on the work of the Shaw Commission on compensation, February 1922 to September 1925.

2. PRINTED PRIMARY SOURCES

Books and Pamphlets

Barry, Tom, *Guerilla Days in Ireland* (Naas, 1978, 6th impression).
Bowen, Elizabeth, *The Last September* (London, 1929).
Hughes, Olivia, *Fethard and its Churches* (Conmore Press, undated) Privately published by Robert McCarthy, Dean of St Patrick's Cathedral, Dublin.

Newspapers

National Library of Ireland, Dublin
Clonmel Chronicle.
Cork Examiner.
Evening Telegraph.
Freeman's Journal.
Nenagh Guardian.
The Witness.

Online Digital Archives

The Irish Times.

Representative Church Body Library

Church of Ireland Gazette.
Preachers's books from Nenagh, Thurles, Newport parishes.
Crockford's Clerical Directory 1936.
Crockford's Clerical Directory 1937.

The Irish Church Directory and Year-Book for 1920 (Dublin, 1920) and *The Irish Church Directory and Year-Book for 1930* (Dublin, 1930) J.B. Leslie (ed.).

Registers of Documents Sealed.

Parliamentary Records

Dáil Éireann Debates, Office of the Houses of the Oireachtas, Leinster House, Dublin (http://historical-debates.oireachtas.ie) (14 July 2012).

Hansard (Houses of Parliament Debate), Hansard 1803–2005, Hansard Digitisation.

Project, Hansard Millbank Systems (http://hansard.millbanksystems. com) (16 July 2012).

3. PRINTED SECONDARY SOURCES

Books and Articles

Abbott, Richard, *Police Casualties in Ireland 1919–1922* (Dublin, 2000).

Akenson, Donald Harman, *Small Differences. Irish Catholics and Irish Protestants, 1815–1922: An International Perspective* (Dublin, 1991).

Akenson, Donald Harman, *An Irish History of Civilisation* Vol. 2 (London, 2006).

Ambrose, Joe, *Seán Treacy and the Tan War* (Cork, c2007).

Augusteijn, Joost, 'Irish Civil War', in S.J. Connolly, *The Oxford Companion to Irish History* (Oxford, 2007), 277.

Augusteijn, Joost (ed.), *The Irish Revolution, 1913–1923* (Basingstoke, 2002).

Augusteijn, Joost, *From Public Defiance to Guerrilla Warfare: The Experience of Ordinary Volunteers in the Irish War of Independence, 1916–1921* (Dublin, 1996).

Barry, Tom, *Guerilla Days in Ireland* 2nd edition (Merica Press, 2013).

Bartlett, Thomas, *Ireland: A History* (Cambridge, 2010).

Bence-Jones, Mark, *Burke's Guide to Country Houses, vol. 1: Ireland* (London, 1978).

Bew, Paul, *Ireland: The Politics of Enmity, 1789–2006* (Oxford, 2007).

Bew, Paul and Henry Paterson, *Sean Lemass and the Making of Modern Ireland* (Dublin, 1982).

Bielenberg, Andrew, *Exodus: The Emigration of Southern Irish Protestants during the War of Independence and the Civil War, Past and Present.*

Bielenberg, Andrew, *The Irish Diaspora* (Essex: Pearson Education, 2000).

Blake, Tarquin, *Abandoned Mansions of Ireland* (Cork, 2010).

Borgonovo, J., Spies, *Informers and the 'Anti-Sinn Fein Society', the Intelligence War in Cork City 1920–1921* (Dublin, 2007).

Bowen, Kurt *Protestants in a Catholic State: Ireland's Privileged Minority* (Dublin, 1983).

Boyce, D.G., *Nationalism in Ireland* (London, 1980).

Brennan, Niamh, 'A Political Minefield: Southern Loyalists, the Irish Grants Committee and the British Government, 1922–31', in *Irish Historical Studies*, xxx, no. 119 (May 1997), pp. 406–19.

Buckland, Patrick, *Irish Unionism I: the Anglo-Irish and the New Ireland, 1885–1922* (London, 1973).

Burke-Plunkett, Elizabeth, *Seventy Years Young, Memories of Elizabeth, Countess of Fingall* (Dublin, 1991).

Butler, David J., *South Tipperary, 1570–1841: Religion, Land and Rivalry* (Dublin, 2006).

Butler, David and Joseph Ruane, *Identity, Difference and Community in southern Irish Protestantism: The Protestants of West Cork. National Identities* 11(1) (2009), pp. 73–86.

Butler, Hubert, *Grandmother and Wolfe Tone* (Dublin, 1990).

Campbell, Fergus, *The Irish Establishment 1879–1914* (Oxford, 2009).

Clark, Gemma, *Everyday Violence in the Irish Civil War* (Cambridge, 2014).

Coffey, Leigh-Ann, *The Planters of Luggacurran, County Laois: A Protestant Community, 1879–1927* (Dublin, 2006).

Comerford, R.V. , *Inventing the Nation: Ireland* (London, 2003).

Cooney, Dudley Levistone, *So Civil a People: A Story of Methodists in the Irish Midlands* (Tullamore, undated).

Crawford, Heather K., *Outside the Glow: Protestants and Irishness in independent Ireland* (Dublin, 2010).

Davis, Richard, *Arthur Griffith* (Dundalgan Press, 1976).

Delaney, Enda, *Demography, State and Society: Irish Migration to Britain, 1921–1971* (Liverpool, 2000).

Donnelly, James S. Jr, 'Big House Burnings in County Cork during the Irish Revolution, 1920–21' in *Eire–Ireland* 47: 3&4 Fall/Win 12.

Dooley, Terence A.M., *The Decline of the Big House in Ireland: A Study of Irish Landed Families, 1860–1960* (Dublin, 2001).

Dooley, Terence A.M., 'IRA Veterans and Land Division in Independent Ireland 1923–48', in Fearghal McGarry (ed.), *Republicanism in Modern Ireland* (Dublin, 2003), pp. 86–107.

Dooley, Terence A.M., *'The Land for the People': The Land Question in Independent Ireland* (Dublin, 2004).

Dooley, Terence A.M., *The Plight of the Monaghan Protestants, 1912–1926* (Dublin, 2000).

Dooley, Terence A.M., 'Land and Politics in Independent Ireland, 1923– 48: The Case for Reappraisal' in *Irish Historical Studies*, xxxiv, no. 134 (Nov., 2004).

Dudley-Edwards, Ruth, *Patrick Pearse: The Triumph of Failure* (London, 1977).

Dudley-Edwards, Ruth, *The Seven* (London, 2016).

Elliott, Marianne, *When God Took Sides* (Oxford, 2009).

English, Richard, *Irish Freedom: The History of Nationalism in Ireland* (London, 2006).

Fanning, Ronan, *The Irish Department of Finance, 1922–58* (Dublin, 1978).

Fanning, Tim, *The Fethard-on-Sea Boycott* (Cork, 2010).

Fedorowich, Kent, 'Reconstruction and Resettlement: The Politicization of Irish Migration to Australia and Canada, 1919–29' in *English Historical Review*, November 1999.

Ferriter, Diarmaid, *The Transformation of Ireland* (New York, 2005).

Fitzpatrick, David, 'The Geography of Irish Nationalism 1910–1921', in *Past and Present*, no. 78 (Feb. 1978), pp. 113–144.

Fitzpatrick, David, *Politics and Irish Life, 1913–1921: Provincial Experience of War and Revolution* (Dublin, 1977).

Fitzpatrick, David (ed.), *Terror in Ireland 1916–1923* (Lilliput Press, 2012).

Fitzpatrick, David, *The Two Irelands 1912–1939* (Oxford, 1998).

Fitzpatrick, 'Protestant Depopulation and the Irish Revolution' in *Irish Historical Studies*, November 2013, p.659.

Flanagan, Francis, *Remembering the Revolution* (Oxford University Press, 2015).

Fleming, Lionel, *Head or Harp* (London, 1965).

Foster, R.F., *Modern Ireland 1600–1972* (London, 1988).

Foster, R.F. 'Something to hate' in *Irish Review* (2003).

Foster, R.F., *Luck and the Irish* (London, 2008).

Garvin, Tom, *Nationalist Revolutionaries in Ireland* (Dublin, 1987).

Garvin, Tom, *Preventing the Future* (Dublin, 2004).

Griffin, Victor, *Mark of Protest* (Dublin, 1993).

Griffin, Victor, *Enough Religion to Make us Hate* (Dublin 2002), p.2.

Hailsham, Lord, *A Sparrow's Flight* (London, 1990).

Hallinan, Michael, *Tipperary County: People and Places: An Anthology of the Evolution of County Tipperary, Some Historic Events and the History of the Principal Towns in the County* (Dublin, 1993).

Hart, Peter, 'The Geography of Revolution in Ireland 1917–1923', in *Past and Present*, no. 155 (May 1997), pp. 142–176.

Hart, Peter, The IRA and its enemies: violence and community in Cork, 1916–1923 (Oxford, 1998).

Hart, Peter, *The IRA at War, 1916–1923* (Oxford, 2003).

Hayes, B. and Fahey, T. , 'Protestants and Politics in the Republic of Ireland: Is Integration Complete?' in M. Busteed, F. Neal and J. Tonge,

Hindley, Reg, *The Death of the Irish Language* (London and New York, 1990).

Hobsbawn, Eric, *On History* (London, 1998).

Howe, Stephen, *Ireland and Empire* (Oxford, 2000).

Hopkinson, Michael, *Green Against Green: The Irish Civil War* (Dublin, 1988).

Horne, J. 'Our War, Our History', in J. Horne (ed.), *Our War: Ireland and the Great War – the 2008 Thomas Davis Lecture Series* (Dublin, 2008)

Jeffery, Keith, *Ireland and the Great War* (Cambridge, 2000).

Jackson, Alvin, *Home Rule: An Irish History, 1800–2000* (London, 2003).

Keane, Barry, *Massacre in West Cork* (Cork, 2014).

Kennedy, Dennis, *The Widening Gulf: Northern Attitudes to the Independent Irish* (2003), pp. 557–589.

Kennedy, Liam, Unhappy the Land, (Merrion Press, 2015).

Lambe, Miriam, *A Tipperary Landed Estate: Castle Otway 1750–1853* (Dublin, 1998).

Leeson, David, *The Black and Tans: British Police and Auxiliaries in the Irish War of Independence, 1920–1921* (Oxford, 2011).

Longley, Edna *Untold Stories* (Dublin, 2002).

Lynch, Michael, *Below Aherlow* (Waterford, 2002).

Lyons, F.S.L., *Ireland Since the Famine* (London, 1973, 2nd rev. ed.).

Lyons, F.S.L., *Culture and Anarchy in Ireland 1890–1939* (Oxford, 1979).

Maguire, Martin, 'A Socio-Economic Analysis of the Dublin Protestant Working Class, 1870–1926', in *Irish Economic and Social History*, 20 (1993), pp. 35–61.

Marnane, Denis G., *Land and Violence: A History of West Tipperary from 1660* (Tipperary, 1985).

McCall, Ernest, *The Auxiliaries: Tudor's Toughs* (Newtownards, 2012).

McDowell, R.B., *Crisis and Decline* (Dublin, 1977).

Meleady, Dermot, *John Redmond, The National Leader* (Sallins, Co.kildare, 2014).

Moffitt, Miriam, *The Church of Ireland Community of Killala and Achonry, 1870–1940* (Dublin, 1999).

Midleton, Lord, *Ireland – Dupe or Heroine* (London, 1932).

Moloughy, Kathleen, *Roscrea, My Heart's Home* (Roscrea, 1992).

Murphy, Gerard, *The Year of Disappearances: Political Killings in Cork, 1920–1921* (Dublin, 2010).

Myers, Kevin, *Ireland's Great War* (Dublin, 2014).

Nolan, William and McGrath, Thomas (eds), *Tipperary: History and Society: Interdisciplinary Essays on the History of an Irish County* (Dublin, 1985).

O'Brien, C.C., *Ancestral Voices: Religion and Nationalism in Ireland* (London, 1994).

O'Connor Lysaght, D.R., 'County Tipperary: Class Struggle and National Struggle, 1916–1924', in William Nolan and Thomas McGrath (eds.), *Tipperary: History and Society: Interdisciplinary Essays on the History of an Irish County* (Dublin, 1985), pp. 394–410.

O'Halpin, Eunan, *Defending Ireland: The Irish State and its Enemies since 1922* (Oxford, 1999).

Patterson, Henry, *Ireland Since 1939* (Dublin, 2006).

Prittie, Henry Cornelius, *5th Baron Dunalley, Khaki and Rifle Green* (London, 1940).

Regan, J.M., 'The "Bandon Valley massacre" as a Historical Problem'" *History* 97, no.325, January 2012.

Ruane, Joseph, *Ethnopolitics,* Vol. 9, No.1, March 2010, p.130.

Ruane, Joseph, and David Butler ,'Southern Irish Protestants: An Example of De-Ethnicisation?', *Nations and Nationalism*, 13 (4), pp. 619–35.

Seaver, George, *John Allen Fitzgerald Gregg, Archbishop* (Dublin, 1963).

Sexton and O'Leary, *Building Trust in Ireland: Studies Commissioned by the Forum for Peace and Reconciliation* (Belfast, 1996).

Stanford, W.B., *Faith and Faction in Ireland Now* (Dublin APCK).

Stanley, Alan, *I met Murder on the Way – The Story of the Pearsons of Coolacrease* (Carlow, 2005).

Tanner, Marcus, *Ireland's Holy Wars: The Struggle for a Nation's Soul 1500–2000* (London, 2003).

Stewart, A.T.Q., *The Narrow Ground: Aspects of Ulster, 1609–1969* (London, 1977).

Thornley, David 'Patrick Pearse – the Evolution of a Republic' in

F.X. Martin (ed.), *Leaders and Men of the Easter Rising: Dublin 1916* (Norfolk, 1967).

Tillinghast, Richard, *Finding Ireland* (Indianna, 2008).

Tobin, Robert, *The Minority Voice* (Oxford, 2012).

Townshend, Charles, *Political Violence in Ireland: Government and Resistance since 1848* (Oxford, 1983).

Townshend, Charles, *The Republic: The Fight for Irish Independence, 1918–1923* (London, 2013).

Trevor, William, *The Story of Lucy Gault* (London, 2003).

Trew, Johanne Devlin, *Leaving the North* (Liverpool University Press, 2013).

Ungoed-Thomas, J., *Jaspar Wolfe of Skibbereen* (Cork, 2008).

Vaughan, W.E. and Fitzpatrick, A.J., *Irish Historical Statistics: Population 1821–1971* (Dublin, 1978).

Walker, Brian M., *A Political History of the Two Irelands – From Partition to Peace* (Basingstoke, 2012).

Wall, Tom, 'Getting Them Out, Southern Loyalists in the War of Independence' (*drb*, Issue 9, Spring 2009) www.drb.ie/essays/getting-them-out - See more at: www.drb.ie/essays/a-house-builton-sand#sthash.G53VpqEj.dpuf.

White, Jack, *Minority Report: The Protestant Community in the Irish Republic* (Dublin, 1987).

Wills, Clare, *That Neutral Island* (London, 2007).

Journal

Tipperary Historical Journal.

4. UNPUBLISHED THESES

Brennan, Niamh, 'Compensating Southern Irish Loyalists after the Anglo-Irish treaty 1922–32' (Ph.D. thesis, University College Dublin, 1994).

Buckland, Patrick, 'Southern Unionism, 1885–1922' (Ph.D. thesis, Queen's University of Belfast, 1969).

Clark, Gemma, 'Fire, boycott, threat and harm: social and political violence within the local community: a study of three Munster counties during the Irish Civil War, 1922–23' (D.Phil., Queen's College, Oxford, 2010).

Index

Also from The History Press

IRELAND
AT WAR

The
History
Press
Ireland

Also from The History Press

Irish
Women

The
History
Press
Ireland

Made in the USA
Las Vegas, NV
29 August 2021